Surnames of Ireland

Origins and Numbers of Selected Irish Surnames

Edward Neafsey

Edward Neafsey was born in 1943 in Lancashire, England. His paternal grandfather was born in Knock, Co. Mayo and his paternal grandmother in Camlough, Co. Armagh. He is English on his mother's side. He read Geography and Economics at the University of Liverpool. His career began in town and country planning in Liverpool and Warrington. He worked thereafter in development planning and since 1982 has been in practice on his own account. He has published a number of articles on planning, including a chapter in a textbook whose other contributors were from the USA and UK. He has also published amateur articles on subjects of Irish interest.

Notice
Published by the Irish Genealogical Foundation.
Comments should be directed to our monthly:

Journal of Irish Families
Box 7575
Kansas City, Missouri, 64116 U.S.A..

www.Irishroots.com
Free Catalogue on Request.
ISBN: 0-940134-97-7

©2002. Irish Genealogical Foundation. Box 7575, K.C., MO. 64116

To Jean, my wife

To Giles, my son

Foreword

... Across the gaunt years
Across the lonely crag of time,
fragile as a thread
kinship stirs ...1

The author came for a concert in Ballyhaunis and moved on to a search for his ancestors and their ancestral place. A genealogical, historical and geographical quest took him to Counties Mayo, Donegal and Derry. Along the way he discovered that his surname, a transliteration of the gaelic cnáimhsighe or cnáimhseach, refered to a mountain heather or bearberry.

... The sounds of Ireland,
that restless whispering
you never get away
from, seeping out of
low bushes and grass,
heatherbells and fern ... 2

It could be said that he literally found his roots among the heathers and bracken of an Irish hillside!! Comparing the distribution of the heather with the distribution of families with his name, it is hardly surprising that he came up with the novel idea of plotting the clusters and spread of surnames on a map of Ireland.

For him, the community of the concert and the shared interest in the music led to the need for a wider understanding. Like the author, all those who seek their roots are in a sense embarking on a communal and spiritual journey.

Cnáimhseach is a gaelic byname for midwife. He found the bearberry had medicinal properties to assist in labour. For Eddie Neafsey, this wonderful book is clearly a labour born of love.

Joe Byrne
Achadh Mór
Ballyhaunis
Co. Mayo
Ireland

Bealtaine 2001

1. 'Thread', by John Chambers, 'New Workings from the West', Ed Val Mulkerns, Berry's, Westport, 1988.
2. 'Windharp', by John Montague, 'Slow Time - 100 Poems to Take You There', Niall McMonagle, Marina Books, 2000.

Preface

The idea for a surname distribution map came to me in 1992 in Ballyhaunis, Co. Mayo. The occasion was my uncle's concert at the Augustinian Abbey. There had been interest in how those of us from England related to families in Ireland, and how our surnames had come to be spelt differently. There was talk of doing a family tree, but to me the mystery was what had been the meaning of my surname Ó Cnáimhsighe and why had it been translated- or pseudo-translated - into English as Bonner. I had always been interested Ireland and Irish names. I knew Irish accents and I also knew standard English and the village dialects around where I lived in Lancashire. This gave me an interest in languages and dialects generally. As someone with a background in geography and town planning, I thought a map of the distribution of the surnames derived from Ó Cnáimhsighe might throw more light on the subject than trying to work on a family tree for our own variant.

Returning to England after the concert, I found the Oxford University Press' 'Dictionary of Surnames'. It had been published in 1988. Looking at its entry for Bonner, I could see that there was material I had not encountered before. I then found myself plotting the Ó Cnáimhsighe derivatives at the same time as I was pursuing new leads on the meaning of the name. It all meshed together and I went on to map other surnames. This book is a consolidation of that work.

My purpose is to enumerate families with particular surnames within Ireland and to present maps of the distribution of the names. Where I have been able to suggest an explanation for the distribution, I have done so. I have assumed that readers will look up individually those entries that interest them. The maps were produced individually. The commentary with each map is self-contained. Each page therefore needs no other reference to any other except perhaps with the maps of the whole population at 1991 or 1841.

For the meanings and histories of Irish surnames I have relied principally on the works of Woulfe and MacLysaght. The history and meaning on my own surname is supplemented from leads I found in the dictionary of the Royal Irish Academy. Fuller details appear in an article 'The Children of Kneafsey and the Shrine at the Pictish Fort' which is on the web.

I hope my maps and data add value to the information Woulfe and MacLysaght provided on individual names. The fact that many names have been mapped means that some common features have become apparent that would have been less obvious to them. I have discussed these observations below.

Introduction

To provide a perspective on surname history, I should begin by saying that it is not unusual for Irish surnames go back even further than 1095, which was when my own surname was first recorded. The most thoroughly researched family tree would not be able to reach back for nine hundred years or more and would not look like a tree if it did. It is accepted that there are four generations to a century. It may be said of each of us that a hundred ago there were eight people who came together to become our great-grandparents. A hundred before them there were 64 who were their great-grandparents. Continue back through nine centuries and we all have 134 million ancestors! Yet 900 years ago Ireland had only 400,000 people, and the British Isles as a whole had only 2.5 million. Bring in Normandy, and even Scandinavia for the Vikings and there would still be under five million. So, if we could track them all, most of us, within a small number of generations, would find the same ancestors on both sides of our family tree and that we are related to everybody else in the same neighbourhood. Looked at in this way, we are all related.

To put Ireland itself in perspective, at 31,800 square miles, 82,000 sq km, the island's 32 counties make up about the same area as South Carolina. The Republic accounts for 84% of it, making the 26 counties a little more than the size of West Virginia and about the same size as Tasmania. Northern Ireland is the same size as Connecticut.

Few surnames have an even distribution over the whole country. There are 1.5 million households in Ireland. MacLysaght's works cover 4,000 surnames. It follows that the average surname has only 375 families and that many Irish names are rare. Families belonging to the 203 surnames covered in this book account for 28% of all the families in Ireland. It follows that the 3,800 surnames not covered will average 285 families each.

In 1992, results of the 1991 census were beginning to come on stream for both the Republic and the North of Ireland. They would provide a background against which surname numbers could be measured. I decided to use the island's telephone directories and so designed a brief for a computer program to analyse surname entries by their phone-code areas. The University of York, England, produced the program. There were seven regions on the island each with its own level of phone ownership. The program grossed up the results in each region to approximate the total number of families with a particular name within each code area. The settlement pattern of any name could then be plotted on a map of the whole island. I used one thousand dots to illustrate the distribution. Where there were fewer than a thousand families, I used the actual number without adjustment.

These are modern distributions. As the Famine caused a great dispersal of families away from Ireland, so many people are interested in population dispersal at that time. I have therefore included distribution maps of the total population of Ireland. These are at two dates: one calculated from the 1991 census and one from 1841, the census preceding the Famine. For the 1991 map, a thousand dots represents the whole population, or one dot represents 0.1%. For Northern Ireland, though it is the county boundaries that are shown, the data collection areas were the 26 district councils which replaced the six counties in 1973. For the Republic, the data collection areas were the counties, except that the Dublin telephone area was used to define Greater Dublin. The 1841 map uses census data for the 32 counties. It has 1,600 dots to reflect the higher population before the Famine. One dot on either map represents 5,100 people.

At this stage I needed whatever meaning and history for the names was available and so turned to the recognised authorities on surnames in Ireland. The Rev. Patrick Woulfe had published his 'Irish Names and Surnames' in 1923. Woulfe's motivation was to help meet the demand by Irish students for the Irish form of their names. He had begun collecting Irish names in a Lancashire industrial town in the late 1890s. He wrote that at that time in most of the industrial towns of England, there remained a good sprinkling of Irish speakers, exiles of the Famine years half a century before. Nearly all of them were from the West of Ireland. Over two to three years Woulfe took down from them most of the names westward of a line drawn from Limerick to Sligo. By 1923 Woulfe was sure that all the people he had spoken to were dead. He drew attention to the difficulty he faced with trying to ascertain meanings of names, in advance of the publication of the Royal Irish Academy Dictionary, with its intended coverage of Old and Middle Irish. Dr Edward MacLysaght came on stream in 1957 with his 'Irish Families' and 'Surnames of Ireland'. His background was heraldry and genealogy. His motivation was to correct the errors people were making in accounting for the origins and meanings of their names and in selecting coats of arms.

As Ireland in general and Ulster in particular has many Scottish and English surnames, I refered to Dr. George F. Black's 'Surnames of Scotland', published in 1946. It was the product of 40 years' work, much of it whilst working at the New York City Library. English language Professor P. H. Reaney published his 'A Dictionary of British Surnames' in 1958. As many British surnames are place-names, I refered also to place-name authorities.

Bonner/Kneafsey proved to be a name clustered in and around Co. Donegal. I went on to map names historically associated with other parts of the country. I then selected different types of surname to see how they varied in their settlement patterns. These include 'single ancestor' surnames; gallowglass; Gaelicised Scandinavian; Anglo-Norman; English and Scottish, together with surnames based on saints' names and names from trades.

I was soon faced with the choice of plotting names together or leaving them apart. Bonner and Kneafsey are part of the same story and it did not occur to me to do other than to put them on the same map. Smith, Smyth and McGowan are not so completely the same story, but the story would be the poorer for keeping them apart. They are distinguishable by colour, though not in a book such as this. By contrast, McComb means 'son of Tom', but there is no point in merging McComb on a map with Thompson. Similarly, McKeown and McShane, both meaning Johnson, have been mapped separately. Putting names together is a matter of choice, or of resources, as it is more time consuming to analyse more than one name at once.

Spelling differences are probably not significant. Change may have occurred in a new country. It may also be due to improvements adopted in Ireland in relatively recent years, as standards of education and historical awareness have improved. I need look no further than my own name for an example. My grandfather's eldest sister Mary was entered in the Knock Baptismal Book with the surname Navisey. His entry was Neafsey. His birth certificate had Kneafsy. Moving to England, he was married and buried as Neafcy. The family in Mayo have become Kneafsey. In England, we have not been so consistent. I am using Neafsey for this book. Even the Gaelic can change. The original Cnáimhsighe of my name has been simplified in the Donegal Gaeltacht to Cnáimhsi. For some of the entries I have added together spelling variants. For others I have mapped one only.

What seems to be an overall pattern is that the south has fewer names but averages a greater number of people per name. It is strong on names from the heroic era, when virtues such as those in the meanings of Kelly or Murphy were the admired qualities. The northern half of the country has these names too, but examples there do not have the numerical strength of the south. As one moves north, surnames become more numerous and have a greater range of type of origin, even excluding names brought from Scotland and England. The north has surnames based on trades, and on saints' names or on religion in other forms. No doubt the same trades were carried on in the south, but for the religious origin names, it does not matter where the saint lived. For example, the cult of St. Brigid was centred on mid-Leinster, but the surname McBride, in full Mac Gil Bride, is concentrated in the north. Saints' names may be prefixed by 'Mul', devotee of, or 'Gil', servant of. In some forms, the prefixes may have been dropped.

At its simplest, change has meant the abandonment or restoration of the 'Mac' or 'O' prefix. Generally, the North has fewer names with the 'O' prefix than the South. For some names I have made a comparison between those with and those without the prefix, to see if there is a regional explanation for the presence or absence. No two names have had quite the same experience. Generally, the maps show the anglicisation of earlier years to be strongest in the North and in the rural areas in the Republic. Urban areas and the south tend to have gone furthest with prefix restoration.

The impressions one gets from MacLysaght is that unsympathetic British rule caused 'O' and 'Mac' prefixes to be dropped, and that restoration has occurred since British rule has ceased. I have found that at one end of the range, 99% of Shea families have the 'O' prefix. The Murphys do not have it at all, with the possible exception of people who write their name in Gaelic. Both these names are centred in Munster, which therefore has the extremes. In Leinster, 15% of Farrells have the prefix, whilst with their near neighbours the Reillys, 62% do. In Ulster, restoration of the 'O' prefix tends to be from west to east. Some 41% of the 3,000 strong Kane families have the prefix. Those with it are mainly in the west. Keane, the spelling variant predominant in the other three provinces and totalling 3,400 families, has hardly any with the prefix. Keane is an example working against the usual trend.

There obviously is a dynamic to be measured in the restoration, particularly of the 'O'. Gorman is an interesting example. The name was originally McGorman. The prefix fell into disuse. A celebrity with the name erroneously assumed an 'O' and others followed suit. MacLysaght, often working with data of a century ago, found that O'Gorman was found chiefly in Clare, whilst Tipperary was plain Gorman. The distribution I find today is that Tipperary today is also O'Gorman country. The 'O' form is evidently spreading from the south west. However, the immense extent of the range of use of the 'O' prefix, the variation in its use within the same region and between different names in the same region, must cast doubt on the influence the British had on this cultural feature.

Whilst it is not a reintroduction, another paradox arises when comparison is made with an example of the use of the 'Mac' prefix in Ulster. McCartan remains solidly with its prefix in the south east, whereas Carton, Cartin Carten and Cartan are the forms found in the north east and along the north coast of Northern Ireland.

Probably the most striking feature of many of the maps is the tight clustering of many of the names. Within their homelands people have not historically been very mobile. Tight clustering at home in Ireland may seem at odds with a people who have scattered around the world but it is not simply Irish people who have these characteristics. Italy has also produced large emigrant communities. Yet within Italy itself, the evidence shows limited mobility. According to the Istituto Centrale di Statistica of 1997, 70% of single Italian men remain at home with their parents until after their 35th birthday and 42% stay within one kilometre of the parental home.

The tight clusters in Ireland may be taken as an indication that all the families in the area of the cluster, of whatever surname, were similarly of very limited mobility. Nine centuries means 36 generations. A botanist might say that 36 generations is not been much time for dispersal. The dispersal we see may be as much as we could reasonably have expected.

In that many names turn out to be variants of other names, the subject matter is more complex than it seems at first sight, but it does now lend itself to quantification and analysis.

Many more surnames remain to be mapped, but with over a quarter of all families in Ireland covered in these pages, the chances are that many people of Irish extraction should find the family name of at least one grandparent in this book. This makes it I believe an appropriate stage at which to consolidate and publish the findings.

Two questions remain - 'what if' and 'what next'.

Surnames have passed down through the male line. What if it had been female? Other things being equal, the clusters would presumably be much the same. Other things may not have been equal. Recent DNA studies show that the female ancestral population of a given individual is more dispersed than the male. The suggested explanation for this is that men were territorial and kept the house/farmstead, whilst women married into the house from some distance away. No doubt much more information of this sort will come to light in years to come as a result of human genome and other projects. The University of Oxford, England, has a website, 'oxfordancestors.com' which has some fascinating data.

What next? Those of us overseas of recent Irish extraction think of Ireland as a land of emigrants. It has not always been so, though it was at the beginning of historic times. The population implosion of the later days of the Roman Empire drew people inwards from all directions, including Picts from Ireland and also Gaels, who settled in what is now western Scotland and north west and south west Wales. The Gaelic settlement in Scotland was strong enough to introduce the language and place names and surnames. Only one or two names had an 'O' prefix, in line with the reducing trend from south to north. In Wales, nothing remains except that two counties have names whose Welsh form betrayals a Gaelic ancestry.

Some inward migration could have come from slavery - St Patrick was a freed slave who returned to convert the people who had enslaved him. Migration in ensuing centuries brought settlers direct from Scandinavia, who left both surnames and place-names. McLaughlin is an example. Scandinavians also carved out the Duchy of Normandy in France, became French speaking, conquered England and then Ireland, and brought into Ireland Norman names including FitzGerald. As the Normans brought with them retainers from Wales, many families were called Walsh. This name is probably the best marker of Anglo-Norman settlement in Ireland. The Tudor and Stuart era brought in a new wave of settlers, with names from England, Scotland and Wales. In the early eighteenth century, refugees from the Rhineland Palatinate were settled in Ireland.

There have been changes since I began work on the maps in this book. In the early 1990s, Ireland was one of the poorest countries of the European Union. It is now one of the most prosperous. This means that Ireland has again become a destination for immigrants, putting it for the first time alongside the rest of the English speaking world as a favourite destination, with people arriving from former communist Europe, the Middle East, Asia and Africa. As migrants are predominantly young and predominantly male, we may expect from this an infusion of surnames new to Ireland. They may also be new to the world, as some cultures at home manage without surnames but adopt them when they find themselves where surnames are expected.

Edward Neafsey
Mayfield
East Sussex
February 2001

EdNeafsey@compuserve.com
Ed.Neafsey@Virgin.net

1   Adamson
180 families

In the late Medieval England Adam was the second or third most popular name for a boy, and was particularly pre-eminent in the north. It was popular in Scotland, where it gave rise also to the pet forms Aidy and Eadie. As the surname Adams is mostly found in Ulster, it is likely that Adamson and other names there derived from Adam were of British origin. Names derived from Biblical and vernacular saints were more popular amongst the Irish in Ulster than elsewhere in Ireland. MacAdhaimh was found Co. Cavan. This is a variant pronounced and now spelt McCaw.

Adamson indicates relationship to a forebear called Adam more precisely than Adams does. The latter could mean 'son of Adam', but could also be 'atte Adams', meaning someone living with the household of someone called Adam.

The map shows the distribution of some 132 households called Adamson in 1992. Allowing for homes without telephones, there were likely to have been about 180 families altogether. Though Northern Ireland is pre-eminent, having 71% of the families, and though the Belfast, Antrim, Lisburn area at 24% has more than double the national average representation in this area, Adamson families are at their greatest density south of Lough Neagh rather than east of it. Their strength in Dublin at 23% is the same as the national average. Ulster names are usually weak in this area. It may mean direct settlement from England. There is an unexpected cluster around Athlone. The Adamson settlement pattern is therefore unusual in several respects. Adamson is a variant of Adam not discussed by MacLysaght. It was perhaps too rare.

Alcorn
150 families

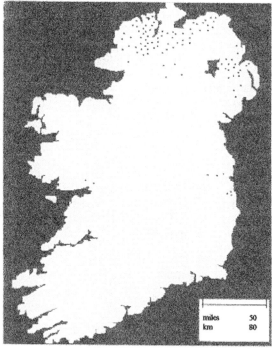

Alcorn is an English name, from ald corn, old corn. It has been fairly prominent in Ulster since the mid seventeenth century and has been particularly associated with Co. Donegal. According to Black's 'Surnames of Scotland', it is probably derived from Alchorne, a parish in the manor of Rotherfield, in Sussex, England.

In Old English, corn refered to the main cereal crop of the area. In England it would mean wheat, in Scotland, oats. Alcorn does not appear in Reaney's 'Dictionary of British Surnames'. In Scotland, the mill of Kethyk was leased to John Awldcorn in 1446. Two years later it was re-let to his son Adam Aldcorn. The name thereafter appears in various parts of Scotland, as Aldcorne, Auldcorne and Alcoirne. In the seventeenth century it is found in Edinburgh, in Castlemilk, Dumfriesshire and in Kelso, which is close to the English border at the confluence of the Teviot and Tweed rivers.

The proximity to the English border may account for the appearance of the name in Ireland. After the union of the crowns of England and Scotland, many families on both sides of the border
found themselves without a role and left to live in Ulster.

The map shows the distribution of 98 families with telephones in Ireland in 1992. Allowing for homes without phones, there were probably 150 families altogether. Co. Donegal remains the most important locality, with 38% of the families living there, mostly in the central part. Another quarter live across the north coast from Co. Tyrone to Co. Antrim. The name is not found in Inishowen. At 13%, the name is slightly stronger in the Belfast area than the national average of 11%.

Only 10% of the families in Ireland live outside Ulster. These are located either in or close to Dublin or in Co. Galway.

Archer
260 families

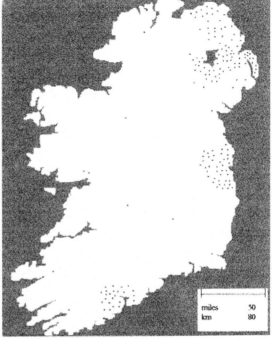

Archer is from the Old French 'archier', Anglo-French 'archer', meaning an archer or professional bowman. It is recorded in England from the eleventh century and in Scotland from the thirteenth.

In Ireland the name was first recorded in Dublin in 1190, where Ralph Larcher (le Archer) was a burgess. It has been most strongly associated with Kilkenny, where an Anglo-Norman family became wealthy and influential enough to be one of the 'Tribes of Kilkenny'. Near the city of Kilkenny there are the place-names Archersgrove, Archersleas and Archersrath. In Co. Wexford, the name has been rendered as Orchard.

The map shows the distribution of some 165 families with telephones in 1992. Allowing for homes without telephones, there were likely to have been about 260 Archer families altogether. The distribution was not typical of the Anglo-Normans. Settlement along the south coast was confined to the Cork area where there was an important cluster. Historically prominent in Kilkenny, the name was virtually unknown there in 1992 and may never have been numerous. It was virtually unknown in Wexford, whether as Archer or Orchard.

The proportion of Archer families in Greater Dublin exceeded the national average of around a quarter. This is normal for an Anglo-Norman name. At 12% in the Belfast, Antrim and Lisburn area, it was about the same as the national average and was high for an Anglo-Norman name. Many of the remainder in Northern Ireland were in eastern Ulster, suggesting that the Archer settlement pattern in the North came from migration from Scotland and the Plantation of Ulster rather than from medieval colonisation.

Northern Ireland had a third of all Irish families. It had about half of Ireland's Archer families.

McAteer
1440 families

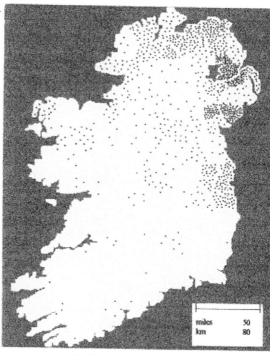

Mac an tSaoir, 'son of the craftsman' became MacIntyre in Scotland. In Ireland, McAteer is found as well as McIntyre. Ballymacateer is near Lurgan, whilst Carrickmacintyre is in Co. Mayo.

The map shows the distribution of some 1,440 Mac an tSaoir families in 1992. Ten dots make up 10% of the total. McAteer accounts for 35%. and McIntyre for 65%. Though some of the Ulster McIntyres may be of planter origin, a Scottish origin for many of the McIntyres in Ireland may be discounted: the name is too widespread. Some 40% of McIntyre families live outside Ulster. Further, the highland home country of the Scottish MacIntyres, Nether Lorn, in Argyll, is an improbable origin for a demographically significant number of settlers. For the most part McAteer and McIntyre are likely therefore to be Irish variant spellings of the same name. The existence of the Scottish name may have caused substitutions for McAteer.

There is a cluster of families in Mayo, which for many names is an indicator of population shift from Ulster or elsewhere.

Like other 'craft' surnames, Mac an tSaoir is scarce in the southern half of the island. McAteer is very much an Ulster name. Some 86% of McAteer families live there. Over most of the province McAteers are mingled with McIntyres, but a quarter of all McAteer families in Ireland live in a cluster in south Armagh and south Down which has very few McIntyres. That this area was south of the Plantation of Ulster may account for the Irish rather than Scottish name form. There is a corresponding McIntyre cluster in north Antrim.

In Dublin it has been rendered 'Carpenter'. In Scotland and in Fermanagh it has been translated as 'Wright'. In Ulster there are many Wrights, a name of lowland Scottish and northern English origin which took the place of Carpenter in those areas. Elsewhere in Ireland, because 'saor' has a secondary meaning of 'free', it has become 'Freeman'. In relation to McAteer and McIntyre, Carpenter and Freeman are not numerous names.

Woulfe and MacLysaght treat McAteer as the citation form of the name, no doubt because it is exclusively Irish whereas McIntyre will include some Scottish origin families.

Barrett
2250 families

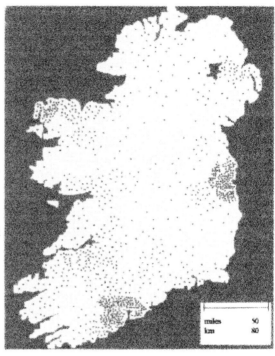

The map shows the distribution of some 2,250 Barrett families in 1992. Each dot represents 0.1% of the total. As with most families, Dublin is now a prominent cluster.

Baréid in Connaught and Baróid in Munster, the name Barrett came to Ireland with the Anglo-Norman settlement. A 1588 pedigree of the Mayo Walshes shows that they were descended from Walynus who came over with Maurice FitzGerald to Wexford in 1169, and that Walynus had a brother called Barrett, from whom were descended the Barretts of Mayo. These became lords of Tirawley. The Conaught Barretts became more completely gaelicised than their more numerous Munster namesakes.

Where the Normans got the name from is disputed. Though there are Anglo-Saxon and Frankish possibilities, the origin is probably from the old French 'barat', to do with commercial dealing. If so, it would be equivalent to the English Chapman and the German Kaufmann. Occasionally it may have been from the French 'barrette', a type of cap. Headgear provided one of medieval England's most common surnames, Hood, and there was an early French royal dynasty called Capet.

The Barrett distribution differs from Walsh, a six times more numerous Anglo-Norman surname, in that it has strong local concentrations, a feature typical of many of the Gaelic septs.

With 7% in Northern Ireland, the Barretts have the highest proportion of all the Anglo-Norman surnames, though numbers there may have been supplemented by later Barretts from England. At 20%, their representation in Dublin is slightly less than the national average. In no county are they sufficiently numerous to amount to 1% of the population.

Bartley
150 families

Parthalán, the forename from which the surname Mac Parthaláin is derived, is regarded as the equivalent of Bartholomew, the name of one of the Apostles. Parthalán is an important figure in Irish mythology, featuring as leading an invasion of Ireland from his native Magna Graecia (modern Sicily) some 300 years after the Flood. The surname has been anglicised in a number of different forms, in Ireland as Mac Parland, MacParlan, MacPartlin as well as Bartley; and in Scotland and thence in Ulster as MacFarland and MacFarlane.

In the 16th century MacParlan appears chiefly in Co. Leitrim where, with Armagh, it is principally found today. It was listed in the 'census' of 1659 as a principal Irish name. It occurs frequently in the Armagh Hearth Money Rolls of 1664.

Though Bartley looks like an English place-name, it does not appear in Reaney's 'A Dictionary of British Surnames'. It is not listed in Black's 'Surnames of Scotland. It is very rare in Ireland.

The map shows the distribution of a hundred Bartley families with telephones in 1992. Allowing for homes without telephones, there are likely to have been about 152 families altogether. The proportion in the Greater Dublin area is about 22%, similar to the proportion of the whole of Ireland's population living in this area. The proportion in the Belfast, Antrim, Lisburn area is 11%, again matching the national average proportion resident there. This is is unusual and so to is the distribution in the rest of the country. Glengormley is more important than Belfast itself. The name is widespread for a rare name. It is hardly represented in Armagh and not at all in Leitrim. After Dublin and Belfast, the main clusters are around Navan, Fermoy and Limerick. It is unlikely that the scatter reflects a dispersal. It may be that unconnected Mac Parthaláin families adopted Bartley.

Beattie
1380 families

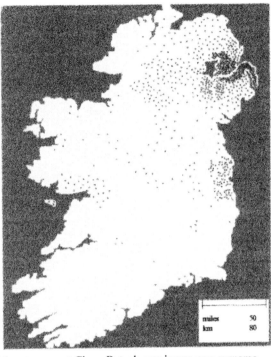

For most of the families of this surname in Ireland, its origin is from Scotland where it was an abbreviation of the Christian name Bartholomew. It is found also as Batey and Batty in England. In Ireland Beattie and Beatty predominate. There is single telephone directory entry for Beatie and three for Betty.

The other origin is from the Gaelic biadhtach, from betagh, food. It has the sense of an hospitaller, a public victualler, or someone providing hospitality. In the 13th and 14th centuries, the betagii, as they were called in the Latin of the time, rendered food as the feudal dues for the land they held. This applied in the parts of the country under effective Anglo-Norman control, much of Leinster, part of Connaught and Munster except Clare. Betagh was in use as a surname but is now almost extinct. In the late 19th century it was still used synonymously with Beattie around Athlone.

The map shows the distribution of some 1,380 families in 1992. Like many names of Scottish origin, the name is found in strongest concentration in south Antrim and north Down. Beattie is well distributed throughout Northern Ireland whose borders are clearly recognisable in the settlement pattern. The history of the name may account for its dispersal in the North. Beattie is common in Galloway and was common in the Borders. The border 'riding clans' were broken in the early 17th century following the union of the Scottish and English crowns and many families came with the Plantation to Ulster and particularly to Fermanagh.

For families whose name is of Gaelic origin, the influence of land tenure under the Anglo-Normans may account for the presence of the name in the Pale - the Greater Dublin area - and in Co. Galway. It does not explain its virtual absence in Munster

Almost four fifths of the families have the spelling Beattie. The spelling variants do not indicate Scottish or Irish extraction, though the two spellings are not uniformly mixed. The closer a family lives to Belfast, the more likely the spelling is to be Beattie. Three quarters of all the families live in Northern Ireland, where only 12% have the spelling Beatty. In the Republic, Beatty is slightly more numerous. In Dublin and Galway about 60% have the spelling Beatty. The representation of the name in Greater Dublin is only half of the national average of one quarter.

Beggs

For most families, the surname Beggs is of Scottish origin, from in the Gaelic 'beag', meaning 'little'. In Ulster, Small was sometimes used as a synonym. For some the origin may have been the English 'Bigg', with the opposite meaning. The pronunciation of 'e' and 'i' is often the same in the Ulster accent. If this has happened, it has virtually eliminated Bigg and Biggs in Ulster. Only three are to be found in the telephone directories. usually the English influence predominates. The final 's' shows this. It is a result of English influence. Many English surnames, particularly monosyllabic names, take an 's', originally as a plural or genitive. There are only 15 Begg families in the Irish telephone directories, of whom 11 are in Dublin one in Limerick, one in Antrim and two in the south of Co. Down.

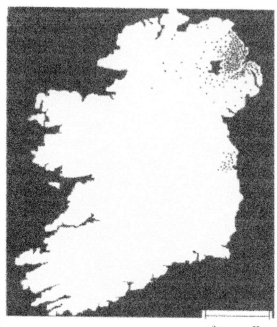

The name is rare. The map shows the distribution of some Beggs 257 families in Ireland in 1992. Allowing for homes without telephones, there are likely to be about 340 families altogether.

For most families today, the Belfast, Antrim and Lisburn area stands out by the density of settlement. This is because the area has become a destination for internal migration since the Industrial Revolution. In the case of Beggs, the settlement occurs at equal density into the Glens of Antrim on the east coast of the county, and into Ards on the east coast of Co. Down. This indicates a settlement that pre-dates the Industrial Revolution.

Beggs is overwhelmingly a surname of Northern Ireland. Few have migrated to the Republic. Greater Dublin has been the most important destination for internal migration in Ireland and now has over 20% of all Irish households. Only 7% of Beggs families live there. All the others live in Northern Ireland.

Bell
2400 families

Black gives four origins for this surname: the Old French 'le Bel', fair or handsome (modern 'beau'); 'atte Bell', not uncommon in Middle English registers, from the sign of the person's public house; a child of Bell or Isabelle; and in Islay and Kintyre, as a translation of Mac Illinamhaoil, a surname said to be a hybrid of MacMillan and Bell. He considers the first two to be the most important sources.

The name was common on the Scottish-English border area. The union of the crowns in 1603 meant that forceful families there who had watched and made a living from the border on both sides were no longer required. The King broke their power and many, including Bell families, moved to Ulster.

The map shows the distribution of some 2,400 families in Ireland in 1992. Ten dots make up 1% of the total. The fact that the Bells' area of entry into Ireland later became one of the two most important urban centres in the island means that the Bell distribution is one of the most localised. Some 36% of them live in the Belfast, Antrim and Lisburn area. The dense settlement extends into Ards, the addition of which brings the proportion in the core cluster to 45%. It also means that despite their strongly localised representation, Bell families are not numerous as a proportion of all families in this populous area. The total number of households in the core cluster is about 250,000, so that Bell families make up around 0.5% of all families. Elsewhere on the island, such a localised concentration may mean that a familiy's numbers amount to 3% or more of all families in the vicinity.

For many Irish families, Greater Dublin has now become their most important location. About 22% of all families live there. Ulster remains much the most important location for the Bells. Northern Ireland has about a third of all Ireland's households. It has 80% of the Bell families.

Bergin
800 families

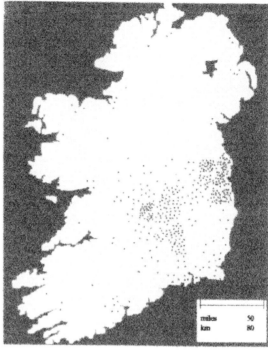

Ó hAimheirgin, O Havergan or O Hamergin, meaning wondrous birth, has long been contracted to Ó Beirgin and Ó Birgin. MacLysaght's sources indicate that Vergin would be a better anglicisation than Bergin or the rare Mergin. However, the 'B' form had become generally accepted in English and Latin by the end of the 15th century. By 1992, the only surviving forms to be found in the telephone directories of Ireland were Bergin, a single example of Bergen, and a few Berrigans. Bergan, the spelling of which would assure a hard 'g' to English readers, is not now in use. Neither is Mergin.

Historically the name is associated with the barony of Geashill, Co. Offaly and with the Leix-Offaly border area.

The map shows the distribution of some 430 households with telephones in 1992. Adjusting for homes without phones, there are probably about 800 families altogether. About 30% of them live in Greater Dublin, a proportion higher than the national average, but not unusual for Gaelic and Anglo-Norman names in modern times. The name occurs in greatest density around the town of Roscrea on the Offaly-Tipperary border. It extends into Kilkenny at much the same density as in Leix. Administrative boundaries often follow watercourses or watersheds. In the case of the name Bergin, it could be said that the historic 'basin' of the name is the Barrow-Nore river system. This is the same territory as the three times more numerous Delaney sept. The historic centre of the Delaneys is not far from Geashill, at Upperwoods at the foot of Slieve Bloom.

Berry
330 families

MacLysaght sees Berry as usually an English name, a variant of Bury, which has been fairly numerous in Ireland since the seventeenth century but widely scattered. In Offaly, the name is an anglicisation of Ó Béara, a family akin to O'Connor and O'Dempsey. Neither MacLysaght nor Woulfe provide a meaning for Ó Béara. The English Bury is from an Anglo-Saxon word for fort, which occurs in many English place-names.

The map shows the distribution of 206 families with telephones in 1992. Adjusting for homes without phones, there are probably some 330 families altogether. For the most part they are to be found in Dublin, Belfast and Wexford, all seaport locations connecting Ireland with England. Small clusters of families live around the ports of Westport and Galway.

The spelling Berry accounts for 88% of the families. Burry accounts for 7% and Bury 5%. Burry families are found exclusively in the Dublin area; and Bury families mainly in Arklow and Wicklow. Bury is almost unknown in the North, despite the seat of a titled family at Greyabbey on Strangford Lough.

Some 14% of all the families live in the Belfast area, a high proportion which confirms the English origin in the North. The Northern cluster extends south westwards into Armagh and north Monaghan. Greater Dublin has almost a half of all the families. The concentration in the Republic's capital will be due to families local to that area, and to families from elsewhere having moved in for work.

Bonner
770 families

St. Columba raised a long dead craftsman from the dead to complete a task he had left unfinished. The man lived on and fathered children. Because he had been cnamhaibh aimsir (foda), a (long) time in bones, his offspring were called the 'Clann Cnáimhsighe. 'Cnáimh' is the Irish for 'bone', in the genitive form. The time was about 573 AD and the place, Duncrun, Co. Derry. The story is recorded in the Irish language 'Life of St. Columba', compiled in 1532 from earlier sources by Manus O'Donnell. A thousand years later, this legend prompted the adoption of Bonner as the anglicised version of the surname. Bonner, and the other three spellings, are all pronounced 'Boner'.

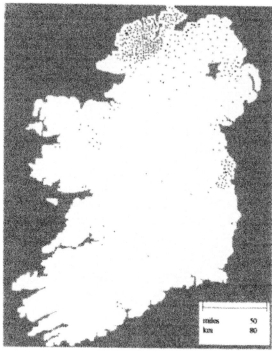

The map shows 446 families in the 1992 telephone directories whose surnames are derivatives of Ó Cnáimhsighe. There are about 770 famiilies altogether. Bonner accounts for 88%. The 12% retaining Gaelic forms are split between Kneafsey in various spellings - two thirds, located in Connaught, and Crampsie in various spellings - one third, located in north Donegal.

Ó Cnáimhsighe was first recorded in 1095. Cnáimhsighe is a plural of which the singular is Cnáimhseach. This was sometimes used as a personal name for a woman, and sometimes as a byname for midwife. O'Donnell may have had satyrical reasons from his own time for the 'miraculous' explanation. The ultimate origin appears to be the bearberry, a mountain heather, cnaimhseag in Scottish Gaelic. In Ireland, the plant is found in much the same area as the surnames derived from Cnáimhsighe - north Antrim through Donegal to the Burren. It is oxytocic, and oxytocin is a drug given today to women in childbirth. As a woman's personal name, Cnáimhseach was an old Irish equivalent of Heather.

Some Bonners in Ireland are not of Cnáimhsighe origin. Scots whose Anglo-Norman name means 'courteous' came from the seventeenth century, mainly to Ulster; and Rhineland Germans with a name recalling the city of Bonn moved to Limerick in the early eighteenth century. Neither of these has left a discernible imprint on the map.

Boyle
3300 families

An old Irish word, baigell, meaning having profitable pledges, may well have produced the surname which in modern Irish is rendered Ó Baoighill. Long associated with the north west of Co. Donegal, the family gave their name to the barony of Boylagh. Warfare in the reign of Elizabeth I caused dispersal throughout the country.

Another origin of the name is a town in Normandy near Caen, Beauville, or Boyville, the name of which was taken to Britain by Norman settlers and adopted by local people, particularly in Scotland. The name appeared in Ireland with the 'New English' in Munster in 1588, and with the much more intensive Plantation of Ulster shortly thereafter.

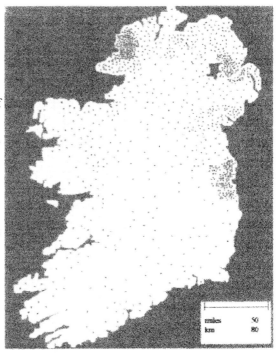

The map shows the distribution of 3,300 families in 1992. Some 16% of them have the 'O' prefix, 84% do not. Ten dots make up 1% of the total. Almost a quarter of all the families live in Co. Donegal where they make up 2% of the population. The Belfast area accommodates about 11% of all the households in Ireland. Some 9% of Boyle and O'Boyle families live there. Greater Dublin has about 22% of all Irish households. Around 12% of the Boyle and 12% of the O'Boyle families live there.

In Mayo and Sligo, over 40% of families have the 'O' prefix. In Donegal, heartland of the sept, only 3% use it. The Dublin area has about the same proportion with the prefix as the national average. Belfast has slightly more than the national average, which is unusual for the northern conurbation. A small area around Ballymena has more than a half with the prefix. A local need to distinguish between Gaelic and British Boyles may be the explanation of the Ulster O'Boyles.

Northern Ireland has a third of all Irish families. It has the same proportion of the Boyles.

Brady
3400 families

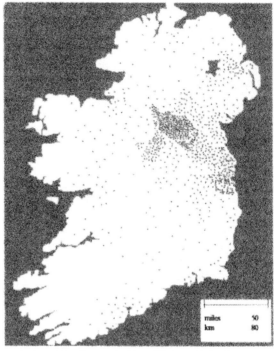

In Irish the name is MacBrádaigh, which is possibly from bradach, meaning spirited. A few families now use MacBrádaigh, but Mac with the anglicised form, Brady, is unknown today. The MacBradys were a powerful sept of Breffny, their chiefs holding sway over a territory centred on Stradone, about six miles east of Cavan town.

The map shows the distribution of some 3,400 Brady families in 1992. Each dot represents 0.1% of the total. The historic heartland of the sept appears very clearly. Outside this area, with the exception of Greater Dublin, their distribution is thin for a clan of this numerical strength. The Dublin area has 22% of all Irish families. Some 26% of the Bradys live there, reflecting the proximity of Breffny to the Republic's capital. About 14% of them live in Co. Cavan, where they make up 3½% of the population. They account for 1% in neighbouring Co. Longford.

Records show that a leading family of the O'Gradys of Co. Clare changed their name to Brady, possibly to distance themselves from the local O'Grady sept for political advantage. Whatever the historical importance of this change, the map shows that the numbers that could have been affected by it are now insignificant in relation either to the rest of the Bradys, or to the local population.

Even though Cavan is an Ulster county, Brady representation in the rest of Ulster is low. They make up almost 1% of the population of Co. Monaghan, but are not in significant strength elsewhere in the Province. "Bold Phelim Brady the Bard of Armagh" came from a county where his sept amounted to only one family in four hundred. Northern Ireland has a third of all Irish households. It has only 10% of the Brady families.

Brennan
4900 families

'Bran', raven, produced a number of surnames, one of which was Mac Branáin. Of the several meanings of the Irish 'braon', sorrows is the most likely origin of Ó Braonáin. Both these surnames became Brennan on anglicisation.

For three centuries from 1159, a succession of Mac Branáins were chiefs of a territory in eastern Roscommon. The Mac prefix was used until the seventeenth century Gaelic eclipse.

The principal Ó Braonáin sept was in Ossory, the Kilkenny and Carlow area. Chiefs of Idough in north Kilkenny, their influence waned in the face of increasing English power. Some families retained their estates. Some progressed, without much loss of glamour,

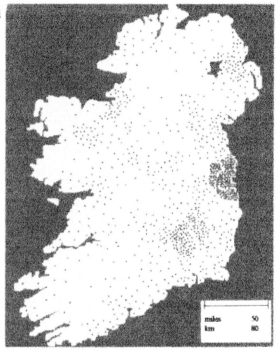

from being rapparees - irregular soldiers armed with pikes - to being freebooters and highwaymen. Several infamous bands of Leinster tories were led by Brennans.

There were three other unrelated Ó Braonáin septs. One was in Westmeath; one in east Galway and one in Kerry. Brennan densities remain slightly greater in these parts than in surrounding areas.

The map shows the distribution of 4,900 Brennan families in 1992, including a very few with spelling variations. Each dot represents 0.1%. In common with many families, the main present day cluster is in Greater Dublin, where 22% of Brennan families live, the same as the national average representation in the Republic's capital area. Northern Ireland, with a third of all Irish households, has only 9% of Brennan families.

Brennans make up the greatest proportion of all families in those parts of the country which are their main areas of historic origin. They are about 2% of the population in Kilkenny and Carlow, and 1% in Roscommon and Sligo.

McBride
1700 families

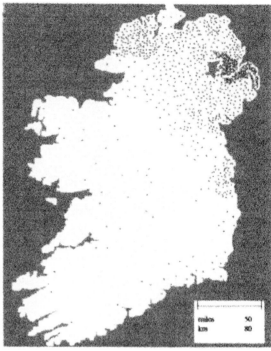

The surname McBride is from the Irish Mac Giolla Bhrighde, son or daughter of a devotee of St Brigid. Scottish MacBrides have the same origin. The use of Brigid as a woman's Christian name, was not usual before the end of the sixteenth century.

St Brigid was the abbess of Kildare who died in 525 AD. With St Patrick and St Columba, she is one of the three most important saints of Ireland. Despite the probable southern origin of the surname's founder, like other surnames derived from saints' names, whether Scriptural or Irish, McBride is mainly found in the North. Several members of the sept became Bishops of Raphoe in Co. Donegal.

The map shows the distribution of the 1700 McBride families in Ireland in 1992. Each dot represents 0.1% of the total. About a fifth of the families live in Donegal, where they make up nearly 1% of the population. Around 55% live in Northern Ireland, compared with 31% of all Irish families. The area of Belfast, Lisburn and Antrim alone has a fifth of all McBride families, which is twice the representation in that area of families generally. Only 5% live in Greater Dublin, the McBrides being much less well represented there than the 22% national average.

Some McBrides in east Ulster are likely to be of Scottish origin.

O'Brien
9600 families

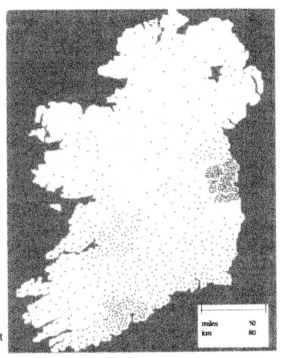

The culmination of High King Brian Boru's career was his final triumph over the Norsemen at Clontarf in 1014, the battle in which he lost his own life. The sept to which he belonged came from Thomond and Brian had built up his power there. Soon after his death, members of his family assumed his name as a surname. Subsequently they divided into several septs, and acquiried land in parts of north Tipperary, Limerick and east Cork. Brian originally meant raven.

The map shows the distribution of some 9,600 O'Brien families in 1992. One dot represents 0.1% of the total. As with most families, Greater Dublin is now the most important cluster. This is because of internal migration to the capital and depopulation in much of the rest of the country since the Famine. Some 22% of the O'Briens live in Greater Dublin, the same as Dublin's proportion of Irish families as a whole.

The area in which the O'Briens make up the greatest proportion of the population continues to be the province of Munster with which they have always been most closely associated. In Cos. Cork, Limerick and Clare, O'Briens account for almost 2% of the population, which is twice the strength they have in the capital area.

Like most Munster septs, the distribution of the O'Briens thins out markedly in the northern half of the island. Only 3% of them live in Northern Ireland, home to 31% of all Irish families.

Brown
3150 families

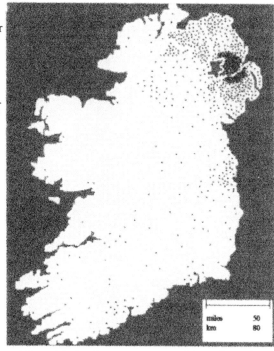

Brown in Ireland may derive from either the English or French language. Old English 'Brun' was a personal name for someone brown of hair or complexion. The Norman 'Le Brun' means the same in French. Brown was also one of the color names adopted by the Lamonts in Scotland when they were 'broken' and forbidden to use Lamont. In the Scottish Highlands, the Gaelic names Mac a' Bhriuthainn, son of the brehon (judge) and Mac Ghille Dhuinn, son of the brown lad, were widely anglicised as Brown.

In the Republic of Ireland, the Anglo-Norman influence brought in Le Brun, which became erroneously De Brun, and was anglicised as Browne. Browne remains the most numerous spelling in the Republic to this day. Browne was one of the Tribes of Galway. The Browne settlement pattern is different from that of Brown and is not shown on the map.

The spelling Brown in Ireland usually indicates a name a name of Scottish and English origin in Ulster, being associated with the Protestant settlement. However, Catholic Scots were sometimes planted as a buffer between the Irish Catholics and the Presbyterian Planters. The map shows the distribution of some 3,150 Brown families in Ireland in 1992. Ten dots represent 1% of the total. Some 86% of the families were resident in Northern Ireland, with 36% being concentrated in the Belfast, Antrim and Lisburn area alone.

The Northern Ireland settlement density extends into the Republic's Ulster county of Cavan, but does not do so into Donegal. Some of the families in the Republic may be Brownes who have lost their final 'e', but those in Carlow and possibly Kildare could be plantation settlers.

Burke
5800 families

Around 1185, William de Burgh, known as the Conqueror of Ireland, arrived in the country. He was a brother of Hubert de Burgh, who would later become 'the most powerful man in England next to King John'. He was made Governor of Limerick, married a daughter of Donal Mór O'Brien, King of Thomond, and wrested control of Connaught from the reigning O'Connors. He succeeded Strongbow as Chief Governor, founding one of the most important Anglo-Norman families.

The map shows the distribution of some 5,800 Burke and Bourke families in 1992. About four fifths have the spelling 'Burke'. Each dot represents 0.1% of the total. There are in addition a few families called de Burgh or de Búrca. In its various spelling guises, Burke is the most numerous of the surnames proper arising from the Anglo-Norman settlement. The most numerous arising from this conquest is Walsh, the name applied to the Welsh retainers of the Norman lords. The Burkes became the most completely hibernicised of the Anglo-Normans. They adopted Brehan Law, formed several septs and proclaimed chiefs after the Irish fashion.

First identified with Connaught, Burke is today found in all the provinces of Ireland. About 5% of the Burkes live in Northern Ireland, quite a high proportion for an Anglo-Norman name. Some 31% of all Irish families live in the North.

As with most surnames, the main cluster today is in Greater Dublin. About 17% of Burke families live in the area, as compared with 22% of Irish families generally. The West remains the area in which the Burkes have the greatest proportion of the population. They account for about 1½% of all families in Cos. Galway and Mayo.

Byrne
9900 families

The Irish Ó Broin is derived from Bran, meaning Raven, a son of an eleventh century King of Leinster. The Byrnes have long been one of the foremost septs of east Leinster, noted for resistance to English rule. The celebrated 'Leabhar Branach', or 'Book of the Byrnes,' is a collection of Irish poems by 35 authors dating from about 1662, most of which are about the exploits of the sixteenth century O'Byrnes.

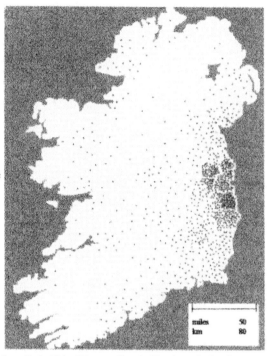

The map shows the distribution of some 9,900 Byrne families in 1992. Each dot represents 0.1% of the total. Their east Leinster origin is evident today in that the Byrnes are the most strongly represented in the Greater Dublin area of all the major Irish families. Over a third are there, where they account for over 1% of the population. Only 5% of Byrnes live in Northern Ireland, as compared to 31% of all Irish families.

Though they were dispossessed from their original north Kildare patrimony by the twelfth century Anglo-Norman invasion, and from their subsequent stronghold in the Wicklow mountains in 1628, Byrne families continue to be strongly represented in these areas, and in neighbouring Co. Carlow.

There are in addition some 400 families who have restored the prefix 'O', including some who have reverted to the Irish form Ó Broin. As O'Byrne families have no distinct locational bias, and as they would constitute only 6% of a combined total, their inclusion would not affect the distribution shown on the map. The families with the prefix are slightly more concentrated in the main urban centres than those without.

Caldwell
540 families

Caldwell in Ireland may be of English, Scottish or Irish origin. Its English meaning remains obvious, being 'cold well', from the Old English 'ceald wielle'. There are several Caldwell place names in England. Scottish surnames derive from Caldwell in Renfrewshire. In Ireland, Colavin and Cullivan families of Connaught and Cavan adopted the name, as did Horish and Houriskey families of north Tyrone. This was a pseudo-translation, under the mistaken impression that the Gaelic word 'uisce', meaning water, formed part of Ó hUaruisce, the Gaelic form of the name. Castle Caldwell in Fermanagh was the home of a Scottish origin family from Ayrshire.

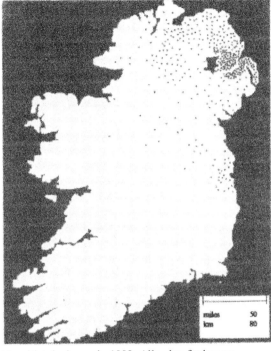

The map shows the distribution of some 385 households with telephones in 1992. Allowing for homes without telephones, there were likely to have been about 540 families altogether at that date. The Scottish origin of many of the families is apparent by the concentration in Co. Antrim and north Co. Down. English and Irish origin may account for the presence of the name in more westerly parts of Ulster. Connaught does not appear as a significant location for Caldwell families at the present time. Fermanagh and Cavan too have little representation. There is a cluster of families in Meath as well as the presence in Dublin, which is usual for almost all names.

Caldwell remains very much an Ulster name. Northern Ireland has about a third of all Irish families. It has 76% of Caldwell families. Greater Dublin has just over a fifth of all Irish families. It has only 6% of the Caldwells.

McCandless
210 families

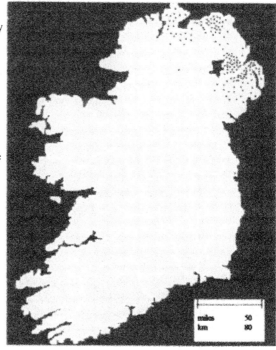

From the Gaelic Mac Cuindlis, this surname normally appears as McCandless in the English spelling. A variant McAndles appears to have died out. Families of this spelling have perhaps been re-absorbed by McCandless as people learned of the origin of the name.

The name is rare. The map shows the distribution of some 150 families with telephones in 1992. Allowing for homes without telephones, there were probably about 210 families altogether.

The settlement pattern is unusual. There are two clusters. One, comprising 39% of the families, extends along the north coast of Ulster from Co. Antrim to the Inishowen peninsula in north Co. Donegal. With the exception of a few in central Co. Antrim and one in Dublin, all the other McCandless families live in south east Ulster. The area centred on Belfast Lisburn and Antrim has about 11% of all the families in Ireland. It has a third of the McCandless families. The same density of settlement extends into Ards. Co. Down has a sparser settlement.

Greater Dublin has over a fifth of all the families of Ireland. McCandless is virtually unknown there, or in Ireland generally outside Ulster.

Edward MacLysaght's 'The Surnames of Ireland' includes a reference to McCandless but it does not indicate whether it is Scottish or Irish. The high concentration of the name in the Belfast area and its virtual absence from Dublin suggest a surname of Scottish origin.

McCann
2400 families

MacLysaght gives the origin of the surname MacCana as 'cano', meaning wolf hound or wolf cub. He states that the earlier assumption that it was from MacAnna, son of Annadh, is incorrect.

The name is mentioned in the Annals of the Four Masters in 1155 and in 1260. The MacCanns were lords of Clanbrassil. Donnell MacCanna was still styled as Chief of Clanbrassil in 1598. Clanbrassil was a district on the southern shores of Lough Neagh corresponding to the baronies of East and West Oneilland and Middle Dungannon. Abraham Hume's survey of 1857 found that the McCanns of Antrim were concentrated in the barony of Upper Toome, on the north shores of Lough Neagh.

The map shows the distribution of some 2,400 McCann families in 1992. Ten dots represent 1% of the total. The core settlement area completely surrounds Lough Neagh. It may always have done so, though the extent of the build up to the east of the Lough is probably due to the industrialisation there. Families would have moved in for the job opportunities. About 17% of all McCann families live in an area bounded by Belfast, Lurgan and Antrim. This is much more than the national average of 11%. It is a high proportion for a name of Gaelic origin and reflects the local heartland of the McCann sept.

Greater Dublin has likewise exerted an attraction, but at about 16% of McCann families, its attraction has not ben so strong.

Limerick has a rare name Mac Annaidh which has been anglicised as Canny, but which may also be the origin of some of the few McCann families in Munster. McCann is an Ulster name, with 60% of all the families living in its nine counties, the great majority of them in the five counties bordering Lough Neagh.

Carlin
300 families

Carlin is derived from the Gaelic Ó Cairealláin, which is a diminutive of Cairell, or Carol. Ó Cairealláin was chief of the Clan Diarmada, whence comes the name of the parish of Clondermot in Derry. In Donegal, the sept were erenaghs of the church lands of Clonleigh in the barony of Raphoe. The name was first rendered into English as O'Carolan. The medieval ecclesiastical records of Derry and Raphoe contain the names of many priests called O'Carolan.

Another Ulster sept, Ó Cairbhalláin, also produced O'Carolan, together with the English forms Carlan(d) and Carleton. Ó Cairbhalláin is however a separate sept, located chiefly in Cavan and Monaghan, from whence they crossed into the Leinster county of Meath. The celebrated bard Turlough O'Carolan was of this sept.

In modern times Carlin is the usual anglicisation of Ó Cairealláin and Carolan is the usual form of Ó Cairbhalláin.

The map shows the distribution of some 217 Carlin families with telephones in 1992. Allowing for homes without telephones, there were likely to have been 300 families altogether.

Typically of many names in modern times, a high proportion of the families live in the Belfast, Antrim and Lisburn area, which has been a destination for internal migration. About 14% of Carlin families live in this area, well exceeding the national average of 11%. There are a few families in Dublin, Waterford and Cork, which again may be the result of modern work opportunities in urban areas. However, the historic heartland of the sept emerges clearly on the map. About 70% of the families live in Derry, Tyrone and north Donegal. There is a definite concentration in the mid part of this area.

Carlin is very much an Ulster name, with around 90% of all families living there.

Carmody
375 families

Woulfe states that Carmody is an old and well known Thomond surname, derived from Ó Cearmada, descendent of Cearmaid, which is a very ancient Irish personal name. MacLysaght advises that the stress in pronunciation should be on the first syllable, but other than that adds only it is found chiefly in its original habitat, east Clare, and also in Kerry and Limerick.

The map shows the distribution of 202 families with telephones in 1992. As with most families, Greater Dublin is evident in the settlement pattern, but only 13% of the Carmody families live there as compared with the national average of 22%. Apart from the Limerick area, the country's urban centres have had little attraction for the Carmodys.

Thomond approximates to the modern counties of Clare, Limerick and north Kerry. The name is widely distributed in the area. However, there is a break in central Limerick and there is a cluster in Kerry which is more dense than would have been expected from MacLysaght's description. The Kerry cluster, extending slightly into west Limerick, has fully a third of all the families. This area is not one likely to have been a destination for migrants in modern times. Settlement in the area therefore is probably of long standing. It has perhaps been overshadowed by more notable land ownerships or higher profile personalities in east Clare.

The name is rare. Allowing for homes without telephones, there are probably some 375 Carmody families altogether. As 72% of the families live in Clare, Limerick and Kerry, it means that even in these counties Carmody accounts for only one family in 300. In Ireland as a whole, there is only one Carmody family in 4,200. Apart from Dublin, the name is virtually unknown outside Munster, or even outside Thomond.

Carroll
4500 families

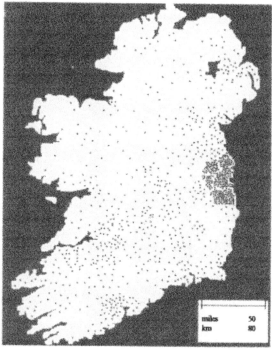

Cearbhall was a very popular Irish personal name. It is the origin of the surnames Ó Cearbhaill and Mac Cearbhaill.

There were several Ó Cearbhaill families, the best known being those of Ely, centred on the Offaly and Tipperary border area, who were descended from a Cearbhall who had fought at Clontarf; those of Oriel, in Monaghan and Louth; those of Lough Lein, around Killarney; those of Ossory, the present Kilkenny; those of Tara; and those of Sligo and Leitrim. As septs, four of the six had disappeared by the end of the thirteenth century, leaving only the O'Carrols of Ely and those of Oriel.

Mac Cearbhaill was the name of a famous family of musicians in Ulster. Some of these were anglicised as Carville, a variant which rarely has the prefix. On the other hand, the McCarrolls were joined by some families called Mac Fhearghail, the 'Fh' and 'gh' being aspirated. Mac Cearbhaill was also found in Leix.

The map shows the distribution of some 4,500 families in Ireland in 1992. Ten dots make up 1% of the total. Its diverse origins make it one of the most evenly distributed names in the country. Carroll families account for 81% of the number; O'Carroll families for 14%; and McCarrolls for 5%. Most of the present day Carroll families are likely to be of O'Carroll origin. Despite the early disappearance of several septs, all the locations with which the name has been associated historically are distinguishable on the map. The presence of the 'O' is likely to be a relatively recent restoration and may have adopted by families that should have a 'Mac'. Comparatively few families in Ulster lack a prefix. McCarroll is almost entirely a name of Northern Ireland.

Representation of the families in Greater Dublin is at about the same level as the national average: 23% live in the area. .

Carson
1050 families

Though it is apparently an English name, Carson does not appear in Reaney's 'A Dictionary of British Surnames'. Black, in 'The Surnames of Scotland' has a long entry, but does not give a meaning for the name. It is an ancient family of Galloway, Scotland, and was found with various spellings: Corsan, Corson, Kersane, as well as de Carsan and Acarson. He says that everything points to it being of native origin. Most of the recorded entries of the name, beginning in the thirteenth century, were in south western Scotland.

The name does not appear in Woulfe's work on Irish surnames, and MacLysaght says only that it is 'A very numerous Scottish name in north Ulster.'

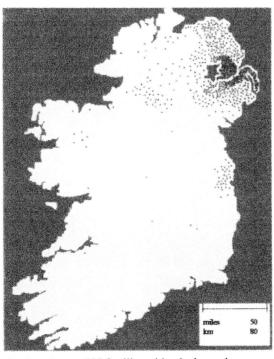

The map shows the distribution of some 775 families with telephones in 1992. Allowing for homes without telephones, there are likely to have been about 1,050 families altogether. The settlement pattern is very definitely Scottish. There is dense settlement in Antrim and Down. It is thinner in Londonderry and Tyrone, and dense again in Fermanagh. The area of greatest concentration is the Belfast, Antrim and Lisburn area, where 36% of Carson families live. The same density is found in the Ards peninsula, where another 8% live.

Northern Ireland has a third of all Irish households. It has 92% of the Carsons. Of the 8% who live in the Republic, half are in Dublin.

McCartan
1200 families

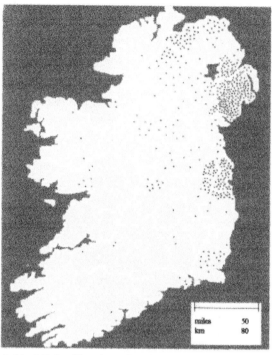

McCartan is from the Irish Mac Artáin, son of Artán, a diminutive of Art. Artán was a grandson of Montán Mac Guinness of Iveagh, in Co. Down. The McCartans were chiefs of Kinelarty in the central part of Co. Down. They were tributary to the O'Neills. Some families have lost the 'Mac' and appear in English as Carton and Cartin, with a few Cartens and Cartans.

Some Cartons have a different origin. Those of the Midlands may be of Ó Cartáin origin. Those of Dublin and Wexford also did not have a 'Mac', the Dublin families having been Huguenots.

The map shows the distribution of some 500 families with telephones in 1992. Allowing for homes without telephones, there are probably 760 families altogether. Some 60% have the 'Mc' prefix. They live mainly in Co. Down and south Antrim. In Cavan and Leitrim, the name is spelt McCartin. Carton and Cartin families, with some other other variants, live mainly mainly in the north of Tyrone, Derry and Antrim, and in the Republic.

The distribution shows the historic McCartan connection with central Co. Down. About a half of all the McCartan families in Ireland live in the county. Many of the remainder live in the now urbanised area in south Antrim.

The Carton distribution is quite distinct. Separate clusters are apparent in Dublin, Wexford, the Midlands and the North. The striking feature of the North is the lack of intermingling with McCartan. The loss of the 'Mac' prefix appears to have been a regional phenomenon. The heartland in south-eastern Ulster has retained the prefix, whilst families in north-western Ulster have dropped it.

Northern Ireland has a third of all Irish families. It has 73% of the McCartans and 29% of the Cartons.

McCarthy
6500 families

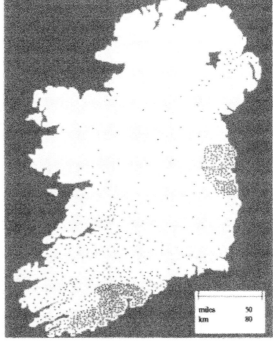

The McCarthys were the chief family of the Eoghanach of Munster, descended from Eoghan Mór, son of a third century King of Munster. They took their surname, Mac Cárthaigh, from Cártac, a lord of the Eoghanach whose tragic death in 1045 was recorded in the Annals. Driven by the Anglo-Norman invasion from Tipperary to the present Cos. Cork and Kerry, the McCarthys remained powerful landowners until the revolution of 1688. They were divided into three main branches, McCarthy More in Kerry; McCarthy Reagh in Carbery; and McCarthy of Muskerry, who built Blarney Castle in 1446.

The map shows the distribution of some 6,500 families in 1992. Each dot represents 0.1% of the total. McCarthy is the most numerous Mac name in Ireland and one of the earliest surnames to be recorded.

Today, about 15% of McCarthy families are resident in Greater Dublin. For many surnames, this would make Dublin the main cluster, but for the McCarthys the present distribution reflects the historic association of the family with Munster. About 40% of them live in Co. Cork, where they make up about 2½% of all families.

Cárthaigh is the Irish for loving. It has also produced the surname Carty elsewhere in Ireland. Equivalent names in the kindred Welsh language are Caradoc and Craddock, familiar in their Latin form Caractacus, from the British Celtic leader who was taken prisoner to Rome around 51 AD.

Carty
560 families

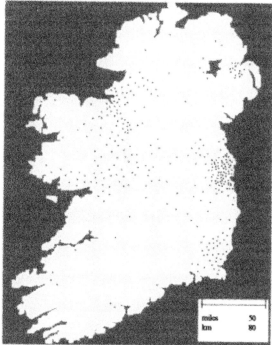

Carty is from the Irish Ó Cárthaigh, descendent of Cárthaich, meaning loving. It is distinct from McCarthy, which has the same derivation. The name is cognate with Caradoc and Craddock in the kindred Welsh language and is familiar in its Latinised form, Caractacus, from the British Celtic chieftain who was taken prisoner to Rome in 51 AD.

Woulfe records the name as being found in Tipperary, Clare and Roscommon, with Roscommon families having extended into Longford, Sligo and Donegal. He states that the name is still common in many parts of Ireland. MacLysaght says that the name is found mainly in Co. Wexford and Connaught.

The map shows the distribution of some 300 families with telephones in 1992. Three per cent of them use the 'Mc' prefix. Allowing for homes without telephones, there are probably 560 families altogether.

The name is virtually unknown in Clare and Tipperary today. In fact, the name is hardly to be found in Munster at all, nor in the neighbouring Co. Kilkenny. This vast area is the home territory of the 7,500 McCarthy families. The impression from the map is that within this area, the Carty name has merged into McCarthy. The pattern that is left to the Cartys is that of an outer arc around the McCarthy core. The greatest density of Carty families is around the famous Loch Cé, on the Roscommon-Sligo border, close to Mayo. This would have been even more so before the Famine.

As the name was originally one with the 'O' prefix, it may be that the small scale adoption of a 'Mac' has been the result of the influence of McCarthy. This has occurred most in Belfast, the most distant part of Ireland from Carty and McCarthy areas and perhaps where local knowledge was weakest.

Northern Ireland has a third of all Irish households. It has only 7% of the Carty families.

McCay
135 families

Edward MacLysaght's 'The Surnames of Ireland' includes McCay as an Ulster variant of MacKay. He states that this is the name of a Scottish clan, some of whom settled in Ulster, and that it is also a synonym for Mac Aodha, the Gaelic for MacHugh. McCoy and McKee derive from the same source.

The MacKays/McCoys were Scottish gallowglasses brought from Kintyre to fight for the MacDonnells of the Glens of Antrim. McCoy is chiefly found in Antrim, Armagh and Monaghan; MacKay in Antrim and McKee in Antrim, Armagh and Down.

The map shows the distribution of some 100 McCay families with

telephones in 1992. Allowing for homes without telephones, there were probably about 135 families altogether. The Belfast, Antrim, Lisburn area has 13% of the McCays, slightly more than the area's average of 11% of all Irish families. This area is not however the centre for the McCays, whose settlement pattern is distinct from that of other Mac Aodha derivatives. It is essentially Counties Derry and Tyrone.

The main Londonderry cluster ends surprisingly abruptly at the border of Co. Donegal. This may be a boundary imposed by spelling, with Donegal rendering Mac Aodha as other variants rather than McCay.

The name is essentially one of Northern Ireland and apparently is more so than other Mac Aodha derivatives. Some 90% or more of McCay families live in the six counties.

Clarke
4900 families

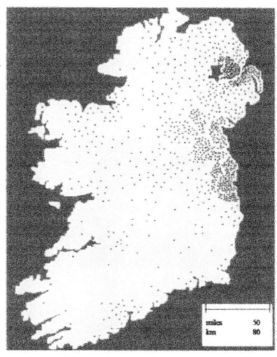

In the Middle Ages all writing was done by the clergy. The Latin 'clericus' therefore came to mean scholar, secretary, recorder or penman. As a surname, it was particularly common for a person who had taken only minor orders. Clarke is its modern English form. In Ireland, the Latin was Gaelicised as 'cléireach', which evolved into the surname O'Clery.

The Plantation of Ulster brought to Ireland many English and lowland Scottish families called Clarke, with some spelling variations. Their numbers were supplemented thereafter both in Ulster and elsewhere in the country by O'Clerys who adopted English forms. As Irish surnames associated with a trade or profession tend in any event to be northern, without a family pedigree or strong family tradition, it is not possible to say whether an Irish Clarke is descended from an O'Clery or a British settler.

The map shows the distribution of some 4,900 families in 1992. Only 3% of them have the spelling 'Clark', the remainder having the final 'e'. Families having the name are more urbanised than Irish families generally. Some 17% of them live in Greater Dublin, compared to the national average of 22%. Some 14% live in the Belfast, Lisburn and Antrim area, compared to a national average of 11%. Most of the families are in eastern counties. The name is not particularly strongly represented in Donegal and Derry, which are the counties historically most associated with the O'Clerys.

Some 37% of the Clarkes and Clarks live in Northern Ireland, slightly more than the national population distribution. Most of the remainder live in the northern half of the island.

McCleary
90 families

McCleary and the alternative spelling of McCleery may be of Irish or Scottish origin. It is common in Scotland where it is derived from the Gaelic Mac an Chleirich, meaning 'son of the clerk'. There were several different families of the name, associated with the clans Campbell, Cameron, Mackintosh and Macpherson. In Ulster, particularly in counties Cavan and Monaghan, there was the name Mac an Chléirigh. This has the same meaning as the Scottish form and it also became McCleary. A northern location is typical of names derived from people in holy orders or from saints' names. In addition, a branch of the O'Haras of Sligo, called Mac Giolla Arraith, anglicised as McAleary, migrated with the O'Haras to Co. Antrim, where they adopted the form McCleary.

There are forms of the name in which the 'Mac' prefix has been dropped. This is true of Cavan, where however the origin may be either McCleary or the Irish O'Cleary without its 'O' prefix. Many McClearys, Clearys and O'Clearys became Clark or Clarke.

The map shows the distribution of some 64 families with telephones in 1992. Allowing for homes without telephones, there are probably 90 families altogether. Most of them live in a cluster extending from Belfast Lough to Portadown. Over two-thirds live in the Belfast, Lisburn and Antrim area, which has 11% of all Irish families. The strength of the McClearys in this area suggests a predominantly Scottish origin. Though McCleary is used as the citation form of the name by authorities on Irish surnames, the variant McCleery is slightly more numerous, with about 95 families overall. The McCleery distribution is much the same as McCleary, but it is even more concentrated around Belfast, Lisburn and Antrim.

McClelland
700 families

McClelland in Gaelic was Mac Gille Fhaoláin, 'son of the devotee of (St) Fillan. It is recorded as numerous in Galloway, in south western Scotland, from the end of the fourteenth century. Its original anglicised form was McLellan.

Sir Robert McClelland of Kirkcudbrightshire was one of the nine Scottish chief undertakers of the plantation of Ulster. His first grant of land was in Donegal, but he sold his property there in 1616. He settled in former O'Neill lands in Down to which he brought many of his McClelland relatives as tenants. He leased lands in Derry which he administered from his castle at Ballycastle in Co. Antrim.

The map shows the distribution of some 521 families with telephones in 1992. Allowing for homes without telephones, there were likely to have been 700 families altogether. The density of the families shows the historic settlement of the clan. About 29% of the families lived in the Belfast, Antrim and Lisburn area. This is almost three times the national average of 11% and confirms the Scottish origin. Ards is settled at the same density. Armagh has a greater density than either north Antrim or Derry.

The name is unknown in Donegal. There are a few families in the other Ulster counties in the Republic, Monaghan and Cavan. Dublin has had only a weak attraction on the McClellands. Greater Dublin has over 20% of all Irish families. It has only 3% of the McClellands.

MacLysaght records an Irish Gaelic sept of the same name derivation, Mac Giolla Fhaoláin, which was based in Co. Sligo. He thought the sept was extinct. The map shows there are no McClelland families in Co. Sligo today.

Clifford
650 families

Clifford is a surname derived from an English place-name meaning ford by the steep bank. It did not necessarily mean the 'cliff' in the modern sense. It is a common surname in England but does not appear in Black's 'Surnames of Scotland'.
   Though the name was recorded in Ireland from the Anglo-Norman period, the first Cliffords permanently resident in Ireland were Elizabethan settlers in Co. Sligo. Unusually for such settlers, the family became Catholic. This family was the only one of the name in Ireland in the 'census' of 1659, but it appears to have had little influence on the numbers and distribution of Clifford families in Ireland at the present day.
   The map shows the

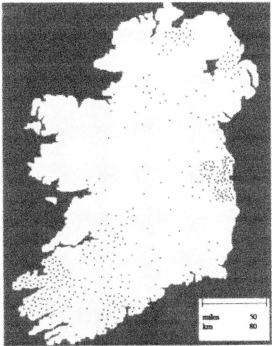

settlement pattern made up by some 435 Clifford families with telephones in 1992. Allowing for homes without telephones, there were likely to have been about 650 families altogether. Sligo has very few, and these may be a dispersal of later English settlers. The Ulster Plantation has had an influence. A greater proportion of the families live around Londonderry (5% of families) than around Belfast (4%). Fermanagh stands out strongly (2½%). Nevertheless, Northern Ireland as a whole accounts for only 14% of the families.
   The reason for this is the adoption of Clifford as an anglicisation of their name by the Ó Clumháin (O'Clovane, O'Cluvane) families of Munster. Half of all the Clifford families live in Munster. Co. Kerry alone has a quarter of all the Cliffords. Greater Dublin has just over a fifth of all Irish families. It has only 16% of the Cliffords, a lower proportion probably explained by the remoteness of Kerry from the Republic's capital. There was an Ó Clumháin sept in Sligo, but this has not survived.

Cochrane
510 families

This surname is derived from a place-name near Paisley, Renfrewshire, now Cochrane but previously spelt as Coueran. The name means 'red brook'. It was first recorded as a surname in 1262 with Waldeve de Coueran. The Cochranes were a sept of the Clan Donald. In Scotland the name was adopted by the Highland MacEacherens when they migrated to the Lowlands.

The name became common in Ulster from the early seventeenth century. It was adopted as an anglicisation in Co. Fermanagh by some of the Ó Corcráin, or Corcoran families. (Corcair means crimson).

The map shows the distribution of some 380 families with telephones in Ireland in 1992. Only three of them have the spelling Cochran, all in Dublin. Allowing for homes without telephones, there are likely to be about 510 families altogether.

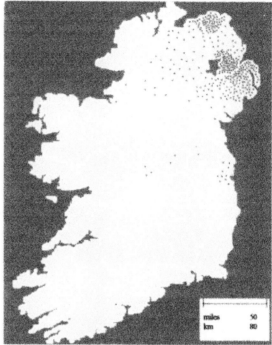

The distribution is unusual in that the Belfast, Antrim and Lisburn area does not have the greatest percentage of families with the name. Some 29% live in the area compared with a national average of 11%, but the cluster in north Antrim has more at 31%. However, the Belfast cluster extends into Ards and central and south Co. Down so that the south east Ulster cluster remains the more populous.

The density of families living in Fermanagh is not sufficient to indicate a sept of separate origin. Those living in the county may be there as a result of dispersal from Co. Down.

Northern Ireland has about a third of all Irish households. It has 90% of the Cochranes. Greater Dublin has over a fifth of all Irish families. Only 5% of the Cochranes live there.

Collins
3900 families

The modern surname is derived from coileán or cuileán, a young dog, by way of the Irish surnames Ó Coileán and Ó Cuileáin. Dogs were highly prized animals in early historic times. Versions of words for them appear in several Irish surnames. The word Cú, hound, appears in the names of many legendary heroes, notably Cú Chulainn.

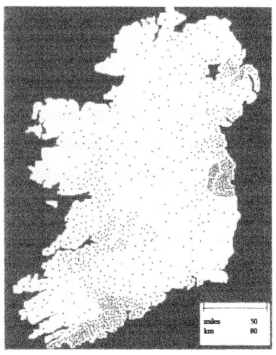

There were distinct families of Ó Cuileáin in Cork, Galway, Tyrone and Tipperary, and perhaps also in Clare and Sligo.

The principal sept was the Ó Coileáns of south west Limerick, who were lords of the baronies of Upper and Lower Connello and of Claonghlas. The Geraldines expelled them, first from Connello in 1178, and from Claonghlas about a century later. The main part of the clan moved to west Cork, near the territory held by their kinsmen, the O'Donovans. The local Ó Cuileáin sept there would have merged with them.

The map shows the distribution of Collins families in 1992. Each dot represents 0.1% of the total. The various septs have given the Collins name a wide distribution throughout the country. At 3,900, Collins has the same numerical strength as FitzGerald. Though both are mainly south western, each has a distinctive settlement pattern. Collins families are still well represented in the original Ó Coileán heartland in Co. Limerick, but there is a marked concentration in Co. Cork, where they make up almost 1% of all households. As with many families today, Greater Dublin is a prominent cluster. Some 16% of Collins families live there.

Northern Ireland has a third of all Irish households. It has about 13% of Collins families.

McComb
375 families

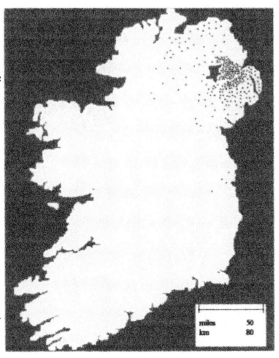

McComb today is the most numerous form of the Gaelic MacThom, son of Thomas. It is accepted that names of Scriptural origin were amongst those brought to Ireland by the Anglo-Normans. Surnames based upon Scriptural names, however, appear to be overwhelmingly northern, a part of Ireland least affected by the Anglo-Normans. Whether Scriptural or native, the North appears to be the area where most saints' names are based. Even McBride, from the native St Brigid, is northern, though the cult of the saint was centred in mid Leinster.

MacLysaght gives McComb as a branch or sept of the Scottish clan MacKinnon. This clan name derives from MacFhionghuin or MacFhionnghain, fair born, and was closely associated with Iona. The religious connection may account for the Scriptural Thom(as) being used as a family name. In Gaelic, consonants becoming aspirated lose their normal sound, so MacThom became McCom. The 'b' was introduced in the late seventeenth century. Forty percent of the families now also have a final 'e'.

There are in addition some variants of the name. The 's' of Thomas is most evident in McComish, and there are also a few McCombs and one or two McComas families. A form 'Tommy' has produced McCombie.

The map shows the distribution of 276 McComb and McCombe families with telephones in 1992. Allowing for homes without phones, there are likely to be 375 families altogether. Four fifths of them live in the Belfast area, four times the national average, a proportion which confirms the Scottish connection. Though as MacCom and MacCome it appeared in the 16th century in Sligo, Leitrim and Louth, only 4% of McCombs today are found in the Republic.

Thomas has also produced the surnames Thom(p)son and Holmes, though the English Holmes has a different origin.

McConnell
600 families

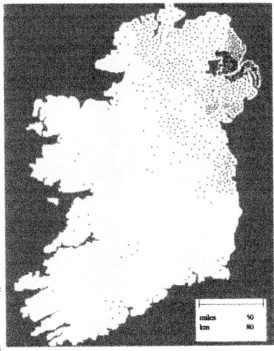

The Gaelic MacDhomhnall, meaning son of Daniel, is by far the most important source of the surname McConnell. The name is of Scottish origin. It is a sept of the McDonnells who are the Glens of Antrim branch of the Clan Donald. The 'h' after the 'D' of MacDhomhnall made the 'D' silent so that the name sounded like Mac'onnell. This pronunciation was sometimes retained in the spoken language when a written form of McDonnell was in use. The other source of the name was MacConaill, from Conall, an ancient personal name cognate with the Welsh Cynvall and the British Cunovalos, meaning high ruler. This origin is very rare. In addition, some families of the Oriel sept of MacCannon or MacConnon anglicised to McConnell.

The map shows the distribution of some 1,400 families in Ireland in 1992. Ten dots represent 1% of the total. Some 27% of the families live in the Belfast, Lurgan and Antrim area. This is more than twice the national average and is indicative of the Scottish origin. The cluster of dense settlement extends from this core along the east coast of Antrim and into the Ards Peninsula of Down and accommodates 40% of all the McConnells in Ireland. A further 32% live in the remainder of Northern Ireland. Many of the families in the Republic live either in the three Ulster counties in the Republic or in north Leinster.

Greater Dublin is now the most important location for many Irish families. Over a fifth of all Irish families live there. The area has only 6% of the McConnells, a reflection of the importance of Belfast to this Ulster name.

The number of families of McConnell origin has been reduced by the loss some who abandonned the initial 'Mac'. The extent to which this has happened nationally is not clear because many O'Connell and Ó Conail, families, who are centred in Munster, also lost their prefix and became Connell.

O'Connor
10700 families

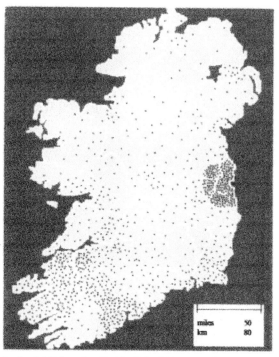

In Irish Ó Conchobhair or Ó Conchúir, the map shows the distribution of some 10,700 families in 1992. One dot represents 0.1% of the total. There were six septs, from Ulster through Connaught and Offaly to Clare and Kerry.

The Connaught septs derive their name from Conchobhar, a King of Connaught who died in 971. He was of a long line of Kings who needed to be champions to maintain their position, champion being the meaning of the name. O'Connor Don of Connaught was the last High King of Ireland. The Connaught branches of O'Connor Roe and O'Connor Sligo have since faded out. O'Connor Faly was descended from Conchobhar, son of Fionn, lord of Offaly, who died in 979. O'Connor of Corcomroe in north Clare was descended from a Conchobhar who died on 1002. O'Connor Kerry ruled an extensive area known as Iraghticonor, and was chief of the O'Connors of Munster until the Norman invasion.

The O'Connor Keenaght sept of Ulster are said to be descended from the third century King of Munster, Oilioll Olum, who was an ancestor of many Gaelic families. This sept largely disappeared after a war with the O'Kanes. Only 4% of O'Connor families live in Northern Ireland.

Though the urbanised areas of Dublin and Cork are now important settlement clusters, the areas of the country historically associated with the O'Connor name are, with the exception of Ulster, still apparent by their density of settlement. About 15% of O'Connor families live in Co. Kerry, where they make up about 5% of all families. Over a quarter of them live in greater Dublin, where they represent almost 1% of all families.

Families of the name have to a great extent either retained or restored the prefix. Only 8% of the families shown have the name Connor. A further 2% have Connors.

McConville
580 families

McConville is a well known Ulster surname. The Gaelic Mac Conmhaoil, son of Conmhaol, has been rendered also as McConwell, a spelling form now almost obsolete. MacLysaght indicates that the name is mainly found in Counties Armagh, Down and Louth.

Six McConvilles in Co. Down are recorded as having been attainted with loss of their lands after the defeat of King James II in 1690.

The map shows the distribution of some 423 McConville families with telephones in 1992. Allowing for homes without telephones, there would probably have been about 580 families altogether.

The settlement pattern is distinctive. The McConvilles live at greatest density on the border between Armagh and Down. Like the McAteers, their main cluster does not extend into Co. Louth. It ends abruptly along what is now the border between the Republic of Ireland and the United Kingdom.

The Belfast, Antrim and Lisburn area has 11% of the population of Ireland. McConvilles strength in the area is also 11%. This is a low proportion in view of the proximity of the McConville heartland to Belfast. It is possibly explained by the Irish Gaelic origin of the families.

Greater Dublin has over a fifth of all Irish families, but only 6% of McConville families live there. A few families live between Dublin and the Northern Ireland border and a few live in Co. Cork. Overall, only 17% live in the Republic.

The name is rare. In part this may be due to its meaning, son of Conmhaol, or high chief. In part it may be because names of this ancient type in the northern third of the island have given ground over the years to surnames based on the names of saints or on trade names.

Copeland
210 families

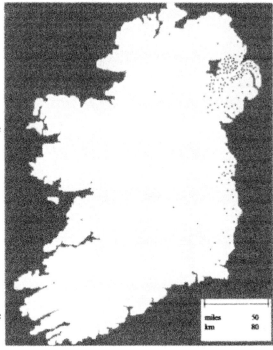

The most probable origin of the surname Copeland is the Cumbria place-name of the same spelling which is derived from the Old Norse 'Kaupaland'. This means 'purchased' land, as compared with 'othalsjorth', which is land acquired by law. Copeland is the district wherein is located Whitehaven, a small port now but which once rivalled Bristol. Copeland is situated due east of the Ulster coast. Another possibility is the Northumberland place-name of Coupland in Kirk Newton, whence came many of the Scottish families called Copeland.

MacLysaght's 'More Irish Families' includes the name amongst those of English origin present in Ireland at the time of the 1659 census, though not numerous enough to be counted as 'principal names'. The map shows the distribution of some 155 families with telephones in Ireland in 1992. Allowing for homes without telephones, there would have been about 210 families altogether. The name is very much concentrated in and around Belfast and in the Ards peninsula. The Belfast, Lisburn and Antrim area has a third of the families. This is three times the national average and is indicative of Protestant settlement. Ards has 7%, and 23% live in east Down and adjacent parts of Armagh.

Greater Dublin has over a fifth of all Irish families. It has 11% of the Copelands, which is quite high for an Ulster family. Another 7% live on the Munster coastal area south of Dublin. This may be accounted for by the plantation in Wexford made by King James I.

Copeland remains very much an Ulster surname. Northern Ireland has a third of all Irish families. It has three quarters of the Copeland families.

Corrigan
1100 families

According to Woulfe, Ó Corragáin means descendent of Carragán, a diminutive of Corra, a widespread personal name. MacLysaght considers it as one sept, primarily belonging to Fermanagh. He notes it as being widely scattered as early as the sixteenth century, when it appeared in localities as far apart as Offaly, Roscommon, Meath and Monaghan. There is a place-name, Ballycorrigan, near Nenagh, north Tipperary, indicating that a leading Corrigan family was seated there not later than the middle of the 17th century.

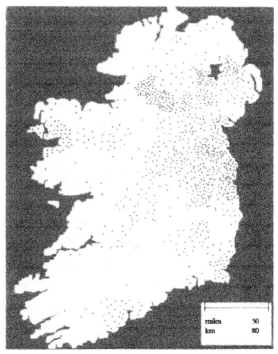

The map shows the distribution of some 1,100 Corrigan families in 1992. One dot represents 0.1% of the total. About 9% of the families live in Fermanagh, where they make up almost 1% of the population. In addition to Offaly, Roscommon, Meath Monaghan and north Tipperary, there are prominent clusters of the family in Carlow, Cork, Kildare, Mayo and Wexford.

About 18% of the families live in Greater Dublin, whilst only 4% live in the Belfast area. Northern Ireland has a third of all Irish households. About 27% of the Corrigans live there.

MacLysaght sees the sept as of the same stock as the Maguires. There is a similarity in the representation of the two names in Fermanagh. Some 10% of the 3,700 family strong Maguires live there, where they make up 2½% of the population. Elsewhere, however, the two distributions are very different. The Maguires are much more heavily represented in Dublin and Belfast, and apart from those areas are strong only in Cavan and Meath. About 29% of them live in Northern Ireland.

Costello
1800 families

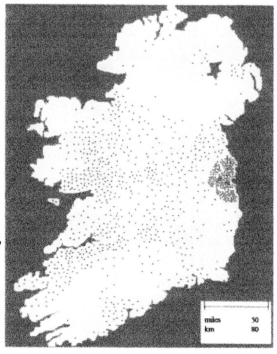

The first reference to the forebears of the Costellos was in the Annals of the Four Masters in 1193. They were called the sons of Oisdealb, himself a son of Gilbert de Nangle, or de Angulos, a pre-eminent Anglo-Norman. So was produced the surname Mac Oisdealbh, later Mac Oisdealbhaigh. It was also written Mac Goisdealbh, Mac Goisdealbhaigh and Mac Coistealbhaigh.

Woulfe says that Oisdealb means shaped like the god Os. MacLysaght cites Curtis' view that the eponymous ancestor was Gocelin (Jocelin). In English, it became MacCostello. It is the first recorded instance of an Anglo-Norman family adopting a Mac name. The prefix however was soon entirely dropped, so that the barony called after the family was Costello. They retained control there to the end of the 16th century. The county boundaries put most of the barony in Mayo with a smaller part in Roscommon. In 1565, the chief seat was in Ballaghadereen in what is now Roscommon.

There are many tales of the feuds between the Costellos and their neighbours the MacDermots, based at Coolavin. The saga has its own Romeo and Juliet in the 17th century persons of Thomas Costello, baron of Costello, and Una, daughter of MacDermot, Prince of Coolavin. They lie in adjoining graves beside the ruined church on Trinity Island in Loch Cé.

The map shows the distribution of some 1,850 families in 1992, including 17% with the spelling Costelloe. Ten dots make up 1% of the total. The pattern is typically Anglo-Norman, though much weaker along the south coast than many such names. Well over a quarter of the families live in Greater Dublin. Before the Famine, their density in north Connaught would probably have been much the same as the south of the province.

Northern Ireland has a third of all Irish households. It has under 3% of the Costellos.

Cowan
450 families

Cowan may be of Scottish or Irish origin. In Scotland. The name is common throughout the Lowlands of Scotland, especially Ayrshire and Dumfriesshire. There, many of the name Colquhoun (pronounced Cahoon), adopted Cowan. Families were also found in Fife and Argyllshire. The name derives ultimately from St. Comgan either directly, or, especially in the south of the Highlands, from Mac Gille Chomgháin, 'son of the servant of (St) Comgan'.

The Irish origin is from the Ulster name of MacCoan or MacCone, in Irish MacComhdháin. These names were very numerous in Armagh in the seventeenth century, as shown in the Hearth Money Rolls and elsewhere. Where the name occurs in Connaught, it may be assumed to be a substitute for Coyne or Coen. This substitution is now rare.

To a large extent MacCowan has been absorbed by McKeown. It is an example of a less familiar surname being absorbed by a more familiar one. The 'dominant' name need not be the more common. The Donegal name of O'Dermond was completely replaced by the better known McDermot. Cowan nevertheless continues to survive.

The map shows the distribution of some 320 families with telephones in 1992. Allowing for homes without telephones, there are about 450 families altogether. Northern Ireland has a third of all Irish families. It has three quarters of the Cowans. Almost a third of them live in the Belfast, Lisburn and Antrim area, which is three times the national average. Greater Dublin, which for many families today is the most important location, has only 14% of the Cowans.

The Cowans are much more concentrated than the McKeowns, half of whose 2,300 families live in Northern Ireland; 23% live in the Belfast, Lisburn and Antrim area; and 20% in Greater Dublin.

Crowe
900 families

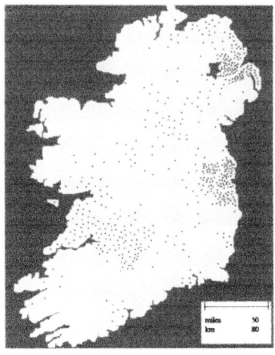

There are several explanations for the surname Crowe in Ireland. Woulfe derives it from Mac Conchradha, son of Conchradh, a rare Irish personal name. This was first rendered in anglicised form as MacEnchroe, which is the name used on the transportation certificates of the 1650s. Reaney has Crowe as an English surname from 'crow' from the twelfth century. For the Isle of Man and Ireland, he has it as a translation of Mac Fiacháin, son of the crow. Black has it from the place-name Croy in Inverness, Scotland.

MacLysaght says that the great majority of Crowe families in Ireland are of MacEnchroe origin, from Thomond, the modern Cos. Clare, Limerick and Tipperary. The sept there was subordinate to that of O'Dea. He considers the considerable numbers in the Belfast area to be of British planted stock.

The map shows the distribution of some 530 families with telephones in Ireland in 1992. Allowing for homes without telephones, there are likely to have been 900 families altogether. About a quarter of the families lived in Greater Dublin. This was slightly more than the national average of 22%. It reflects internal migration in relatively recent times. About 10% of the families lived in the Belfast, Lisburn, Antrim area. This was much the same as the national average and too high a proportion to be explained by families of Thomond origin. The strength of representation in the Ards Peninsula and the coast of Co. Antrim confirms a British and probably Scottish origin for Northern Ireland. A third of all Irish families lived in the North. About 23% of all Crowe families lived there.

Apart from the historic concentrations in eastern Ulster and Thomond, there is a cluster centred on Co. Cavan. Families in this area may be there as a result of Stuart Plantations, or they may be Reaney's Mac Fiacháins, for whom he does not give a location within the country.

McCullough
1350 families

The Ulster Gaelic Mac Cú Uladh or Mac Con Uladh, which mean 'Son of the Hound of Ulster', produced the present spelling McCullough and other variants. The name is also Scottish. It may represent Scottish settlers in Ulster whose own forebears were from Ulster. Another explanation is Scottish Gaelic Mac Cullaich, 'Son of the Boar'. In Ulster, about one third use the 'agh' ending and most of the remainder use 'ough'. McCullow and McCulloch are also found, amongst others.

In Petty's 'census' of 1659, MacCullough was listed as one of the 'principal Irish names' in several Co. Antrim baronies. However, many of the families must have been Scottish.

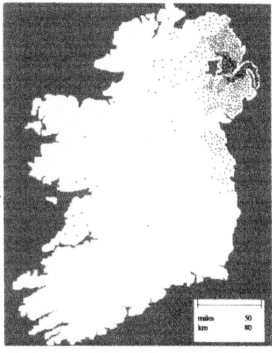

The map shows the distribution of some 1,350 McCullough families in 1992. Ten dots represent 1% of the total. The families are concentrated in Cos. Antrim, Down and Armagh, an area corresponding to the historic Uladh. Outside this area, there is a sparse representation in Co. Tyrone. There is an unexpected absence of McCulloughs in the north of Co. Louth. It may be that one of the other spelling variants was adopted there. The name becomes strong again in the south of Co. Louth and adjacent parts of Meath. There is a thin scatter of families in Cos. Clare and Galway.

Greater Dublin has a fifth of all Irish families. It has only 2% of the McCulloughs. The strength in the Belfast, Antrim and Lisburn area is almost four times the national average at 41%. Another 14% of the families live in Ards. Northern Ireland has a third of all Irish families. It has 94% of the McCulloughs.

Daly
4500 families

Ó Dalaigh is derived from Dálach, meaning someone who holds or frequents an assembly, or dáil. Daly families are descended from Maine, a son of Niáll of the Nine Hostages, and are of the southern Uí Néill. The territory of the parent sept was located in what became the barony of Magheradernon, Co. Westmeath. They progressed to achieve pre-eminence throughout Ireland as a bardic family.

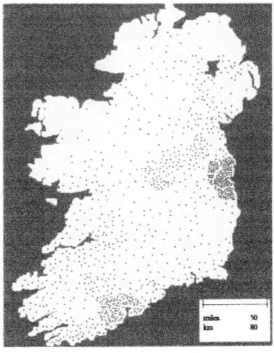

The first to become famous for his learning was CuChonnacht na scoile, who died in 1139. Thereafter poetry became a profession for the Dalys. The most famous was Donogh Mór O'Daly, the Irish Ovid, whose death was recorded in 1244, and who was first in a line of poets in north Clare. Some of Donogh's family settled in Burren, where they became poets to the O'Loghlens. In the latter part of the fifteenth century some of them went on to settle in Úi Maine, modern Galway and Roscommon. Another branch settled in Cavan and became poets to the O'Reillys. Other branches became poets to the O'Neills, and to the O'Connors of Connaught. Ragnall Ó Dalaigh had settled in Desmond in the twelfth century and became chief poet to McCarthy. Diarmuid Og O'Daly was made official poet to the McCarthys of west Cork, and thereby acquired lands in the barony of Carbery.

The map shows the distribution of 4,450 Daly families in 1992. One dot represents 0.1% of the total. As with most families, the main cluster today is Greater Dublin. About 19% of Dalys are resident there, compared to 22% of all Irish families. Cos. Westmeath and Cork, the principal areas with which they have been associated historically, are apparent by greater density of settlement. The county in which the Dalys make up the greatest proportion of the population is Westmeath, where they are over 1%.

The Dalys are not numerous in northern parts of the country. Only 6% of them live in Northern Ireland, as compared to 31% of all Irish families.

Davison
420 families

Davison means 'son of Davy', a pet form of David, which also produced Davis and Davies. In Ireland these names and Davidson stem overwhelmingly from the northern Scottish Clan Davidson. Dawson and Mac Daid were also Davidson septs. The clan descends from David Dhu, fourth son of Muiriach of Kingussie, Chief of the Clan Chattan. As such, it was an important part of the Clan Chattan federation. The main families were of Cantray in Inverness-shire and of Tulloch in Perthshire.

In addition to the Clan Davidson, there were two other origins of Davison and Davidson. One was the Clann Dáidh, a much less numerous Scottish riding clan of the border area of Roxburgh. The other was the Donegal sept of Mac Daibhéid. Though most of these families become (Mac) Davitt or (Mac) Devitt, some, in Donegal, Derry, and Tyrone, were anglicised as Davison.

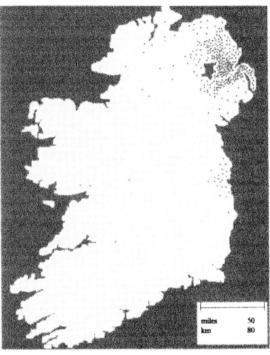

The map shows the distribution of some 316 Davison families with telephones in 1992. Allowing for homes without telephones, there were likely to have been about 420 families altogether. A third of the families live in the Belfast, Antrim and Lisburn area, three times the average representation. This is evidence of the Scottish origin of the name. Further, the core cluster extends outwards at the same density into the Ards peninsula, and at almost the same density to the south and north of Lough Neagh. Settlement in the Glens of Antrim is slightly less dense.

Families in the west of Ulster may be outliers of the main Clan Davidson cluster, or they may represent Donegal origin Mac Daibhéid families. In either case, they are very few. Typically of a Scottish origin surname, Greater Dublin has not been attractive to the Davisons. The Republic's capital has 22% of all the families in Ireland. It has only 6% of the Davisons.

Northern Ireland has a third of all Irish families. It has 90% of the Davisons.

Delaney
2100 families

A topographical riddle is posed by the Irish surname Ó Dubhshláine. In English it means 'descendant of black of the Slaney'. The map shows clearly the present day heartland of the Delaneys. It corresponds closely with a river catchment area, but it is not that of the Slaney. The main Delaney cluster, Dublin apart, is around the Barrow and Nore river system, which extends from Slieve Bloom south to the sea. Delaneys have been associated with this area throughout recorded history. Perhaps, in an era before records began, those already living around the Barrow and Nore rivers called people moving in from the south east after the territory the newcomers had left behind.

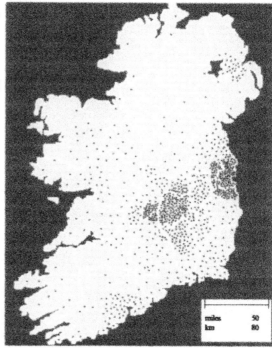

The map shows the distribution of 2,100 families in 1992. Each dot represents 0.1% of the total. Internal migration in modern times has made Greater Dublin the principal location for many Irish surnames. The Republic's capital area accommodates 22% of the population of Ireland. Delaney families, typically of those of Leinster, are more strongly represented. Some 26% of them now live there.

The Delaneys make up the greatest proportion of the population in the area where they have their historic links. Some 15% of them live in Co. Leix, where they account for 1½% of the population. They are probably at the same strength in adjacent parts of Co. Offaly, and they are at half of it in Co. Kilkenny.

Delaney is a name where the 'O' prefix has not been restored. Except in Northern Ireland, a sizeable minority of the families use the spelling Delany, probably slightly more so in Dublin than in the heartland.

Northern Ireland has about a third of all the households in Ireland. Only 3% of Delaney families live there.

McDermot
1850 families

McDermot families may be of one of two origins. Of much the longer standing are the McDermots of Connacht. Their head is an authentic chieftain, entitled to be called The MacDermot. The family is descended from Diarmaid, grandson of Tadhg O'Connor, an 11th century King of Connacht. In the mid 14th century they divided into two main septs. That having precedence, headed by The MacDermot, is at Coolavin, with a fortress at the Rock of Lough Cé, near Boyle, Co. Roscommon. The other, that of MacDermot Roe (Red), is at Kilronan, Co. Galway.

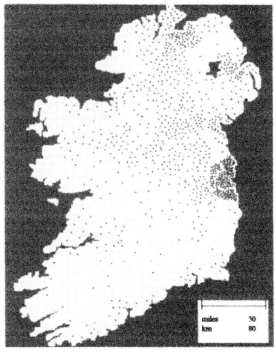

The name Dermot derives from 'di' meaning without, and 'airmit' meaning injunction, giving the name the sense of 'free man'.

The map shows the distribution of some 1,850 families in 1992. Ten dots make up 1% of the total. About 24% of the families live in Greater Dublin, as compared with the national average of 22% Another third live in the rest of Leinster, Munster and Connacht. A further third live in the nine counties of Ulster. Only 4% live in the Belfast area.

The story of the second family to take the name is necessary to explain this distribution. The reason why Ulster has a third of all McDermot families is that Ó Duibhdhiorma, meaning descendant of the black trooper, often shortened to Ó Diorma and in English O'Dermond, a name not now in use, was anglicised as MacDermot. The family were once lords of Bredach in Inishowen. Being a family of Cinel Eoghain, the clan name of the O'Neills who were based in Tyrone and parts of Derry, it may be that the anglicisation of O'Dermond extended to families in southern and western Ulster and possibly into Leinster. It is not possible from the map to distinguish between these families and the original MacDermots.

Devine
2000 families

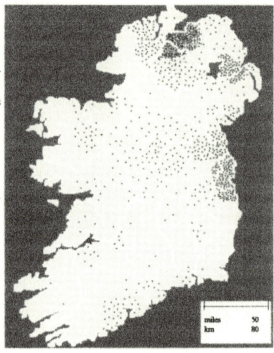

Many old Irish names were inspired by a quality associated with an animal or bird. In Irish Devine is Ó Daimhín, from damh, an ox or stag. It is not from dámh, a poet. The O'Devines and the Maguires were septs founded by Cormac, a son of Cairbre Dam Argait, King of Oriel. The O'Devines took their name from Daimhín, Cormac's brother, who died 966. They were lords of Tirkennedy, Fermanagh and a leading sept of the county until the 15th century, when the power of the leading family was broken by the O'Neills to their north and the Maguires to their south.

The map shows the distribution of some 1,000 families in Ireland in 1992. Ten dots make up 1% of the total. A small number of Devin families, from the same source, are included, a spelling found mostly around Drogheda. About 40 families with a spelling Davin, a variant found in southern Connaught and scattered across the south east of Ireland, are not included.

The Devine settlement pattern is unusual. Whether a result of the 15th century power struggle or for some other reason, Fermanagh is almost depopulated of Devine families, as is southern Donegal and most of Monaghan. There is a break in the distribution across southern Ulster, from the west coast almost to the east.

There is a heavy concentration of Devine families in a cluster in north Tyrone and north Derry, where over a quarter of them live. Another 12% live in the adjacent parts of Donegal, south Tyrone and south Derry. This means that Devines are under represented in the Belfast, Lisburn and Antrim area, at 8% as compared to the national average of 11%, and also in Greater Dublin, at 12% against 22%.

About a third of all Irish families live in Northern Ireland. Some 48% of the Devines live there.

McDevitt
420 families

The Gaelic Mac Daibhéid, son of David, has been anglicised as McDaid and McDevitt. Some families have lost the 'Mac' to become Davitt and Devitt.

The principal sept was of Inishowen, where their ancestor was David O'Doherty, a chief of Cenél Eoghain, who died in 1208. MacLysaght says that MacDaids and MacDevitts are numerous in Co. Donegal and adjacent parts of Derry and Tyrone, but are seldom found elsewhere; and that MacDaids outnumber MacDevitts by three to one.

The map shows the distribution of 295 families with telephones in 1992. Allowing for homes without telephones, there will be about 420 families altogether. Some 40% of the families which do not have the prefix. Neither form is numerous. Typically for a surname deriving from a saint's or Biblical name, McDevitt is northern.

The McDevitts accord with the description given by MacLysaght, except that Inishowen in north Donegal is almost devoid of McDevitt families. The cluster extends from west Donegal through north Tyrone to north Derry. There has been some dispersal beyond this area, but only 7% of McDevitts live in the Belfast, Antrim, Lisburn area, as compared to 11% of all Irish families. Some 14% of them live in Greater Dublin, also well below the national average of Irish families living in that area.

The Devitt distribution differs completely from McDevitt. Over a third of them live in Greater Dublin, well over the national average. This is a large proportion relative to the other cluster extending from west Clare into Tipperary, so that the two may have different origins. The evidence of the map indicates that the Devitts are not northern McDevitts who have lost the 'Mac'. There is no separate discussion of Devitt by MacLysaght or Woulfe.

Doherty
5000 families

Ó Dochertaigh is derived from dochartach which means obstructive. Like their neighbours and rivals the O'Donnells and O'Neills, the Dohertys were descended from the early fifth century Niall of the Nine Hostages. Owners of Inishowen until 1603, their leader did not join the earls of the other two clans in their Flight to Italy in 1607. Cahir O'Doherty stayed on to collaborate, then to defy and die at 21.

The map shows the distribution of some 5,000 families in 1992. Thirteen percent of them have the 'O' prefix, including a a small number who use the Irish form Ó Dochertaigh. Ten dots make up 1% of the total.

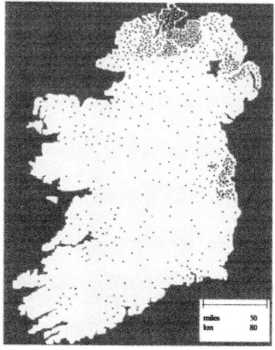

Long associated with Donegal, some 29% of all the families live there, where they make up about 5% of the population. Inishowen, the historic heartland of the sept, has 16% of all Doherty families and remains paramount. South of Inishowen, there is a larger area of slightly less dense settlement on both sides of the border. Greater Dublin, which has 22% of all the families of the island of Ireland, has only 10% of the Dohertys.

The 'O' prefix is generally a twentieth century restoration and is typically urban and southern. Some 31% of families in the Dublin area have the prefix. The few in the Cork area exceed this at 40%. It is only 8% in Northern Ireland. Further north than Northern Ireland, but even so in the Republic, it is only 2% in Inishowen.

Northern Ireland has 31% of all Irish families. It has a third of Dohertys, but only a fifth of the O'Dohertys.

Donaghy
860 families

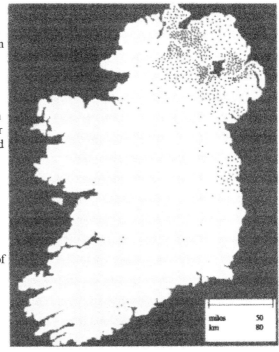

Donaghy is one of several surnames in Ireland and Scotland that have their origin in the personal name Donnchadh, meaning 'brown warrior'. Other derivatives are Duncan, McConaghy, McConkey and McDonagh. There has also been some fusion with names of other origins. Donnchadh in Derry and Tyrone produced MacDonnchaidh, which was first anglicised as MacDonaghy and then Donaghy. In Fermanagh it is said that most Donaghys descend from Donnchadh Ceallach Maguire, who led the Maguire conquest of Clankelly in the mid fifteenth century.

The map shows the distribution of some 624 families with telephones in Ireland in 1992. Allowing for homes without telephones, there will be about 860 families in total. Donaghy has a distinctive settlement pattern. Its core area could be described as Armagh, Tyrone, Derry together with the Inishowen area of north Donegal. With the exception of Inishowen, the boundaries of main Donaghy settlement coincide unusually closely with the county boundaries. The name is also well represented in Antrim and to a lesser extent in Down. Despite the historical association, the name is scarce in Fermanagh. Perhaps the plantations that took place after the fifteenth century caused some reduction in numbers, though the form McDonagh, the variant usual in Connaught, is better known in Fermanagh than Donaghy.

As is usual for an Ulster family, the area centred on Belfast, Lisburn and Antrim has attracted significant numbers of Donaghy families. Some 14% live there, compared to 11% of all Irish families. Only 4% of the families live in Greater Dublin, compared to 22% of all Irish families.

McDonald
2300 families

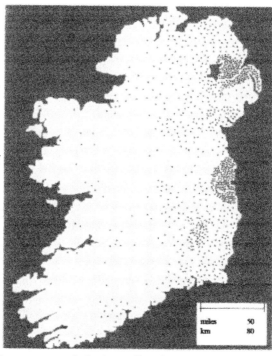

Sumarlidi was the Old Norse for 'summer sailor', a name given to Vikings who arrived in the Isles of what is now western Scotland with the easterly winds of early summer and returned with the prevailing westerlies later in the year. This is the apparent origin of the personal name Somerled, Gaelic Somhairle, of a mid 12th century chief of the Isles. Of the ancient Clann Colla, Somhairle married a daughter of the King of Norway, wrested control from the local Norwegians and became Lord of the Isles. His offspring founded several clans. His grandson, Domhnall or Donald of Islay, founded the clan MacDhomhnuill. McDonald lands in Scotland came within 20 miles of the coast of Ulster. Some of Donald's sons came to Ireland as gallowglasses. As reward the McDonalds obtained estates in Leix and Wicklow and were well established in Leinster by the mid 15th century.

In addition to the McDonalds of the Isles, there were Mac Domhaill septs in Fermanagh and Thomond.

The map shows the distribution of some 2,300 McDonald families in Ireland in 1992. Ten dots represent 1% of the total. The name is numerous throughout Ulster, except Donegal. Some 14% of the families live in the Belfast, Lisburn and Antrim area. The same high density of settlement extends into the Ards Peninsula. Typically of the numerous Leinster names in the present day, a high proportion, about 19%, live in the Greater Dublin area. Perhaps reflecting the maritime connection with the Vikings, families are found all along the east coast, an area of mixed Irish and Norse place-names. Outside Dublin, the main Leinster settlement cluster is in Co. Carlow. The Mac Domhaill septs of Fermanagh and Thomond do not appear to have adopted the form McDonald in significant numbers.

Northern Ireland has about a third of all Irish households. It has 38% of the McDonalds.

O'Donnell
3750 families

Ó Domhnaill has an original meaning of 'world-mighty', a popular name amongst the ancient Gaels, and found also in Donald and MacDonald.

The map shows the distribution of some 3,750 O'Donnell families in 1991. Ten dots on the map represent 1% of the total. As with many families, Dublin is now a most important cluster. This is because of internal migration to the capital and depopulation in much of the rest of the country since the Famine. Remote from Dublin, they are, however, at 13%, much less well represented there than the 22% of Irish families generally. Co. Donegal remains paramount with a quarter of all O'Donnell families being resident there.

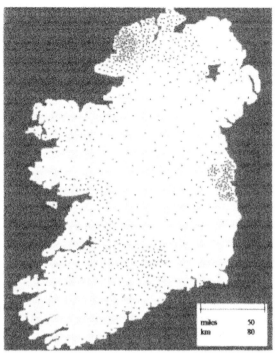

O'Donnell is one of the most famous families in Irish history. The Donegal sept is descended from Niall of the Nine Hostages through his son Conal Gulban, from whom Tyrconnell, the old name for Donegal, takes its name. Though only about 11% of O'Donnell families live in Northern Ireland as compared with 31% of Irish families as a whole, the Northern Ireland border is not reflected in a marked reduction in density.

There are various other historic O'Donnell septs, most notably in Thomond and Uí Maine - approximating to Clare, mid Galway and Roscommon. The name remains well represented in these areas, but no less so today than Co Limerick and south Tipperary.

Donnelly
2000 families

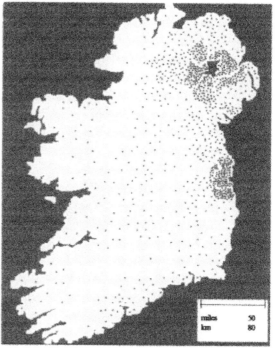

Practically all families with the name Donnelly today may be regarded as of the Ulster sept of Ó Donnghaile of Cinel Eoghan. They derive their name from Donnghaile, fourth in descent from Domhnall, King of Aileach and brother of the Niall who gave his name to the O'Neills.

The O'Donnellys were originally centred at Drumleen, just north of Lifford, Co. Donegal. They were displaced from there by the Cinel Conaill and moved to the eastern part of Co. Tyrone. Ballydonnelly, a settlement 3½ miles west of Dungannon, was called after them. Their chief was hereditary marshall of O'Neill's military forces. One of the most famous of them, Donnell O'Donnelly, died in the service of O'Neill at the battle of Kinsale in 1603. After the 1607 Flight of the Earls, the administrator of the forfeited O'Neill estates, Sir Toby Caulfield, was given Ballydonnelly and renamed it Castlecaulfield.

The map shows the distribution of some 3,000 Donnelly families in 1992. Each dot represents 0.1% of the total. As with many families, there are now more of the name in Greater Dublin than anywhere else - 17% live there. About 12% live in the Belfast, Lisburn and Antrim area, slightly over the national average and a high proportion for a Gaelic Irish surname. The original heartland on the east side of Lough Neagh remains clearly apparent, and it is there that the Donnellys make up the greatest proportion of the population. They are almost 1% of the families of Cos. Tyrone and Antrim. The number of Donnelly families who have restored the 'O' prefix is negligible.

Northern Ireland has a third of all the households of Ireland. It has 51% of the Donnellys.

O'Donovan
3100 families

Donovan is derived from two Gaelic words: 'donn', brown, and 'dubh', black. In modern Irish the name is spelt Ó Donnabháin. The Donovans are one of Ireland's best chronicled families. The eldest branch has a verified pedigree from Gaelic times, when they held a semi-Royal position. Their place of origin is Co. Limerick, whence they were forced to migrate to south west Co. Cork after the arrival of the Anglo-Normans. The 'Chief of the Name' lives in Skibbereen. A branch of the sept settled in Kilkenny and Wexford.

The map shows the distribution of some 3,100 families in Ireland in 1992. Ten dots make up 1% of the total.

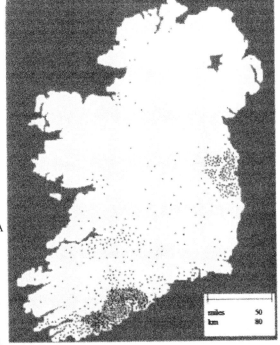

Donovan families are amongst those who have made a significant restoration of the prefix. Referring to 1890s' data, MacLysaght put the proportion of families with the prefix at that time at 2%. A century later, it is three quarters. Often, the urban areas and the south lead the way in the restoration of the prefix. This trend is evident with O'Donovan, except that Dublin remains a stronghold of families without it. It is the families dispersed away from the main south Cork cluster who have not restored the prefix. Families overseas descended from 19th century emigrants also will be unlikely to have it.

With or without the prefix, the name is virtually unknown in Northern Ireland.

Doran
1600 families

Doran is derived from the Irish Ó Deoráin, formerly Ó Deoradháin, from a word for an exile or stranger. It is the name of two families in Ireland, one originally of Co. Leix and one of Co. Down.

Originally one of the Seven Septs of Leix, the Leix family was described as 'the great brehon family of Leinster'. For generations its members were custodians of one of the three manuscript copies of the 'Tripartite Life of Saint Patrick.' Their association with Co. Wexford is recorded from 1540 when they were seated at Chappell. In 1608 they were listed among the principal gentlemen of Co. Wexford, though in the following year leading Leix members were transplanted to Kerry.

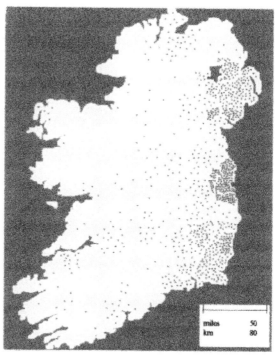

The map shows the distribution of some 1,600 Doran families in 1992. As with most families today, Greater Dublin is the most important location for the Dorans. About 19% of the families live there, as compared to 22% of all families. About 7% live around Belfast, Antrim and Lisburn, lower than the national average, but as such, typical for a Gaelic family.

\there is thin Doran settlement in Leix. This may be a result of the Queens County plantation, or it may be that that social prominence was not accompanied by numbers of people on the ground. The Leinster sept is now clearly centred on Carlow, Kilkenny and Wexford.

There are small settlement clusters around most of the ports: Derry, Cork, Limerick, Galway, and even Belmullet and Westport, which may be explained by economic migration, but the group around Listowel and Tarbert on the Kerry-Limerick border may be a trace of the 17th century transplantation.

Dorans are well represented on both sides of the border, with 28% of them living in Northern Ireland, as compared to about a third of all Irish families.

Doyle
1600 families

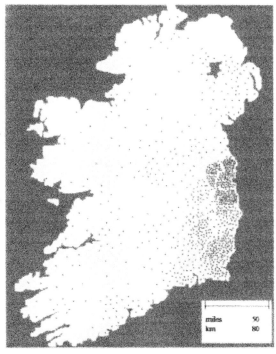

The Irish dubh ghall, dark foreigner, was a name given to Viking settlers, who were recorded as Dubhghall in the Annals between 978 and 1013. They called themselves Ostmen, meaning eastmen. The Scandinavians were not necessarily related to each other, so that by the time surnames came into being in the eleventh and twelfth centuries, it is likely that several distinct families were called Ó Dubhghaill. Their main area of settlement was on the Leinster seaboard, where they had founded Dublin in 841 AD. They were well established long before the Anglo-Norman invasion. MacDugall is a name of the same origin used in Scotland and later introduced to Ireland where it has become McDowell.

The map shows the distribution of some 6,400 Doyle families in 1992. One dot represents 0.1% of the total. Despite some dispersal, the initial area of Scandinavian settlement is still apparent. The first town-dwellers in Ireland, English forms now disguise early place-names. The famous 'Vik-' appears in Wicklow, where 'ló' was the Norse equivalent of the English 'lea'. Vadrefjord, meaning wether (male sheep) inlet became Waterford. Escirfjord became Wexford. (Escir is the Irish for a glacial ridge). The names Leinster, Munster and Ulster were coined by the Ostmen from Irish elements. Dublin was called after the Irish for a black pool in the Liffey.

Greater Dublin is now the main area of settlement for the Doyles, as it is for many families. About 30% of them live there, where they make up almost 1% of the population. The Doyles make up the greatest proportion of the population in east Leinster outside of Dublin. They account for about 3½% of the population of Cos. Wexford and Carlow.

About 7% of the Doyles live in Northern Ireland, as compared with 31% of all Irish families.

Duff
680 families

Dubh is the Gaelic for black, with the sense of black-haired. Woulfe says that it was a description that supplanted the original name, which is now lost. The name occurs in Scotland as well as Ireland. MacLysaght indicates that Duff has no particular location and that MacDuff is Scottish.

According to Woulfe, MacIlduff and MacElduff are variants of Mac Giolla Dhuibh, meaning 'son of the black (haired) youth'. This name was common in several parts of Ireland and also in Scotland. In particular, the name was associated with three families, one centred in Co. Cavan, one in Co. Galway and one in Co. Sligo.

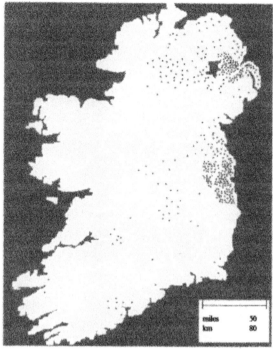

The name may have lost ground by translation to Black. It may have gained by the absorption of some Duffin and Duffy families.

The map shows the distribution of some 420 families with telephones in Ireland in 1992. Allowing for homes without telephones, there were probably 680 families altogether. Some 85% of the families are called Duff or McDuff; 13% are called McElduff and McIlduff accounts for the remaining 2%.

The Duff families are mainly to be found in Cos. Antrim, Down, Louth and Westmeath; and in Greater Dublin. They are also represented in the Midlands. The island's two capital areas stand out. Over a third of the families live in Greater Dublin and 20% live in the area from Antrim through Belfast to Ards. The McDuffs account for only one in a hundred of the combined Duff and MacDuff total and are dispersed rather than clustered. This perhaps suggests a modern restoration of the prefix.

The McElduffs and McIlduffs are clustered and neither is associated with the areas found by Woulfe. The McIlduffs are exclusively Antrim and Down and therefore perhaps of Scottish origin. The McElduffs are predominantly Co. Tyrone families.

Duffy
3600 families

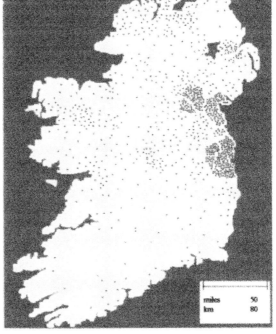

There were several Ó Dubhthaigh families. The Duffys in Donegal were kinsmen of the seventh century St. Dubhtach, and were abbots and priors of the saint's foundation in Raphoe for 800 years. The sept in Connaught provided notable church leaders and was responsible for the famous Cross of Cong. Its territory was close to Strokestown, Co. Roscommon. That centred on Monaghan was notable not so much for its high dignataries, but for the number of parish clergy it provided.

The map shows the distribution of some 3,600 Duffy households in Ireland in 1992. Each dot represents 0.1% of the total.

Duffy is relatively thin on the ground across the country south of the Shannon estuary, and in Ulster in Antrim and south Donegal. This may be because the Irish Ó Dubhthaigh, which means black, probably black-haired, has also been rendered into the English in Munster as Doohig and Duhig, and in Ulster as Doohey or Dowey. In Mayo, families called Ó Doithe, or O'Diff, joined the Ó Dubhthaighs in assuming Duffy as the anglicised form of the name.

As with most surnames, the main present day cluster is in Greater Dublin. This is because the Republic's capital has been a destination for internal migration since the Famine, whilst much of the rest of the country has suffered depopulation. Greater Dublin has 18% of Duffy families, compared to 22% of all families. Duffys have the highest proportion of the population in Co. Monaghan, where they are around 2% of the total.

Some 16% of Duffy families live in Northern Ireland, as compared with 31% of Irish families generally.

Duncan
510 families

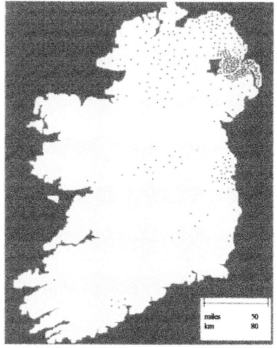

Duncan is a Scottish name derived from the Gaelic Donnchadh. The second part of the name means warrior. The first element probably means 'brown', though 'dun' a word meaning 'fort' is a possibility. The same Gaelic source produced other variants in Scotland, together with Donagh and Donaghy and a number of variants in Ireland, sometimes with a 'Mac'. Some in Ireland adopted Duncan. The name was introduced into England in early times from both Scotland and Ireland.

The map shows the distribution of 364 families with telephones in Ireland in 1992. Allowing for homes without telephones, there were probably 510 families altogether.

Almost a third of the families live in the Belfast, Antrim and Lisburn area, three times the national average. The cluster extends into Ards, where a further 8% live. This concentration is evidence of the pre-eminence of the Scottish origin in the present mix of Duncan families. The settlement extends through all of Ulster with the exception of Cavan and Monaghan.

Greater Dublin in modern times has over a fifth of all Irish families and is now the most important location for many families. It has had little attraction for the Duncans. Only 7% live there.

The name is scarce in the south of Ireland. The few in Cork may be from recent dispersal, but may be from the Irish McDonaghs. Most of these however adopted McCarthy from the strength of that name in the south west. The origin of the Duncan cluster in Westmeath is unclear.

The name is very much one of Ulster. Northern Ireland has a third of all Irish families. It has 65% of the Duncans. Another 9% live in Donegal.

Dunlop
665 families

This surname has its origin as a place-name in the district of Cunningham in the Scottish county of Ayrshire. In Gaelic it is Dùn Làpach, meaning 'muddy hill'. The first record of it as a surname was a Willelmus de Dunlop in 1260. The weak pronunciation of the 'n', which sometimes occurs in Scotland, is evident from the earliest days, as Dunlopp and Dullope appear in the 13th century as alternative spellings for the same person. Delap is therefore established as a long standing variant of the name. Around 1900 Delap was being used interchangeably with Dunlop in parts of Cos. Antrim and Fermanagh.

In the early 17th century Dunlops from the Isle of Arran settled in north Antrim in Ireland. A Bryce or Brian Dunlop married a Stewart of the neighbouring Isle of Bute acquired a grant from the McDonnells of land to the west of Ballycastle on the north Antrim coast.

The map shows the distribution of some 495 families with telephones in 1992. Allowing for homes without telephones, there were likely to have been some 665 families altogether. the name is closely associated with the county of Antrim.

About 35% of the families live in the Belfast, Antrim town and Lisburn area. This is three times the national average and is confirmation of the Scottish origin of the name. Greater Dublin has over a fifth of all the families of Ireland, having been the major centre for internal migration. It has only 3% of the Dunlops.

Londonderry is a county of secondary settlement for the Dunlops. However, John Dunlap, who printed the Declaration of Independence of the United States, was born in Strabane in the county. Perhaps because of his example, the spelling Dunlap is usual in the USA. It is not found in Ireland.

Dunne
4500 families

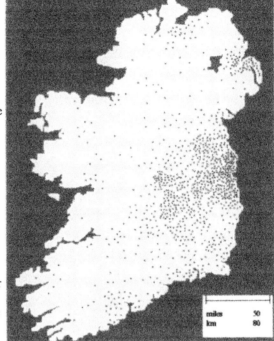

Dunne, descendent of Donn, meaning brown, is associated historically with only two areas of Ireland.

One Ó Duinn family was based at Tara, Co. Meath, and was dispossessed soon after the Anglo-Norman invasion. The head of the other was lord of Ui Riagain, or Iregan, in Co. Leix, an area which was co-extensive with the present barony of Tinnahinch. This family was specially mentioned in mid-sixteenth century official orders as hostile to English interest.

The English language also has a word 'dun', also meaning brown. This became a surname in England. Notably for Irish history, some English families of the name were of the 'riding clans' along the Scottish border, who were broken by James I in 1603. Many went to Ulster.

Northern Ireland normally differs from the Republic in having fewer names with a Mac or O prefix. Though the O has not been restored by a significant proportion of Dunne families on either side of the border, there is a difference in the proportion without the final 'e'. Some 91% of all families live in the Republic, and of these, under 2% have the spelling Dunn. Most of them are in Dublin. By contrast, of the 9% who live in Northern Ireland, almost three-quarters do not have the final 'e'. A 'riding clan' origin may be the explanation.

The map shows the distribution of 4,500 families in 1992, including those with the spelling Dunn. Ten dots represent 1% of the total. As is usual with Leinster families, the main cluster is now Greater Dublin. At 30%, the Dunnes well exceed the national average representation in this area. The area where they constitute the greatest proportion of the population is the area of their historic origin. Dunnes are almost 2% of the families in Co. Leix.

Elder
150 families

MacLysaght considers Elder to be an English name, saying that it has been mainly associated with Cos. Derry and Donegal. The surname signified the elder of two bearing the same forename. It has been recorded in England since the thirteenth century and in Scotland since the fifteenth.

Under his heading of 'Elder', Black refers also to MacNoravaich, from the Gaelic Mac an fhoirbhich, meaning son of the elder. The Gaelic 'foirbheach' means an elder of the church. The 'h' after the 'f' means the 'f' is aspirated to sound as an 'h'. As McGowan, son of the smith, is known to have been been rendered into English as Smith, there must be a possibility that MacNoravaich has been translated into English as 'Elder'. If so it would mean the name is Scottish rather than English.

The map shows the distribution of some 109 households with telephones in 1992. Allowing for homes without telephones, there would be about 150 families altogether. This is a rare name in Ireland.

Rather than Derry and Donegal, the name is mainly found in Antrim and Derry, This settlement pattern could equally suggest a Scottish as an English origin for most of the Elder families

Northern Ireland has a third of all Irish households. It has 80% of Elder households. The few in Donegal bring the proportion in Ulster to 84%. Over half of the families resident in the Republic live in Dublin.

McElroy
940 families

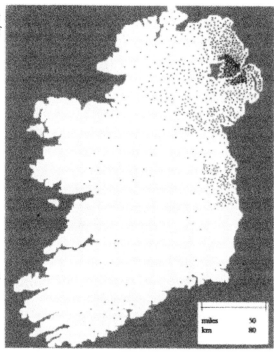

McElroy and McIlroy are considered to be variants of the same name. MacLysaght gives the origin for MacElroy as Mac Giolla Rua, son of the red haired youth. Black gives the origin for both as MacGhille Ruaidh, with the same meaning.

The MacElroy sept originated on the east side of Lough Erne in Co. Fermanagh, where the place-name of Ballymacelroy is found. There is a Ballymackilroy in Co. Tyrone and a Ballymacilroy Co. Antrim. In Scotland the name was first found in Dumfriesshire in the fourteenth century. It has long been associated with Ballantrae, Ayrshire. Many of the Plantation settlers came from these south western counties.

The map shows the distribution of some 940 families in Ireland in 1992. Ten dots make up 1% of the total. The name McElroy accounts for 53%.

Fermanagh and Tyrone are still important counties for the McElroys, but their settlement is at its most dense in Monaghan, Louth and the southern parts of Armagh and Down. McIlroy is much more localised. It is overwhelmingly a name of Co. Antrim and north Co. Down. It is virtually unknown in the Republic. There is an extensive area of overlap of the two variants and possibly there has been some confusion of the two forms, particularly in these localities. There is a clear geographical distinction between the two forms, suggesting that McIlroy was more likely to be of Scottish Gaelic origin. The same polarity is to be found with the much rarer McElduff and McIlduff families.

Just over a fifth of the McElroys live in Greater Dublin Under 1% of the McIlroys lived there. The Belfast, Antrim and Lisburn area has 5% of the McElroys. It has 43% of the McIlroys. Northern Ireland has 38% of the McElroys and 93% of the McIlroys.

English
720 families

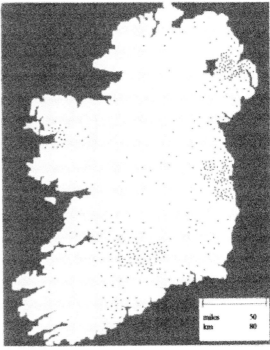

The surname 'English' in England arose to distinguish between English and other races in the country, notably Danes or Normans. In Scotland and Wales it distinguished English from local families.

In Ireland the name has two origins. In the south, found mainly in Tipperary and Limerick, it is Anglo-Norman. It probably served to distinguish its families from fellow Anglo-Norman settlers of French or Welsh origin. In the north, it is a mistranslation of the Irish surname Mac an Gallóglaigh, son of the gallowglass. They were a Donegal sept, later more associated with Tyrone. Not all them adopted 'English'.

There were frequent references to the name in Leinster up to the mid 17th century. Thereafter it became more closely identified with Munster. In the 13th and 14th centuries the name was recorded in variants such as L'Englys, L'Anglys and Lenglais. 'Inglis' is a variant in use today.

The map shows the distribution of some 466 English families with telephones in 1992. Allowing for homes without telephones, there would be about 720 families altogether. In the areas historically associated with the name, there is a cluster in Tipperary and Limerick. This exceeds the 14% in Greater Dublin. A fifth of the families live in Ulster. They are likely to be of Mac an Gallóglaigh origin, as little Anglo-Norman settlement occurred in the province. There is little trace today in either Donegal or Tyrone. Some 11% live in the Belfast, Antrim and Lisburn area, the same as the national average. A further 2% live in neighbouring Ards.

McEvoy
1310 families

Woulfe and MacLysaght give three Irish names as origins of McEvoy.

Mac Giolla Buide, a name of the north west of the country, was normally anglicised as McElwee and McGilloway. Mac a' bhuide was a familiar form of this, and produced McAvoy and McEvoy.

Mac Fhiodhbhuidhe, pronounced Mac-ee-vwee, was a corruption of Mac Fhiodhbhadhaigh, son of Fhiodhadhach, meaning 'of the wood', or 'woodsman'. Chiefs of this sept at first had lands in Westmeath, but there was early settlement in Leix where McEvoy became one of the 'Seven Septs of Leix'. In 1609, leading members of the sept were transported to Co Kerry.

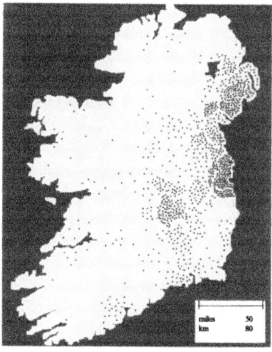

Mac an Bheatha, which produced McVeagh as well as McEvoy, was from a personal name meaning 'son of life'. It was located in Oriel - south east Ulster and Louth areas.

The map shows the distribution of some 1,310 McEvoy families in Ireland in 1992. One dot represents 0.1% of the total. There are few examples of the name in north west Ulster, which indicates that McEvoy was not adopted by significant numbers of the Mac a' Bhuide sept. The heartlands of the other two septs remain evident. Though the Oriel sept is generally considered to have assimilated its name to that of Leix, the McEvoy settlement is less dense in Leix.

In common with most families in modern times, Greater Dublin is now the most important single location. Some 19% of the McEvoys live there. This is close to the 22% national average and may be because both present day McEvoy septs are strongly represented in areas close to the Republic's capital.

Only 4% of the families live in the Belfast area. Gaelic origin names are usually under represented here, but at less than half the national average, this is low in view of the McEvoy strength in Co Down.

McFall
350 families

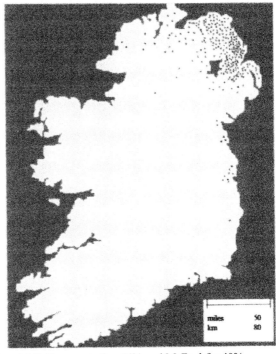

Most of the families in Ulster with the surnames McFall, McFaul and McPhail are of Scottish origin. Their names are derived from the Gaelic Mac Pháil, son of Paul. The exceptions were families called Ó Maolfabhail, meaning descendant of the devotee of (St) Fabhail. Most of these were anglicised as Lavelle, but some, in Inishowen, north Donegal, became McFaul and a few in central Donegal became McPaul. The surname Paul is also found in Ulster, but this is of English origin. A few of the McFaul families have the spelling McFaull.

The map shows the distribution of some 265 families with telephones in 1992. Allowing for homes without phones, there are likely to be about 350 families altogether. McFall accounts for 56% and McFaul for 40%. The remainder are split evenly between the McPauls and the McPhails.

The McFall and McFaul families are intermingled in their core area of Antrim and Derry. It is probable that individual families throughout history will have been recorded inconsistently. However, it is evident that McFall is the preferred spelling in central and south Antrim and north Down including Ards; whereas McFaul is the predominant spelling along Antrim coast and in Derry.

The minority spellings of McPhail and McPaul are on the fringes of the main population cluster. The McPhails are on the east coast and are mainly outside Ulster. The influence of the McFaul spelling in Derry has apparently influenced the anglicisation of the Ó Maolfabhails of Inishowen

McFall in its various forms is very much a name of Northern Ireland. About 90% of all the families live there.

Farrell
4300 families

From the Irish Ó Fearghail, descendent of a man of valour, Farrell became the name of several distinct families. The most prominent of these were the O'Farrells of Annally. Other families of the name were seated in Wicklow and Tyrone.

The chief of the Annally family lived at Longphuirt Ui Fhearghail, or O'Farrell's fortress. The sept maintained its independence until 1565 when Annally was reduced to shire ground by the Lord Deputy. Longford became the name of the town and the county. It suffered from the plantation schemes of James I.

The map shows the distribution of 4,300 families in 1992. Some 14% have the 'O' prefix. Ten dots make up 1% of the total. As with most families today, particularly those of Leinster, the main cluster is in Greater Dublin. Some 28% of the joint total live there, comprising 23% of the Farrells and 35% of the O'Farrells.

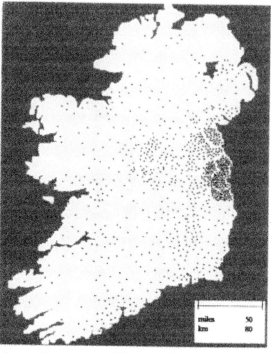

Of the areas with which they are associated historically, the Farrells make up the greatest proportion of the population in Longford. They are 1¼% of the population of the county. The connection with Tyrone is not evident from the modern distribution. The whole of Northern Ireland, which has about a third of all Irish households, has only 7% of Farrell families. The part of Co. Wicklow outside Greater Dublin does not indicate a strong Farrell presence, but Farrell's are almost 1% of the population of neighbouring Co. Carlow.

The distribution of the less numerous O'Farrells has a typical urban and southern bias. Over 50% in Cork have the prefix. In Dublin it is 18%. In Northern Ireland the prefix is rare.

Farrelly
1100 families

Woulfe explains Ó Faircheallaigh as a descendent of Feircheallach, meaning super-war. The family has long been associated with Cos. Cavan and Meath. MacLysaght indicates that in parts of Ulster Farley is used as a synonym of Farrelly, leading to confusion as Farley is a common English name.

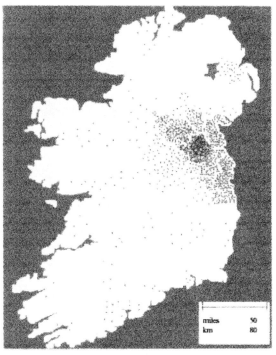

The map shows the distribution of some 1100 Farrelly families in 1992. Ten dots make up 1% of the total. A quarter of the families live in Greater Dublin, as compared to a national average of 22%. The higher than average proportion in the Republic's capital area may be explained by the fact that the traditional heartland of the Farrellys abuts Co. Dublin. Some 4½% of the Farrellys have the prefix 'O', mainly in the West.

There was a second sept in the neighbourhood of Duntryleague in eastern Co. Limerick which Woulfe thought probably extinct. The map shows a continuing Farrelly presence in east Limerick which may be survivors if not recent movers from north east Leinster.

At only about 90 families, the Farley families would make up only 7% of a joint total. The scope for the confusion anticipated by MacLysaght appears likely only in Monaghan. Elsewhere it appears that Farley is a feature of the planted areas. They appear to be rural and have not been proportionately attracted by the urbanisation opportunities of Belfast area, where only 9% of them live. This is less than the national average and low for an English origin name, particularly one whose numbers may have been supplemented by name-change Farrellys. More surprisingly, a quarter of the Farley families live in Greater Dublin and 8% live in Cork.

Intermixture of Farrelly and Farley occurs mainly in Belfast and Monaghan. Belfast is likely to have both names as a result of economic migration in industrial times.

Northern Ireland has about a third of all Irish families. It has only 3% of the Farrellys, but 37% of the Farleys.

Flanagan
2200 families

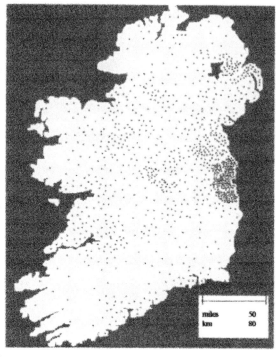

The Irish Ó Flannagáin means descendent of Flannagan, a diminutive of Flann, red. It was the name of at least five distinct families in different parts of Ireland. One of these was around Toorah in the barony of Magheraboy in Co. Fermanagh; another was located in Co. Roscommon around Elphin; a third were lords of Comair and Teffia in Westmeath; a fourth were chiefs of a territory approximating to the barony of Ballybrit of Offaly. The fifth had been based in the north west of Co. Waterford, but were dispossessed by the Powers after the Anglo-Norman invasion.

The map shows the distribution of some 2,200 Flanagan families in 1992. Each dot represents 0.1%. As a result of internal migration since the Famine, Greater Dublin is now the most important location for many Irish families. Some 22% of all Irish families live in the Republic's capital area. The same percentage of the Flanagans lives there. The name is widespread throughout the country. Long associated with the name, the counties of Fermanagh, Roscommon, Offaly and Westmeath are still apparent by the density of Flanagan settlement, but only in Roscommon do Flanagans approach 1% of the total population.

At about 6%, those having retained or restored the prefix 'O', or who use the Irish form Ó Flannagáin, are not shown separately. Their predominantly urban and southern distribution is a usual feature of names using the prefix. Half of them are in Dublin. Virtually all the families in the Republic have the spelling Flanagan. Those in Northern Ireland have a significant proportion of variations, but none have the prefix.

Northern Ireland has a third of all Irish households. It has about 16% of the Flanagans.

Fleming
1750 families

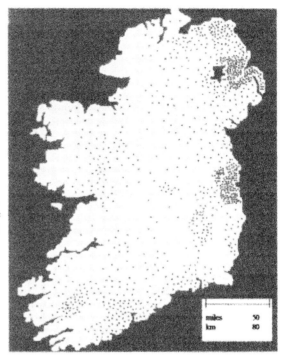

Towards the end of the eleventh century parts of Flanders were lost to flooding by the sea. Many families moved to England where they were allowed to settle on the Scottish border. The name Fleming thereafter has been chiefly associated with Scotland, though shortly afterwards some were moved by Henry I and settled along the coast of South Wales.

Families from South Wales entered Ireland with the Norman invasion and acquired estates, notably in Meath. Fleming appears amongst the names of prominent churchmen, one having been Archbishop of Armagh in the fifteenth century and one Archbishop of Dublin in the seventeenth. Christopher Fleming, Lord Slane, held the castle of Slane in the seventeenth century, but the family's support of the Stuart cause led to their ruin.

The map shows the distribution of some 1,750 families called Fleming in Ireland in 1992. Typically of an Anglo-Norman name, there is a swathe of settlement along the south coast and a strong representation in Connacht. There is a pronounced cluster in Carlow.

About 14% of Fleming families live in the Greater Dublin area, which is slightly less than the national average.

The distribution shows a feature which is not typical of Anglo-Norman settlement. Fleming also has a strong representation in Northern Ireland. A third of the families live there, which is the same proportion as of Irish households as a whole. This is a consequence of settlement from Scotland as part of the Plantation of Ulster.

Flynn
5250 families

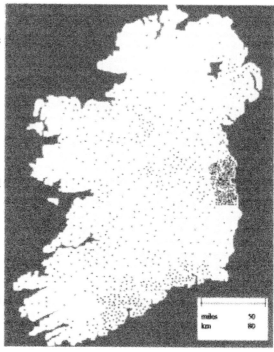

The surname Ó Flionn appeared in several parts of Ireland from the Gaelic personal name Flann, meaning ruddy. The map shows the distribution of 5,250 families in 1992. About 15% of them have the 'O' prefix. Ten dots make up 1% of the total.

The distribution brings out the two main areas associated historically with the name: Cork and Waterford; and Cavan, Leitrim and Roscommon. There is another prominent cluster in Westmeath.

The distributions of Flynn and O'Flynn are distinctly different. The most striking feature of the Flynns is their concentration in Greater Dublin. A third of them live there, putting them in the same league as notable east Leinster families such as Byrne, Reilly and Doyle. The national average proportion of 22%. At around 0.5% of all families, the Flynns have the same strength in Greater Dublin that they have in Cos Cork and Westmeath. They account for the greatest proportion of the total population in Leitrim, where they are about 1¾%.

Greater Dublin usually has a higher proportion of surnames with the 'O' prefix than elsewhere. O'Flynns are unusual in that the proportion is only 12%. Some 58% of the O'Flynns live in Co Cork, where an exceptional 60% of families have the prefix: O'Flynns outnumber Flynns by 3 : 2 in the county.

Flynn and O'Flynn are not the only Ó Flionn derivatives. An Ulster sept accounts for 7% of them. Ulster Irish aspirated the initial 'F', so that the surnames Lynn and O'Lynn emerged. This form of the name is mainly but not exclusively Ulster. It extends down the east coast to Dublin, and there is a separate cluster, amounting to about 8% of the Lynns and O'Lynns, in north Mayo and Sligo.

Foran
440 families

Woulfe gives the Irish origin of Foran as Ó Fuarráin and Ó Fuartháin, meaning descendent of Fuarrán or Fuarthán, diminutive of fuar, cold. The first anglicisation was O'Forhane. It subsequently became Foran and sometimes, especially in Cork, Ford or Forde, though this name has a different origin. The name first appeared in Waterford and occurred in sixteenth century records also in Leinster. It is associated historically with Waterford, Cork, Kerry and Limerick. MacLysaght says that Forhan and Fourhane are still extant between Millstreet, Cork, and Killarney, Kerry.

The map shows the distribution of some 238 families with telephones in 1992. Allowing for homes without phones, there were probably 440 Foran families altogether. Some 46% of Forans who now live in Greater Dublin. This is double the national average percentage. The source of this high proportion may be the cluster of families just east of the capital, around the borders of Meath, Offaly and Kildare, for whom a movement to the capital would have been a minor matter.

Whilst the Forans of Leinster are inland of Dublin, the distribution of the families in Munster is coastal. There are gaps either side of Cork. That between Cork and Kerry would, according to MacLysaght, be bridged by Forhan and Fourhane families. In 1992 however, there were no such families in the area with entries in the telephone directories. If the families were coastal, it may be that it was the adoption of Ford/Forde that caused the break, and that the present families in Cork and Kinsale are more recent incomers from Kerry or Waterford.

Foran families have hardly any representation outside Munster and Leinster. There are none in Northern Ireland and indeed none in the nine counties of Ulster altogether,

Gallagher
5000 families

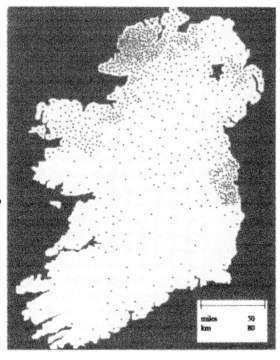

The surname Ó Gallchobair, or Gallagher, implies descent from Gallchobhar, who was himself descended from Maolchobha, a King of Ireland in the early seventh century. Gallchobhar means foreign help. Gallaghers claim to be the senior and most royal of the Cineal Connaill. Their territory extended over a wide area of what became the baronies of Raphoe and Tirhugh. From the fourteenth to the sixteenth centuries Gallagher chiefs were notable as marshals of O'Donnell's military forces. Several Gallaghers became bishops of Raphoe and Derry.

Gallagher is the least numerous but the oldest of the three principal surnames implying foreigner, the others being Doyle (dark foreigner, or Scandinavian), and Walsh (Welshman). It is the most concentrated of the three in its original heartland, probably because of its claim to a single ancestor.

The map shows the distribution of 5,000 Gallagher families in 1992. One dot represents 0.1% of the total. From an area remote from the two conurbations, the Gallaghers are less urbanised than Irish families as a whole. Unusually, Dublin is not the main cluster of the clan: only 12% live in Greater Dublin, as compared with 22% of all families; and only 4% live in the Belfast, Lisburn, Antrim area, as compared with 11% of all families. Almost a third of Gallagher families live in Co. Donegal, where they make up nearly 5% of the population. They are strongly represented also in Mayo and Sligo, where they make up about 1½% of the population.

Northern Ireland, has about a third of all Irish households. Despite the strength of the Gallagher representation in Donegal, only a sixth of Gallagher families live in the six counties.

Gannon
950 families

Gannon is the anglicised form of the Irish Mag Fhionnáin. The aspirated 'f' accounts for the 'Mag' rather than 'Mac', and the meaning is from fionn, fair. Historically, the name has been most associated with Erris, in Co. Mayo. MacGannon also appeared in west Clare, where it originated in as Mag Canann, a variant of Mac Canann, meaning son of Cano or Cana, a whelp, or wolf.

The map shows as green dots the distribution of some 513 Gannon families with telephones in 1992. About 2% have the 'Mac' prefix. The name is rare. Allowing for homes without phones, there are probably about 960 families, which means that Gannons in Ireland account for only one family in 1,600.

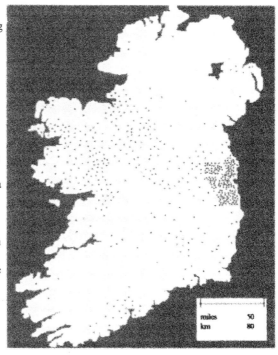

Erris does not appear strongly on the map, though Co. Mayo is, after Dublin, the home county of more Gannon families than elsewhere in the country. One in eight live there, where they make up one family in 275. However, it is in Leitrim where Gannons are relatively most numerous, at one family in 190. In Roscommon they have the same strength as in Mayo.

These counties have suffered severe depopulation since the Famine. In 1991, Co. Mayo had only 28% of its 1841 population. Roscommon and Leitrim have been worse affected, retaining only 20% and 16% of their 1841 populations. Gannon families therefore originated in areas particularly at risk from depopulation. This probably explains why over a quarter of them now live in Greater Dublin.

The presence of the name in south Leinster and around Cork is not subject to comment by MacLysaght or Woulfe. The dispersal suggests long-standing settlement rather than a destination for recent movers.

Garland
210 families

In Ireland Garland is a synonym of Gernon. The Gernons of Gernonstown, Co. Meath and of Killincoole Castle, Co. Louth, are descended from Roger de Gernon, who accompanied Strongbow in the Anglo-Norman invasion of 1172. The consistent use of the 'de' with Gernon suggests that Gernon was a place-name in France. Many other Anglo-Norman surnames in Ireland are more properly 'le'. The transition from Gernon to Garlan is curious, but the subsequent addition of a final 'd' is not unusual.

The map shows the distribution of some 150 families with telephones in Ireland in 1992. Allowing for homes without telephones means there are about 210 families altogether. Eighty-seven percent of the families now have the name Garland. The remainder retain the spelling Gernon.

As with many Irish surnames, Greater Dublin stands out as the most important location today. A third of all the families live there, a proportion which exceeds the 22% national average. The area historically associated with the name also stands out: the border area of Louth, Meath and Monaghan. Here the Gernon spelling accounts for half of the families.

The Belfast area has a quarter of the families, none of which has the Gernon spelling. This proportion is more than double the national average of 11% and is high for an Anglo-Norman name. An intermixture of Garland families of English extraction may account for it. There is an English surname Garland which had two sources. One was from a maker of garlands, which were then circlets for the head adorned with gold or silver rather than flowers. The other was from gore-land, Old English 'gara land', or land of triangular shape.

Northern Ireland has a third of all Irish families. It has the same proportion of the Garlands.

McGarvey
240 families

McGarvey, Gaelic Mac Gairbhith, is almost entirely an Ulster surname. MacLysaght has it as a Donegal name. It is seldom abbreviated to Garvey, families of which name usually being from the distinct septs of O'Garvey, Ó Gairbhith, of Co. Armagh and Co. Down. Both names are derived from 'garbh', meaning rough.

The map shows the distribution of some 166 families with telephones in 1992. Allowing for homes without telephones, there are likely to have been about 240 families altogether at that date.

The distribution is unusual. Co. Donegal less important than would have been expected. It has about 27% of the families. Co. Derry is important, but the main cluster there is not along the Donegal border, but quite separate around the Maghera/Cookstown area. This is the area of densest settlement. The name is also well represented in Co. Tyrone which has 17% of the families.

About 11% of the families live in Belfast, which is the same as the national average. Greater Dublin, which has over a fifth of all Irish families, has only 6% of the McGarveys.

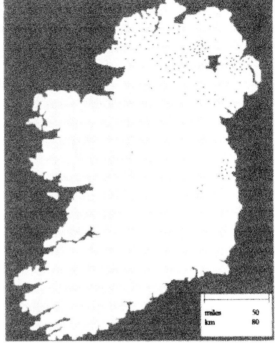

McGee
825 families

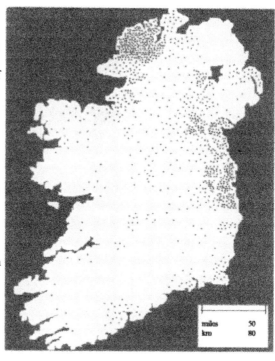

McGee is derived from the Gaelic Mag Aoidha, meaning son of Hugh. It is also derived, particularly in Donegal, from Mac Gaoithe, of the wind, which became Mac Geehee and by translation, Wynne. It is equivalent to the Welsh Gwynn. The McGees historically belong to the country on the borders of Cos. Donegal and Tyrone.

Mag Aoidha has also produced Magee and McGhee. These are families of Scottish origin and are akin to the MacDonnells. They claim descent from Colla Uais, which makes them also ultimately Irish. They are associated with Co. Antrim, where the large isthmus to the east of Lough Larne was once in their possession and is still called Island Magee.

The map shows the distribution of some 825 McGee families in 1992. Ten dots represent 1% of the total. Donegal is much more densely settled than Tyrone and may be taken to be the core area of the McGees. A third of them live there. There is a secondary cluster in Louth and Cavan, extending to Lough Neagh along the Armagh-Tyrone border. Settlement is thin in the east of Ulster. The Belfast, Lisburn and Antrim area has only 2% of the McGees, compared to 11% of Irish families as a whole. On the other hand, Greater Dublin has 14% of the McGees. Beyond these main settlement areas, there are clusters of McGees throughout the Republic.

The McGee distribution differs markedly from that of the 1,570 Magees. Because of the strength in Donegal, the Republic has 86% of McGee families. It has only 26% of the Magees. Most of those are in the Ulster counties of Cavan, Monaghan and Donegal. Some 28% of the Magees live in the Belfast, Antrim and Lisburn area alone. Apart from some families in Dublin, Kildare and Cork, there is hardly any Magee representation in the Republic.

Geoghegan
770 families

Geoghegan is from the Irish Mag Eochagáin, from Eochaidh, a once common Christian name rendered in English as Oghy.

The Geoghegans are not numerous. The map shows the distribution of some 423 families with telephones in 1992. Adjusting for homes without phones, there are probably about 770 families altogether. This is about one Irish family in 2,000. In common with many Leinster families, the Geoghegans have more than average representation in nearby Dublin. Over 40% live there.

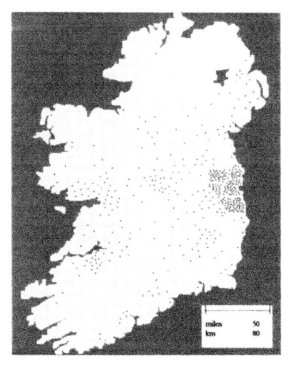

Woulfe and MacLysaght speak in terms of only one sept: the Mageoghegans, who are of the southern Ui Neill and of the stock of the famous sixth century King Niall of the Nine Hostages. The seat of the Chief was near Kilbeggan in Co. Westmeath and various branches of the family held extensive estates in the county. The most important was Castletown, now called Castletown-Geoghegan. The family suffered through warfare and confiscation during the seventeenth century, when most of their estates were lost and their owners outlawed. Members of the family in Westmeath subsequently became Jacobites, and some saw service on the Continent, especially France.

In the course of the confiscations, a branch of the family was transplanted to Galway. The Galway cluster shown on the map is large in relation to that centred on Westmeath, perhaps indicating of the severity of the confiscations. Kilbeggan and Castletown-Geoghegan are now on the eastern edge of the Westmeath cluster. There is a Geoghegan presence in Kildare and Carlow. This now seems separate, but it may once have been joined to Westmeath. The cluster in Limerick suggests either a separate sept, or another migration.

The name is associated mainly with the central parts of the country. A third of Ireland's households live in Northern Ireland, but only 3% of Geoghegans live there.

Geraghty
1070 families

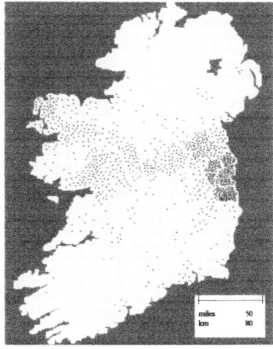

The original surname of this Irish family was Ó Roduibh. Towards the end of the 12th century descendants of Oireachtach Ó Roduibh adopted Mag Oireachtaigh. Oireachtach means a member of a court or assembly. The name produced several derivatives, of which Geraghty accounts for about 80%. The family is of the same stock as the O'Connors, though its settlement pattern is very different from that of the ten times more numerous O'Connors. MacGeraghty was one of four provincial chiefs of Connaught under O Connor Don. They were chiefs of Muinntear Roduibh, Co Roscommon until dispossessed in the mid 16th century. Branches of the family have long been settled in Leinster.

The map shows the distribution of some 1,070 families in 1992. Ten dots represent 1% of the total. A few, in Sligo, retain the 'Mc' prefix. There is a large and continous cluster of families across the country from Belmullet to Dublin, with little representation outside it. In common with most families in modern times, Greater Dublin is now the most important location. About 40% of the families live there. This is a high concentration which for the most part may be explained by the severity of depopulation caused by the Famine in Roscommon and Connaught generally.

The numbers within the cluster would be reinforced with the addition of another 135 and maybe more families with a variety of spellings such as Garty, Garrity, Gearty and Gerety. More than half of these retain the Mc, typically mainly those in Dublin. McGarrity is from Mag Aireachtaigh, an older form of the name, which is found mainly in eastern Ulster. The cluster would be extended into Northern Ireland with the inclusion of the 125 Garrity families there, of whom three quarters have the Mc.

Dublin has about a third of the families of whatever spelling form.

FitzGerald
3900 families

The FitzGerald families of Ireland are said to be descendants of Maurice, son (French 'fils') of Gerald, an Anglo-Norman Constable of Pembroke, South Wales, who accompanied Strongbow in his invasion of 1169.

In 1176, Strongbow rewarded Maurice with the manor of Maynooth, Co. Kildare. The family centred in Kildare became the senior of the two FitzGerald families in Ireland. The other, in Munster, was headed by the Earls of Desmond.

The Desmonds were destroyed as a great family in the sixteenth century. All that remains of their tradition are the knighthoods of Glin and Kerry, created for his sons by Earl John FitzGerald in 1333 under delegated royal powers, and

unique in being hereditary. The family and titles of the Maynooth branch survived to the present day.

The map shows the distribution of the 3,900 FitzGerald families in 1992. Each dot represents 0.1% of the total. As with most surnames, the most important cluster is now in Greater Dublin. About 19% of FitzGeralds live in this area, which accommodates about 22% of Irish families generally.

Despite the more mixed fortunes of the house of Desmond, the FitzGerald name is much more a feature of the south west of Ireland, where Glin and Kerry are located, than it is of Kildare. FitzGeralds are not strongly represented in that county. They have their greatest representation in Cos. Kerry, Limerick and Clare, where they make up about 1¼% of the population.

Typically of Anglo-Norman surnames, there are few FitzGeralds in the northern half of the country. Northern Ireland has a third of all Irish households. It has under 3% of the FitzGeralds.

McGimpsey
70 families

This surname has essentially the same meaning as the much more numerous Dempsey. Both are derived from 'diomsach', meaning proud. In Gaelic, Dempsey is Ó Diomsaigh, whereas McGimpsey is Mac Dhiomsaigh. The 'h' means that the 'D' is aspirated, which would give a pronunciation of Mag Himsey. The 'p' is intrusive, as with Dempsey. There are now no McGimpsey families in the Irish telephone directories without the 'p'. The only spelling variant is McGimpsy, in Newtownards.

MacGimpsy is the citation form of the name in Black's 'Surnames of Scotland'. It appears in a variety of spelling variants, being first recorded in 1529 in Kirkcudbrightshire. The heartland of the name in Ireland and the fact that a man called MacGimpsey was one of the heroes of the defence of Derry in 1689 suggests that the name is of Scottish origin.

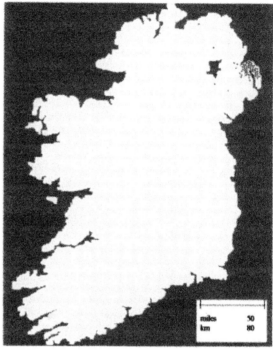

The map shows the distribution of some 54 households called McGimpsey in 1992. Allowing for homes without telephones, there were likely to have been about 70 families altogether. The families form a cluster at the northern end of Strangford Lough in Co. Down. This area often features in the distribution of Scottish origin names, usually also with strong representation in the Belfast area. The Belfast, Antrim and Lisburn area has about 11% of all Irish families. McGimpsey representation there is only at this level, which is surprising given its proximity.

There has been some dispersal westwards into the rest of Northern Ireland, but the name is unknown in the Republic.

Given
110 families

This rare surname has traditionally been associated with northern Ulster, especially the Glenties area of Co. Donegal. Formerly spelt Giveen, it is derived from the Irish Mag Dhuibhín. The 'ín' is a diminutive. The nominative form of the root word is 'Dubh', meaning black. 'Dhuibh' is a genitive, meaning 'of black'. Mag Dhuibhín therefore means 'son of Little Black'. The genitive makes the initial 'D' aspirated rather than pronounced. This means that the normal 'Mac' may become 'Mag' as has happened with this surname. Over time the name pronounced 'M'g hiveen' has become Given. The Mac form persisted, notably in Donegal and Sligo, giving rise to the names McAvin and McKevin, but these appear not to have survived. Present day variants are Givens, Givan and Givans. A terminal 's' is popular with English names, particularly short ones, and English influence in Ulster is likely to account for these variants.

The map shows the distribution of some 78 Given households with telephones in 1992. Allowing for homes without telephones, there are likely to have been about 110 families altogether.

About 12% of the families live in the Belfast, Antrim and Lisburn area, which is about the same as the national average. Greater Dublin has about 22% of all Irish households. In common with other Donegal families, its attraction for Given families has been weak. Only 5% live in the Republic's capital area. Northern Ireland has about a third of all Irish families. It has two thirds of the Given families. Most of the remainder are in Donegal.

Glennon
400 families

Mag Leannáin is a name derived from a diminutive of 'leann', meaning cloak. MacLysaht indicates that the name belongs to the Midland counties, Westmeath, Leix and Offaly. In Co. Roscommon it is probably the Uí Fiachrach name Ó Gloinín, which was absorbed either by the Glennons or the Glynns.

In the 1659 'Census', Glennon was recorded in Westmeath and Roscommon.

The map shows the distribution of some 217 families with telephones in Ireland in 1992. Allowing for homes without telephones, there were probably 400 families altogether. Of the total, 94% had the name Glennon; 3% were Glennane, 2% McGlennon and 1% Glenane. The families with the prefix may well have resumed it relatively recently.

The Glennon settlement runs in a band across the centre of the country with little representation outside it. The name extends further west than is indicated by MacLysaght. About an eighth of the families live in C. Galway. The pattern is similar to that of the 2½ times more numerous Geraghtys, except that their distribution extends into Mayo. The Geraghtys also have only a few families with the prefix.

Almost 40% of the Glennon families lived in the Greater Dublin area. This is the same proportion of the Geraghtys. It is a high concentration. The explanation for both may be the severity of depopulation caused by the Famine in Roscommon and the West generally.

Northern Ireland has about a third of all Irish households. It has only a tenth of this proportion of the Glennons.

McGonagle
510 families

McGonagle, McGonigal and McGonigle are some of the spelling variants derived from the Irish Mac Congail. MacLysaght notes the long standing association of Mac Congail with Co. Donegal and the adjacent parts of Co. Derry. Neither he nor Woulfe provide a meaning for the name.

Some of the sept were followers of O'Donnell, but theys have been most notable for their ecclesiastical connections. MacLysaght has them as erenaghs of Killagtee, Co. Donegal, but Robert Bell says this as an error, with their church being at Killibegs.

The map shows the distribution of some 349 families with telephones in 1992. Allowing for homes without telephones, there were probably 510 families altogether. Inishowen stands out as the most important area for the sept, with the adjacent part of Co. Derry being next most important. Belfast and the Greater Dublin are less important to McGonagle families than to most families. The Belfast, Antrim and Lisburn area has 11% of all Irish families. It has only 7½% of the McGonagles. Greater Dublin has 22% of Irish families, but only 9% of the McGonagles.

Apart from Dublin, there are very few McGonagle families in the Republic.

The spelling McGonigal is very rare. Of the 349 families with the name in all spellings, it accounts for only 8% of those in Dublin. It accounts for only 7% of those in Northern Ireland. It is not found in Co. Donegal or the rest of Ireland.

Gorman
2300 families

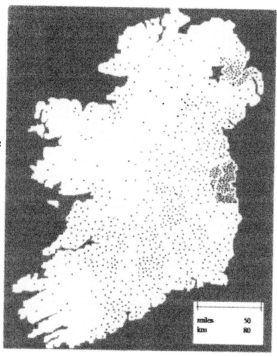

The name in Irish is Mac Gormáin, derived from 'gorm', blue. Originally the sept occupied the barony of Slievemargy in Co. Leix, but they were driven by the Normans to Clare and Monaghan. There are 12 townlands called Gormanstown or Gormanston across the centre of the country from Dublin to Limerick.

Gorman is the famous example of a surname, which, having lost its Gaelic prefix at the days of suppression, put back the wrong one after the restoration of national consciousness. The person probably chiefly responsible for the substitution of 'O' for 'Mac' was the celebrated 18th century Thomas O'Gorman, an exiled vineyard owner in France. Edward MacLysaght, who often used data from the late 19th century, found that Clare was mainly O'Gorman and Tipperary was Gorman.

The map shows the distribution of some 2,300 families in 1992. Ten dots make up 1% of the total. Only 2% remain McGorman, and these are strongest in north Monaghan. O'Gormans now account for 53% of the families, and Gorman 45%. The 1992 picture shows that the 'restoration' of the 'O' has continued since the time of MacLysaght's data. Tipperary is now also O'Gorman country.

About 18% of all the families live in the Dublin area.

Only 13% of the families live in Northern Ireland with 5% living in the Belfast area. The 'O' prefix is still uncommon amongst the families that live in the North: some 78% of the sept's families are Gorman, whilst O'Gorman has 16% and MacGorman 6%.

McGourty
70 families

In his notes to the 'Four Masters', O'Donovan places the MacDarcy sept in the parish of Oughteragh, in what is now Co. Leitrim, under the date 1310. In the 'Annals of Loch Cé', MacDarcy appears as the name of a Co. Leitrim chieftain in the years 1384 and 1410. In Irish, the name is Irish MacDhorchaidh, from dorca, meaning dark.

There were two septs of Ó Dorchaidhe, in Mayo and Galway, which were anglicised as Darcy, sometimes Dorcey. Though the aspirated 'D' of the 'Mac' form would normally have been silent, Fr. Travers considers that MacDarcy has occasionally been anglicised as Darcy in Fermanagh. There are a few Darcy families in the area of the McGourty cluster which could be accounted for in this way.

The map shows the distribution of 53 families with telephones in 1992. The spelling variant McGourkey is not now to be found. A few have the spelling McGorty. The names are evidently the same sept, and the spelling differences are likely to be due to choices in relatively recent times. Allowing for homes without telephones, there are probably 70 families altogether.

The names retain a clear association with Leitrim and adjacent parts of Fermanagh. The cluster in the area accounts for two-thirds of the families. Sometimes names with an Ulster base have a secondary cluster in Connaught as a result of population displacement. McGourty however is virtually unknown in Connaught outside Leitrim. If displacement did occur, families moving to Mayo or Galway may well have merged with Ó Dorchaidhe, thus obscuring any connection.

The name is very rare in Ireland, amounting to only one family in 22,000. About a third are in Northern Ireland.

The same Gaelic root words have produced MacGorth in Scotland, though the word 'Kenelman' with which the Scottish was associated in an early charter may be for 'Cenél Maine', or Maine's sept. If so, it suggests a link with Galway.

McGrath
3400 families

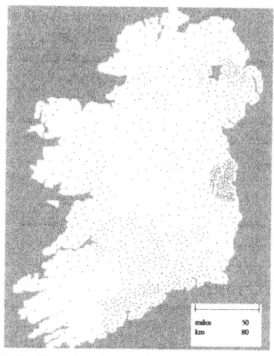

This surname is derived from the Gaelic MacGraith, the personal name being Craith. Despite a standard pronunciation, a number of modern spellings have evolved, of which McGrath is the most numerous. A few families have the spelling Magrath. There is also a form McGraw, particularly in Ulster. In Scotland the main modern form is McCrae, which name also occurs in Ulster, in several spellings. The name means son of grace or prosperity.

Widespread in Ireland today, the McGraths originated mainly from two main septs. One, headed by the hereditary guardian of the monastery of St Daveog at Lough Derg, was Termon MacGrath. This was based in Cos. Donegal and Fermanagh. The other originated in Co. Clare, where for centuries the family supplied poets to the O'Briens of Thomond, recording their lineages and their battles.

The northern sept subsequently extended into Tyrone, and the western sept became established in Cos. Tipperary and Waterford in the sixteenth century. It is in these southern counties where the McGraths now have their strongest representation. McGraths account for about 2% of the population of Co. Tipperary, and just less than 1% of Waterford.

The map shows the distribution of some 3,400 McGrath families in 1992, including a few with the spelling Magrath. As with many Irish families today, the main cluster of McGraths is in the Greater Dublin area - some 16% live there, compared to a national average of 22%. Almost a fifth of McGraths live in Northern Ireland, as compared with about a third of the population of Ireland as a whole.

Greer
845 families

The principal families called Greer came to Ireland in the seventeenth century, the earliest in the Plantation of Ulster and others a generation later. The name occurs many times in the 1669 Hearth Money Rolls for the Ulster counties, particularly Co. Antrim.

Greer derives ultimately from Gregor, a personal name from a Greek word meaning watchful. It became a favourite ecclesiastical name from the third century and was adopted by several early Popes. Greer is an anglicised form of the Scottish MacGregor. Grier and Grierson are from the same source.

The map shows the distribution of some 600 families with telephones in 1992. Allowing for homes without telephones, there were probably 845 families altogether. Families with the spelling Greer account for 92%. Those spelt Grier account for 7%. Grierson families make up 1% of the total.

Greer families in Ireland have an extremely localised distribution. Almost two-fifths of them live in the Belfast, Lisburn and Antrim area. This is well over three times the national average and is strong confirmation of a Scottish origin.

Northern Ireland has a third of all Irish families. Though the name is scarce in Tyrone, Fermanagh, Monaghan and Cavan, the North has 82% of all the Greers. The name is rare in the Republic. Greater Dublin accounts for over a third of the 18% of the families living south of the border. Most of the rest are either in the three Ulster counties in the Republic or in neighbouring counties.

Hackett
615 families

The surname Hackett in Ireland may have any one of three origins. The earliest source was the Anglo-Normans. Haki was a common Scandinavian personal name, brought by the Vikings to northern France in the creation of the duchy of Normandy. Another source was by adoption: in Cos. Tyrone and Armagh, the Irish Mag Eachaidh, McCahey or McGahey, became Hackett from the sound of the Gaelic form. The third source is Scottish, as Hackett was an old spelling of Halkett. As '-et' sometimes meant wood, and as Halket probably had a silent 'l', the name may have been associated with a place-name, Hawkwood, near Strathaven, Lanarkshire.

Soon after the Anglo-Norman invasion, families called Hackett were settled in what are now the counties of Kilkenny, Carlow and Kildare. Hacketstown in Co. Carlow is called after them.

The map shows the distribution of some 350 families with telephones in 1992. Allowing for homes without telephones, there were probably 615 families altogether. The line of settlement along the south coast is typically Anglo-Norman. So too is the presence in the West, though the connection is unusual in that it is through Tipperary rather than through Cork and Limerick. The Tipperary connection is longstanding, as Hacketts were Sheriffs in Tipperary in the sixteenth century.

Almost a third of the families now live in Greater Dublin. This is a normal proportion. The cluster in Ulster is unusual for an Anglo-Norman name. The likely reason is the assimilation of the McCaheys. The proportion in the Belfast, Lisburn and Antrim area, at 4%, is less than half the national average, and suggests that a Scottish origin is unlikely to be a primary source of the name.

Northern Ireland has about a third of all Irish families. It has only 18% of the Hacketts.

O'Hagan
1250 families

O'Hagan is derived from two Ulster names, Ó hÁgáin and Ó hÁodhagáin. Ó hÁgáin is a form of Ó hÓgáin, from the Irish Óg, meaning young, and was the name of a sept of Tullaghogue in Co. Tyrone. They had the hereditary right of inaugurating O'Neill as King of Ulster. The O'Hagans, like the O'Quinns, were of the Clann Feargusa, descendants of Feargus, son of Eoghan, son of Niall of the Nine Hostages. Ó hÁodhagáin is from Aodhagán, a diminutive of Hugh. It was a sept of Armagh. The two septs were so close geographically that they have become indistinguishable.

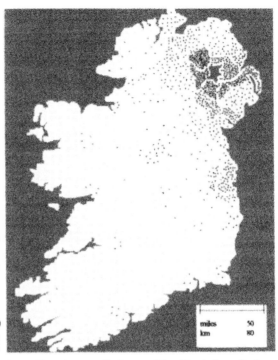

The map shows the settlement pattern of some 1250 families in Ireland in 1992. The distribution is similar to that of the five times more numerous Quinns. There is a small cluster of families in Longford. O'Hagan is an example of a name where the 'O' prefix has been increasingly resumed in the twentieth century. Some 65% of the families had the 'O' prefix in 1992. Ten dots make up 1% of the total. The southern and western fringes of Northern Ireland have gone furthest in the restoration of the prefix, whilst families on the east coast of Antrim and Down remained content to do without it.

The name is overwhelmingly one of the North of Ireland. Some 70% of all the families live there. This is composed of 65% of the O'Hagans and 80% of the Hagans. About 11% of all the families live in the Belfast, Antrim and Lisburn area, which is the same as the national average and high for a Gaelic name. About 12% live in the Greater Dublin area, little more than half of the national average and low for a Gaelic name.

Harley
110 families

Harley is a well known English name, meaning dweller at the hare's wood. It appears as de Harelea in the 12th century and as de Hareleye in the 13th. In Scotland it occurs in Fife and Clackmannanshire. It is considered to be a late incomer from England. Harley occurs as a place-name in Shropshire and Yorkshire.

The name may have been introduced to Ireland by settlers from England and Scotland, but for the most part its presence is due to its adoption as an anglicisation of Ó hEarghaile, a name associated with Donegal and Mayo. Etymologically the name is akin to Farrelly (Ó Fearghaile) and Farrell and Ferrall (Ó Fearghail) with the meaning of 'man of valour'. The aspiration of an initial 'F' occurs frequently in Gaelic.

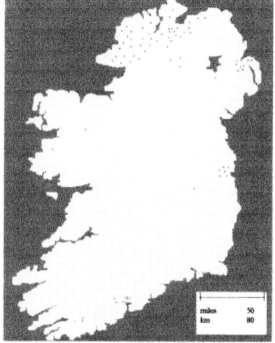

Harley is a rare name in Ireland. The map shows the distribution of some 72 Harley households with telephones in 1992. Allowing for homes without telephones, there were likely to have been about 110 families altogether. By comparison, there were 4,900 Farrells and O'Farrells and 1,100 Ferralls and O'Ferralls. Farley is another derivative. This is rarer than Harley, with fewer than 100 families. The scarcity of Harley and Farley is probably explained by the slight Gaelic trilling of the 'r' sound and because of a tendency in Gaelic to pronounce a vowel between two consonants, here 'r' and 'l', even where none appears in spelling. There is a rare Harrily.

Traditionally associated with Donegal, the county is still home to 40% of the Harleys. their presence in the Belfast area at 7% is weak and only 6% of them live in Dublin. Some 12% live in Cork, but as this county is home to the Hurleys, Harley there may be a local variant.

Northern Ireland has about a third of all Irish families. It has the same proportion of Harley families.

Harrington
1000 families

There are several localities in England called Harrington, which have produced a surname there. Very few Harringtons in Ireland are of English stock, but the Earl of Harrington is based in Co. Limerick.

The Ó hIongardail sept of south west Cork and Kerry at first took the name O'Hungerdell, which was an approximate pronunciation of the Gaelic, but long ago changed to Harrington. Families of two other septs sometimes also adopted the name. Properly anglicised Heraghty, the Ó hOireachtaigh sept belongs to Cos Galway and Mayo. A Ui Maine sept of Co. Galway, the Ó hArrachtáin, were scattered throughout north Munster in the sixteenth century. Their name is recorded as a synonym or alias of Harrington in the Dingle - Tralee area of Kerry.

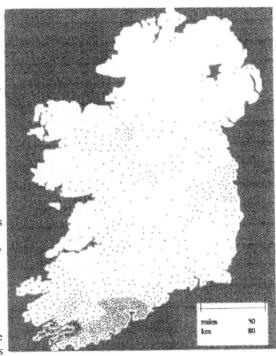

The map shows the distribution of some 1,000 Harrington families in 1992. Each dot represents 0.1%. Found throughout the country, the settlement pattern is distinctive. Greater Dublin, which houses almost a quarter of all Irish families, has only 6% of the Harringtons. Almost half the Harringtons live in Co. Cork. Though they make up only one family in 200 in the populous county as a whole, the concentration of 17% of them around Bantry Bay means that Harringtons account for about 5% of the population in that area. The families in Kerry of Ó hArrachtáin origin are not distinguishable by name form but are likely to be relatively few.

Present in Cos Galway and Mayo, families of Ó hOireachtaigh origin are at their greatest density on the eastern borders of Connaught. Even in Roscommon, they are only at half the strength of the Harringtons of Co. Cork.

Northern Ireland has about a third of all the households in Ireland. Only 1% of Harrington families live there.

Hassett
290 families

Ó hAiseadha in Gaelic, the Hassetts were an old Thomond family whose original homeland was in the barony of Bunratty, Co. Clare. A branch of Clancullen. they were one of the septs that fought in alliance with their kinsman the MacNamaras in the Battle of the Abbey in 1317.

The first English language records rendered the name as O'Hessedy or O'Hassia. The 1659 'census' found it to be one of the principal names in Bunratty and recorded it as O'Hashea. The modern form Hassett made its appearance just a little later, in the Money Heath Rolls of Co. Tipperary of 1665 - 1667.

MacLysaght says that from the mid-seventeenth century it is not always easy to distinguish families of the Gaelic sept from the better known English settlers called Blennerhassett. The plantation of Ulster brought Sir Edward Blennerhassett from Norfolk, to acquire lands in Co. Fermanagh and to call his residence Hassett Castle. Blennerhassett was a place in Cumberland. The Blennerhassetts came to Co. Kerry at the end of the reign of Queen Elizabeth I. They built up land holdings in Kerry as well as in neighbouring Cos. Cork and Limerick.

The map shows the distribution of some 180 Hassett families in 1992. Allowing for homes without telephones, there were probably 290 families altogether. Despite the extensive Blennerhassett land holdings, there is little to suggest origins for the families that are other than Irish. Co. Fermanagh does not feature in the Hassett settlement. Very few of the name live in Co. Kerry and those in Cos. Cork and Limerick seem to belong to distinct local clusters rather than to an expansion from Kerry.

Greater Dublin has about 22% of all Irish families. It has only 14% of the Hassetts. Some 13% of them live around Waterford and Wexford. Neither MacLysaght nor Woulfe refers to this south eastern cluster.

Hasson
215 families

Hasson is the most numerous anglicisation of the Irish Ó hOsáin, which Woulfe translates as descendant of Osán, a diminutive of 'os', a deer, and describes as an old family of Derry and Tyrone. Many old Gaelic personal names were taken from the names of animals admired for their strength or swiftness. The legendary Ossian, or Oisin, is from the same source. Other spellings are Hassan, Hassen and Hassin.

The concentration of the name suggests the sept has been relatively little affected by the disruption in Ireland caused by migration from Britain. Ulster surnames tend to have secondary clusters in Connaught, suggesting population shifts as a result of the Plantation. The clan now known as Bonner, in various spellings, in neighboring Co. Donegal to the west has an offshoot in east Mayo. To the east of Derry, the Antrim family Lynn, an Ulster variant of Flynn, is represented in north Mayo.

There has not been distortion as a result of similar names from Britain. A family called Hasson was recorded in the sixteenth century in Wexford, but leaves no trace today. Hassan is a popular family name amongst followers of the world's billion strong Muslim religion, and a few immigrants into Ireland are now of this origin and name. They are easily distinguished by their eastern given names and are not included in the data from which the map is compiled.

The map shows the distribution of the 160 Hasson, Hassan etc families who had telephones in 1992. Another four families in the Cookstown and Moneymore areas have the spelling Hessin, which is probably the same sept. Adjusting for homes without phones, there are likely to be 215 families altogether. This is a rare name. In Ireland as a whole only one family in 7,000 has the name. Even in its heartland of Derry, it accounts for only one family in 300.

Northern Ireland has a third of all Irish households. Virtually all Hasson families live there.

Hayes
2900 families

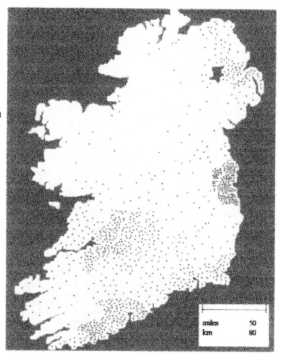

Hayes in Ireland has two origins, the Irish Ó hAodha, and the Anglo-Norman de la Haye. Ó hAodha means descendant of Aodh, or Hugh. La Haye is a placename near Coutance, Normandy, which was brought by a family that settled in Wexford at the time of the invasion and is found only there.

Woulfe translates Aodh as 'fire', and describes no less than thirteen septs with the surname Ó hAodha. The most important of these was a Dalcassian family of Thomond, an area covering most of Clare, Limerick and Tipperary.

Hayes was adopted as the anglicisation of Ó hAodha in the south, the equivalent in the north of the country being Hughes. The map shows the distribution of some 2,900 Hayes families in 1992. Each dot represents 0.1% of the total. Thomond shows up clearly, indicating that this sept chose the name Hayes. Around 16% of the Hayes families live in the Clare-Limerick area where they make up almost 1% of the population. Two of the other septs were in Cork, which also chose Hayes, though a few families there took O'Hea. From the thin Hayes settlement elsewhere in the country, the other nine septs appear to have taken the name Hughes. About 16% of Hayes families live in the Greater Dublin area.

Though there was a sept in each of Donegal, Monaghan and Tyrone, western Ulster has few Hayes families. There was no Ó hAodha family in Antrim or Down to account for the cluster of families now around Belfast. The name there may have come from England with the Plantation of Ulster or have been adopted locally as a result of it. Neither MacLysaght nor Woulfe refers to the name in this area. Northern Ireland has about a third of all Irish households. It has 12% of Hayes families.

Healy
3100 families

The Ó hÉilidhe sept of north Connaught, whose name means 'claimant,' had their seat at Ballyhely on Lough Arrow, Co. Sligo. They came to share the surname Healy with the Ó hÉalaighte sept of Munster, whose name means 'ingenious'. Formerly correctly rendered in English as O'Healihy, this family was based in the barony of Muskerry in Co. Cork. They formed a Protestant branch whose chief took the title of Earl of Donoughmore from a placename in the barony.

The map shows the distribution of some 3,100 families in Ireland in 1992. A few, mainly in Northern Ireland, use the spelling Healey. One dot on the map represents 0.1% of the total.

About 17% of Healy families today live in Greater Dublin, which is a slightly fewer than the 22% of all families that live there. Only 5% live in Northern Ireland, as compared with 31% of all Irish families.

The Healys in Co. Cork are seven times more numerous than those in Co. Sligo, but, at almost 1% of the population, they have the same proportional strength in each county. Though the name remains clearly associated with Munster and Connaught, it is quite dispersed and is well represented also in south Leinster.

Heffernan
1050 families

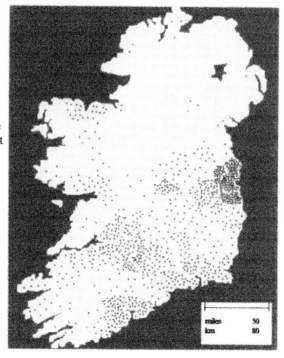

The sept of Ó hIfearnáin, meaning descendent of Ifearnán, were originally of a territory in north Co. Clare near Corofin, called Muintirifernán after them. In early history, they established themselves as chiefs of Owneybeg in the north east of what became Co. Limerick, close to the Tipperary border. They lost control to the Ryans of Tipperary in the 14th century. In 1600 O'Heffernans still featured amongst the most important families of neighbouring Clanwilliam.

There were some 1,050 Heffernan families in 1992. Like the Ryans, none now retains the 'O' prefix abandoned during the era of repression, though one entry in the telephone books has the Gaelic form Ó hEifearnáin.

The map shows the Heffernan distribution. In common with many families in modern times, Greater Dublin is now the single most important area. Over a quarter of the Heffernans live there as compared to a national average of 22%. Few if any families now live in Corofin, but Owneybeg remains in the core area of the family. The Heffernan distribution contrasts with that of the nine times more numerous Ryans. Apart from the cluster in their historic heartland in the Golden Vale of Tipperary and adjacent part of Limerick, only Dublin stands out clearly on the Ryan map. The Heffernan core area along the Limerick/Tipperary border remains clearly in evidence, but there has been dispersal other than to Dublin. Unusually, it has been in all directions. The locations of Cork, Waterford, Wexford, Galway, Ballina and Tullamore are all discernible by density of settlement on the Heffernan map. Heffernan settlement extends through and beyond the Ryan heartland to Waterford and Kilkenny.

Of the four provinces of Ireland, only Ulster does not have a significant proportion of the Heffernans. Most of the few in Ulster are in the three counties belonging to the Republic. Northern Ireland, with about a third of all Irish households, has much fewer than 1% of the Heffernans.

Henderson
1050 families

After the Norman conquest of England, the personal name Henry was introduced to Britain and became one of the most popular Christian names. It derives through Frankish from the Old German Heimric which means home rule or realm. Many nicknames and surname derivatives acquired an intrusive 'd'. The name is well known in Ireland, though little has been written about it as an Irish name.

The map shows the distribution of some 1050 families in Ireland in 1992. Ten dots make up 1% of the total. About 23% of the families live in the Belfast, Lisburn and Antrim area. This is twice the national average and is indicative of a Scottish origin. The density of settlement in this area is however exceeded by that to the north of Strangford Lough and in the Ards peninsula. This small area alone has 11% of all Henderson families in Ireland. The name is well represented over the rest of Down and Antrim. It is strong in Derry and in the Inishowen peninsula of north Donegal. Fermanagh was a destination for families of the 'riding clans' of both sides of the English-Scottish border, who were displaced by King James I after he succeeded to the crowns of both countries.

Some 12% of the families live in Greater Dublin. This is low in relation to the national average of 22%, but exceeds many names of Scottish origin. Some of these families may be of English origin, though numbers will have increased through internal migration in modern times. There is a thin cluster of settlement in mid Leinster. The origin of these families so far from Ulster is not clear. Plantations of James I might provide an explanation. There are several families along the coast of Co. Cork, which might be Cromwellian.

Northern Ireland has about a third of all Irish families. It has 72% of the Hendersons.

Henry
1550 families

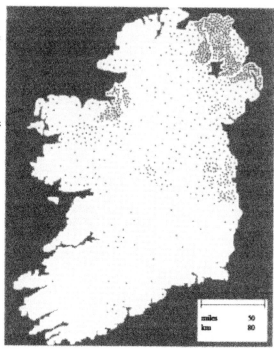

The surname Henry in Ireland may be of Irish, Norman or Scottish origin. In Ulster, there was a sept called Ó hInneirghe, O'Henry, whose head was chief of Cullentra in Co. Tyrone and whose territory once extended to the Glenconkeine valley in Co. Derry. In Munster, there was Mac Inneirghe, McHenry, a sept of the same stock as the O'Donovans and located in the barony of Upper Connelloe, Co. Limerick. The name may also be an abbreviation of FitzHenry, a Norman family chiefly associated with Co. Wexford but with a branch in Connaught. These became Mac Einri in Irish, which became McHenry and Henry. In Scotland Henry is a name with origins in Ayr and Fife. This often took an intrusive 'd' to make Hendry, which is well known in both Scotland and Ireland.

The map shows the distribution of some 1550 families in Ireland in 1992. Ten dots represent 1% of the total. The most notable feature is a concentration in Ulster of unusual pattern. About 12% of the families live in the Belfast, Antrim and Lisburn area. This area is often distinct in its density of settlement, but in the case of Henry the high density continues up to the north coast and into Ards in Co. Down. The Glens of Antrim on the county's east coast are thinly settled. The area of dense settlement thins out abruptly in Tyrone and Down. This pattern suggests the Scottish origin is most important.

There is a second cluster in Connaught, of almost equal density to that in Ulster, centred on Co. Sligo. These families, together with others in Mayo, Galway and Roscommon, may be taken to be of FitzHenry origin. There are few Henry families in Co. Wexford despite the FitzHenry connection. There are few in Limerick, despite the McHenry associations. The families may of course continue in these counties but with the appropriate prefix.

Hogan
2100 families

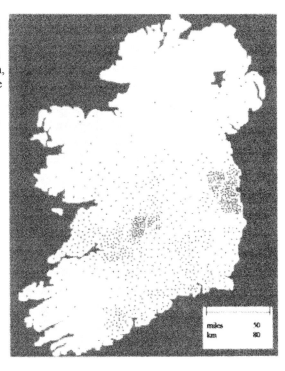

Hogan is from the Irish Ó hÓgáin, from óg, meaning young. MacLysaght describes the origins of the name as Dalcassian, a population group embracing the main septs of Thomond, a territory covering most of Co. Clare with neighbouring parts of Tipperary and Limerick. These Hogans were descended from Ógán, an uncle of Brian Boru. Their chief lived at Ardcrony, near Nenagh, Co. Tipperary, in the extreme north east of Dalcassian territory. Other Hogans were based in Lower Ormond, covering much of Kilkenny and north Tipperary. There are different views on whether these were a separate sept from the Dalcassians. Still more and regarded as a separate sept, were the Hogans of the Corca Laoidhe, in south west Cork.

The map shows the distribution of some 2,100 Hogan families in 1992. Ten dots make up 1% of the total. As is usual in modern times, Greater Dublin has become the most important single cluster. A fifth of the Hogans live there, slightly less than the national average in that area. The historic Dalcassian connection is clearly apparent and an area of high density Hogan settlement extends across from Nenagh to Roscrea. To the east of this area the Hogans are more densely settled in Kilkenny and Carlow than in north Tipperary. If the Lower Ormond Hogans are a separate sept, their centre of gravity is somewhat further east than is suggested by MacLysaght. Though the name is well represented in the centre and east of Co. Cork, there is a notable absence of Hogans in the south west of the county.

The name is virtually unknown in Ulster and much of Connaught. Under 2% of Hogan families live in Northern Ireland.

Hogg
270 families

In his 'Surnames of Scotland', George F. Black says that the surname Hogg is usually explained as a nickname derived from the animal, though he points out that the earliest reference to it - in 11th century England- is in the form 'Hoga', an Old English word for 'careful' or 'prudent'. The name in Scotland historically appears in the central belt, notably Edinburgh and Glasgow. Edward MacLysaght's 'Surnames of Ireland' describes Hogg as an English name, numerous in Ulster, and used occasionally as a synonym of O'Hagan.

The map shows the distribution of some 200 families with telephones in 1992. Allowing for homes without telephones, there are likely to have been about 270 households altogether. In Northern Ireland and in the far south of Ireland, the only spelling is Hogg. In Greater Dublin, a quarter of the families use the spelling 'Hogge'. In Connaught and the Republic's Ulster counties, almost 40% have a final 'e'.

The settlement pattern is typical of many names of English and Scottish origin. The Belfast, Antrim and Lisburn area has 11% of all Irish families. It has twice that proportion of Hogg families. Another 11% live in Ards and the Glens of Antrim. The rest of Cos. Down and Antrim are important areas of settlement for Hogg families. Fermanagh, a county strong in plantation names, stands out clearly on the map.

Northern Ireland has a third of all Irish families. It has three quarters of Hogg and Hogge families. The Republic is correspondingly sparsely settled. There are clusters of settlement in north Connaught, in Westmeath and around Clonmel. Overall, the name is rare both north and south of the border.

Hopkins
480 families

Robert, a Frankish name meaning fame bright, came to the British Isles with the Normans. Hobbe evolved as a colloquial name, perhaps influenced by the French pronunciation of Robert. Hobekinus appeared in the thirteenth century. The diminutive served to distinguish a son from a father, like 'junior' today.

In Ireland, MacObichin appeared in a list of mostly Gaelic-Irish clergy names in Co Mayo. Then the 'census' of 1659 recorded Hobigan as one of the principal names in the barony of Rathcline in Co Longford. In Co Galway a man recorded as Edward Obbykin in 1641 became Edward Hopkins in 1676. In England, a final 's' was often added to names which became surnames. The 's' forms are much later in Ireland, and may be taken to be anglicisations following an earlier presence of the name. The diminutive '-gan' may be an Irish rendering of the English, or it may have evolved independently. The suffix is of common Indo-European origin. It is cognate with the German 'chen' and the Latin 'genus'. However, Black says that '-kin' is English: the name appeared in Scotland at much the same time as in Ireland, as Habkine, Hobkin and Hopkin. As in Ireland, it did not have the final 's'.

The map shows the distribution of some 270 Hopkins families in Ireland in the 1992 telephone directories. Adjusting for non-response means there are about 480 families altogether. There are three concentrations. Greater Dublin has about a third. About 12 % live in the Belfast area, and about 18% live in Co Mayo.

The distribution is unusual. It lacks the representation in the south of the country so characteristic of the Anglo-Norman suggested by Robert. Its strength in the Belfast area is untypical of either a Gaelic or an Anglo-Norman name. MacLysaght says some families in Ireland will be of English stock. This is likely to be so in the Belfast area, though at 15% of its families in Northern Ireland, Hopkins has only half the national average representation there. The strength of representation in the Greater Dublin area suggests that the Republic's capital has been more of a destination for Hopkins families than many others. This is perhaps because Mayo suffered badly from the effects of the Famine.

MacLysaght says that in Connaught, Hopkins is either a Gaelic-Irish or a Gaelicised Norman surname, now spelt MacOibicín.

Hough
134 families

MacLysaght has Hough as derived from Ó hEachach, itself derived from a personal name anglicised as Aghy, once a popular Christian name. He has it as a variant of Haugh, which belongs mainly to Co. Clare. Hough is given as the variant common in Co. Limerick. Ó hEachach is cognate with Mac Eachaidh which produced the surnames McCaughey, McCahey and Mulcahy.

The Old English 'Hoh', meaning a heel, was common in place-names. It had the sense of a spur of land or the ridge of a hill. The nominative singular gives Hough or, in the North of England and Scotland, Heugh. The dative singular became Hoe or Hoo, later Howe. Modern English uses the nominative as the citation case for words from Old English or from modern inflected languages. The dative case however occurs much more frequently in speech. This may well account for the small number of Hough surnames relative to Howe, though this is not a straightforward explanation for the ratios of the name in Ireland.

The map shows the distribution of some 84 families with telephones in 1992. Allowing for homes without telephones, there were probably about 134 families altogether. The name occurs in a cluster from the western part of Co. Limerick, extending across the county into northern Tipperary, and adjacent parts of Galway, Offaly and Roscommon.

This is a rare name in Ireland. There are a few Hough families in Northern Ireland. These may be of English rather than Ó hEachach origin.

Hussey
350 families

Sometimes found as Hosey or Hosie, this surname in Ireland has two origins.

One branch is from the Anglo-Norman family Houssaye, (housé, Latin hosatus, meaning 'hosed' or 'booted'), who arrived with Strongbow and acquired lands through Hugh de Lacy in Meath. Some of this family migrated to Kerry in the mid sixteenth century.

MacLysaht says that the Husseys of Roscommon are presumably of the sept Ó hEodhusa. This was a Cinel Eoghan family, clan name of the O'Neills, descended from Eoghan, son of Niall of the Nine Hostages, and first associated with Tyrone and Derry. They migrated to Fermanagh and hereditary bards to the Maguires. Under the Gaelic submergence, Hussey in Ulster was further anglicised to Oswell and further still to Oswald.

The map shows the distribution of some 229 families with telephones in 1992. Adjusting for homes without phones, there were probably 350 families altogether. Eighty-four percent have the spelling Hussey, and the rest have either Hosey or Hosie. The latter, perhaps reflecting a stronger Anglo-Norman consciousness, are almost all in the former territories of Strongbow and de Lacy. As with most families in modern times, Greater Dublin is the most important location. It has a quarter of all the families, slightly more than the national average.

There are no Northern Ireland telephone directory entries today for Oswell. There are only eight for Oswald, all in eastern Ulster. A change of name therefore does not explain the virtual extinction of Hussey families in Fermanagh, where the Maguire chief was one of the most important in Ulster until the confiscations of Cromwell and William of Orange, where 10% of the 3,700 strong Maguire families still live, and where they still make up 2½% of the population. The Hussey presence in the Connaught county of Roscommon suggests a possible transplantation, which would have needed to be only small scale for the small numbers involved.

Hynes
1040 families

According to Woulfe, the Gaelic Ó hEidhin is from eidhean, ivy. The 'h' following the 'd' indicates that the letter should be aspirated rather than pronounced, hence the early anglicisation of the name as O'Heyne.

The chiefs of the O'Heynes held large areas of land in south Galway from the seventh century into modern times. MacLysaght says the name is still most plentiful in Galway and Clare.

The map shows the distribution of some 1,040 Hynes families in 1992. Ten dots make up 1% of the total. Co. Galway with 23% of the families and Greater Dublin with 19% stand out as areas of high density settlement.

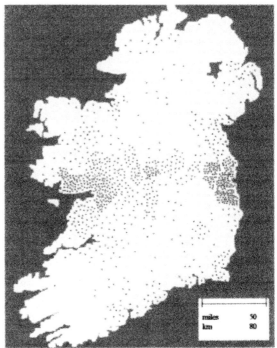

There are seven telephone directory entries for Ó hEidhin. Four are in Galway City, one in Cornamona, Co. Galway, one in Limerick and one in Dublin.

Outside the areas historically associated with the Hynes name, there is settlement between Galway and Dublin; along the south coast; in Carlow; in Mayo and Sligo; in Louth; and in Ulster.

In England both 'hine' meaning a servant and 'hind' meaning a deer became surnames. The English language has a tendency to add a final 'd' after an 'n' and a tendency to add a final 's' to any name: hence Hines, and Hinds, and possibly versions with a 'y'. These 'd' and 's' adaptations could also occur with names of Irish origin.

About 250 families have spellings other than Hynes that may have come from Ó hEidhin or from Hind or Hine. These are Heyne and Heyns; Hind, Hinds and Hindes; Hine and Hines; and Hynd, Hynds and Hyndes. The forms with a 'd' account for 86% and of those 83% live in Northern Ireland. Some 77% of the few without a 'd', live in the Republic. These localisations suggest an English origin for the names with a 'd' and an Ó hEidhin origin for those without.

Irwin, Irvine
2100 families

MacLysaght found Irwin to be almost entirely of British planter stock and interchangeable in spelling over the years with Irvine and with Erwin and Ervine. In fact, the surname Irwin in Ireland could be from any one of four origins. Two were from Britain. The Anglo-Saxon 'Eoforwine' had a meaning of 'boar-friend'. The Scottish place-name Irvine, pronounced to rhyme with Irwin, is thought to be from old Celtic words equivalent to the modern Welsh 'ir', fresh, green, and 'afon', river. From Irish Gaelic, Woulfe has two family names, which he describes as rare: Ó hEireamhóin, O'Hervan; a south of Ireland name; and Ó Ciarmhacáin, O'Kerywokyn, a Munster name, which produced Irwin as well as Carey.

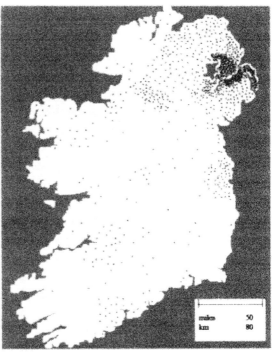

The map shows the distribution of some 2,100 families in 1992. Each dot represents 0.1% of the total. There are about 800 Irvine families, about 38% of the joint total. Only 8% of them live in the Republic, and most of those live in Dublin. This suggests a Northern origin with movement south in relatively modern times. The names Ervine and Erwin, with some spelling variations, each have about 130 families. They are virtually unknown in the Republic.

Irwin differs from the other spellings in its strength and distribution in the Republic. There were 1,300 Irwin families in 1992. As would be expected from the planter element, Northern Ireland stands out by the density of Irwin settlement. Two thirds of all the families live there. A fifth of the total live in the area around Belfast, Lisburn and Antrim, which is twice the national average and points to Scottish and English ancestry. However, fully a third of Irwin families live in the Republic, and only about a fifth of these live in Greater Dublin. This indicates a longstanding settlement pattern.

Irwin is virtually the sole form in the Republic outside Dublin. Therefore MacLysaght's interchangeable planter spelling theory applies only to the North. In the South, the Gaelic origin appears to be more significant than he recognised.

Jennings
900 families

Woulfe gives Jennings as the anglicised form of two similar Irish names. Mac Seinín, son of Jenin, a diminutive of Jean, the French for John; and of Mac Sheóinín, son of Little John. The latter was a patronymic surname assumed by a branch of the Burkes in Connaught from an ancestor named Seóinín, or Little John Burke. The form from the French, for which Woulfe gives no location, was responsible for both names being anglicised as Jennings. (Many English speakers would not have pronounced the 'g' of Jennings earlier than the 20th century.)

MacLysaght points out that Jennings is also an English name and that some families in Ireland may be of English origin. He adds that the name is common in Oriel, the area around Armagh and Monaghan, where it is from a Norse diminutive of Jen or Jan.

The map shows the distribution of some 900 Jennings families in 1992. Ten dots make up 1% of the total. As with many families, the main cluster now is Greater Dublin. About 21% of Jennings families live there, virtually the same as the national average. There is no cluster in Oriel, though there are some families there.

There is a concentration in Connaught, particularly Mayo, where almost a quarter of the Jennings live. They are relatively more concentrated in Mayo than the Burkes, and, judging by relative numbers, it seems that a third of the Burkes of Mayo must have called themselves after Little John. The Jennings settlement pattern differs from that of the Burkes in the strength in Northern Ireland. They are 21% there to the Burkes' 5%. The cluster in Antrim and Down is as dense as Mayo and may be assumed to be of planter origin.

There is a cluster around Bandon, Co. Cork. The Burke origin does not account for this, and families in this location are presumably the Mac Seiníns.

Johnstone
100 families

Johnstone is a variant of Johnston, which itself may be an alternative to Johnson.

In Scotland, the City of Perth was often called Johnston or St. Johnston. There was a Jonystoun, now Johnstonburn in East Lothian Some families took their name from these locations. However, much the most important source was the Johnstons of Annandale in Dumfriesshire, one of the greatest riding clans of the Scottish borders. The ferocity of their feuding, mainly with the Maxwells, produced their ironic nickname of the 'Gentle Johnstones'.

Many riding clan families went to Ulster after the union of the Scottish and English crowns. The Johnstons settled principally in Fermanagh, where their name and that of other riding clans, notably Armstrong, Elliott, Irvine Nixon and Crozier, came to predominate in the county, and where they were strong enough to survive the 1641 rising which destroyed Plantation settlements in other counties.

Some Johnstons had become Johnson even in Scotland. Some Johnsons took an intrusive 't'. Johnston in Scotland was pronounced John's toon. The spelling 'Johnstone' may have been adopted to preserve the long vowel. In many cases it would have shortened anyway.

The map shows the distribution of some 69 Johnstone families with telephones in Ireland in 1992. Allowing for homes without telephones, there were likely to have been almost 100 families altogether. Some 26% of the families live in the Belfast, Antrim, Lisburn area, more than double the national average of Irish families. More surprisingly, 21% of Johnstone families live in Greater Dublin. This is much the same as the national average representation in Greater Dublin and is unusual for an Ulster surname. A direct English origin seems unlikely, unless these families were originally Johnson: England has hardly any place-names beginning with 'J' and no Johnston.

Joyce
1500 families

The source word for Joyce, the French 'joi', was from the Latin 'gaudia'. This was much used in Church Latin and so may have had the sense of joy in worship. In French, the softening of a Latin 'g' is commonplace and so is a middle consonent falling silent.

In 1283 Thomas de Jorse, or Joyce, from Wales, married the daughter of O'Brien, Prince of Thomond, and went with her to Galway. At first the Joyces were tributary to the O'Flahertys, but they established themselves in Iar Connaught on the Galway-Mayo border, an area that became known as Joyce's Country. They had a Chief of the Name in the Irish way, who was based at the barony of Ross, Co. Galway.

The map shows the distribution of some 1,500 Joyce families in Ireland in 1992. Each dot represents 0.1% of the total, except for the Aran Islands in Galway Bay, where for space reasons it is 0.3%.

As a result of internal migration, Greater Dublin, with 22% of all Irish families, is now the most important location for many surnames. Anglo-Norman names are typically well represented there, but Joyce is only 13%.

The Joyce settlement pattern has Anglo-Norman features in its presence the South East, particularly Wexford; in the South and South West; in the West; and in the sparse representation in the North. Its most striking feature is the concentration in Connaught. With a third of the Joyce families living in Co. Galway, they make up 1% of the population there. They are at almost the same strength in Co. Mayo.

In Irish the name is Seoighe, son of Joy. The 's' sound at the end may be because of English usage, where this often happens, but it may be from what is now 'joyous'. In Kilkenny and Cork the name was after a Breton saint, Jodoc, from a place now called St Josse sur Mer. The now silent 'd' is still in evidence in the saint's name and the 'oc' ending looks like a Celtic language genitive.

Northern Ireland has a third of all Irish households. It has under 4% of Joyce families.

Keane & Kane
5350 families

Ó Catháin means descendent of Cathán, a pet form of a now lost name beginning with Cath. The early anglicised form of the surname was O'Cahan, but in modern times Keane and Kane are almost universally used.

There were two great septs of the name. One of them was descended from Niall of the Nine Hostages, fifth century founder of the O'Neill dynasty. O'Cahan was one of the inaugurators of O'Neill. Originally from east Donegal, they won Derry from the O'Connors and remained in ascendancy in Derry until the Plantation of Ulster. The MacCloskeys of Derry are a branch of the O'Cahans, being descended from Bloskey O'Cahan, slayer of Murtagh O'Loughlin, heir to the throne of Ireland, in 1196. A minor branch of the Ulster O'Cahans is thought to have settled in Clare.

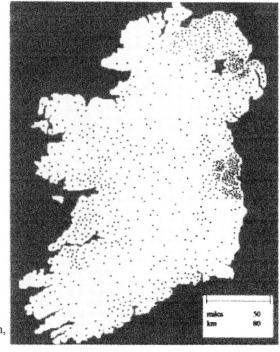

The other O'Cathan sept was a branch of the Ui Fiachrach and was based in Galway.

The map shows the distribution of some 5,350 families in 1992. Keane, which is the predominent form outside Ulster, accounts for 53%. There are hardly any O'Keanes. Ulster by contrast is overwhelmingly Kane country, and the 'O' prefix has regained popularity amongst Kane families. Kane families make up 29% of the total. O'Kane accounts for 18%. Ten dots of any color make up 1% of the total. As with other Ulster names, the restoration of the prefix has gone furthest in the west.

In common with many surnames, Dublin is now the most important location. Some 18% of Keane families live there; as do a fifth of the Kanes and 6% of the O'Kanes. The discrepancy between the proportions of Kanes and O'Kanes in Dublin suggests that in the Republic's capital, Kane may be a variant of Keane. Northern Ireland has about a third of all Irish households. It has 79% of the O'Kanes; 45% of the Kanes and 1½% of the Keanes.

Kelly
14600 families

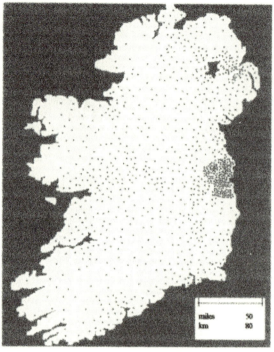

Second in numbers only to Murphy, the surname Kelly has origins in at least seven different parts of the country. With the exception of the septs of Tipperary and Kilkenny, which had a family name of Ó Caollaidhe, in each case they took the surname Ó Ceallaigh after an ancestor called Ceallach. The first recorded Ceallach was a son of a chief of the Uí Maine, or Hy Many, people around 874 AD. This sept was the most numerous and important. Their area covered parts of Galway and Roscommon.

The map shows the distribution of some 14,600 Kelly families in 1992. One dot represents 0.1% of the total. There are in addition almost 600 families, making 4% of a joint total, who have restored the 'O' prefix. These show the typical urban and southern preference for the restoration, two thirds of O'Kellys being in Dublin, Cork and Limerick.

Greater Dublin stands out as clearly the most important present day location. About a fifth of Kelly families live in this area, which contains much the same proportion of all Irish families.

The most probable origin of the name is from 'ceall', meaning battle or strife. As O'Connor and O'Neill are derived from words for champion, Ceallach was perhaps intended to convey the idea of a striver or contestant. Many early names have two themes. Kelly has no second theme to restrict its application. It is probably the most evenly distributed name in the country. Well represented everywhere, it is not numerous even in Cos. Galway and Roscommon. Kelly families make up about 2% of all families in this Hy Many area, which is under half the strength some less numerous surnames have in their heartlands. They are 2% also in Co. Carlow and probably approach this level in many areas.

Some 19% of Kelly families live in Northern Ireland, as compared to 31% of all Irish families.

Kennedy
5800 families

Ó Cinnéide, meaning descendent of Cinnéididh or Cinnéidigh, (helmeted head), was the name of at least two families. One was based in Co. Galway. The other derive their name and descent from Cinnéidigh, a nephew of Brian Boru, and were at first based in the same area as the High King. They were later driven from east Clare by the O'Briens and their marshals, the MacNamaras. They settled in north Tipperary, and from the eleventh to the sixteenth centuries were lords of Ormond. A branch of the sept migrated to Antrim around 1600, where their numbers are likely to have been supplemented by Scottish Kennedys.

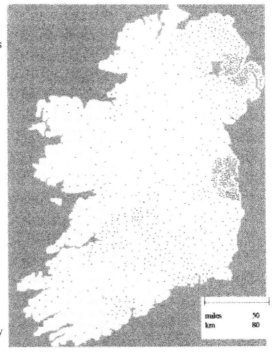

The map shows the distribution of the 5,800 Kennedy families in Ireland in 1992. Each dot represents 0.1%. The importance of the sept descended from Brian Boru is evident. Some 9% of the Kennedys still live in Co. Tipperary, where they make up about 3% of the population. Their strength in Galway is only a tenth of that in Tipperary.

Nowadays the most notable features of the Kennedy distribution are that it is widespread throughout the country and that it is strongly represented in and around the two capital cities. Both cities have been destinations for internal migration. Greater Dublin has around 22% of the all-Ireland population, and Belfast/Lisburn/Antrim has about 11%. About 18% of the Kennedys are in the Dublin area, and 12.5% live in and around Belfast. Northern Ireland has about 31% of Irish families. It has the same proportion of Kennedy families.

Under 2% of the Kennedys are to be found in Wexford, the home county of the family of US President John F. Kennedy.

Kenny
2900 families

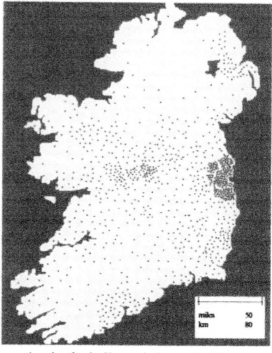

Woulfe gives the Irish Ó Cionnaoith the meaning of 'firesprung'. The main area of origin is Ui Máine - parts of Cos. Galway and Roscommon. In early times there was another sept of the same name in Co. Tyrone. Long established Kennys in Co. Down are probably of the minor Ulster sept of Ó Coinne. (Conn).

By co-incidence, an English family called Kenny acquired lands in the Ó Cionnaoith heartland. These descend from Nicholas Kenny, Elizabeth I's Escheator General for Ireland, who was previously based in Wexford. Such a family is unlikely to have had much demographic weight in the area.

The map shows the distribution of 2,900 Kenny families in 1992. Each dot represents 0.1% of the total. As it is for many families, the most important location for the Kennys is Greater Dublin. Some 22% of all Irish families live there now, and the area accommodates 26% of the Kennys.

A cluster of high density of settlement is evident approximating to the early homeland. The centre of gravity has evidently shifted slightly eastwards to the western part of Westmeath. Kennys make up the greatest proportion of the population in Co. Roscommon, where they account for 1% of the total. They are at almost the same level in Westmeath, but have only half this strength in the more populous Co. Galway. Wexford also stands out by the density of its Kenny settlement. Relative to the county's population, the name has the same strength there as it has in Galway.

Northern Ireland has a third of all Irish households. It has under 6% of the Kennys. Co. Antrim is the main area. Despite historical associations with the name Ó Coinne, Co. Down has very few Kennys in relation to its population. Co. Tyrone is the sole county that does not appear as an area of Kenny settlement.

McKeown
2200 families

Early Irish forms of John produced the surnames Mac Eoghain in Connaught and Mac Eoin in east Ulster. The most frequent anglicisation of them is McKeown. The map shows the distribution of 2,200 families in 1992. Each dot represents 0.1% of the total, which includes some families with the spelling McKeon. This spelling is mainly found in and around Dublin, and is virtually unknown in Northern Ireland.

There are in addition many McGeown families, also mainly in Ulster, and other rarer variants of McKeown and McGeown have been recorded. Mac Eoin has been restored by some families in the Republic, mainly Dublin, but it is virtually unknown in the North.

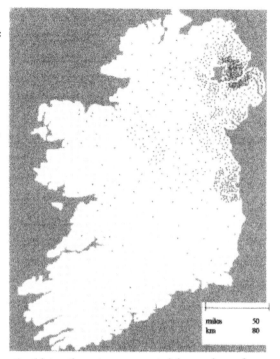

Scottish Bissetts who settled in the Glens of Antrim from the thirteenth century augmented the numbers of McKeowns by adopting the name. On the other hand, McKeown numbers have been reduced by translation and mistranslation into English as Johnson, Johnston and Johnstone.

Another Irish equivalent of Johnson is Mac Seáin, or McShane, which is from a later form of John, introduced by the Anglo-Normans.

With 13% of their number in Greater Dublin, the McKeowns are much less well represented there than the 22% national average. Even though it has a main sept in north Connaught with a branch in Co. Galway, like other surnames derived from saints' names, whether Scriptural or Irish, McKeown is mainly found in the North. Some 23% of McKeown families live in the Belfast/Lisburn/Antrim area, as compared with 11% of Irish families generally; and 53% live in Northern Ireland as a whole, compared with 31% of all Irish families.

Kerr
1800 families

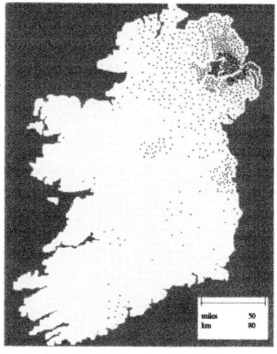

Following the union of the crowns of Scotland and England in the early 17th century, the 'riding clans' of the borders were broken and many families moved to Ulster. Most of the Kerr families in Ireland are descended from Kerrs of the Scottish borders, where they were strongest in Liddesdale and east Teviotdale. They were second only to the Scott family in Middle March. The origin of the name is from the Old Norse kjarr, meaning brushwood in wet ground.

In Ireland the name became confused with the Irish Carr. The two names were still being used synonymously in Coleraine and Lisburn at the turn of the 20th century. In Donegal, Kerr may also be an anglicised form of MacIlhair or a shortening of Kerin, a variant of Kieran. In Monaghan it is often, like Carr, from Mac Giolla Cheara. There have been Irish forms of Kerr in isolated cases in Munster from the 14th century, from various Irish sources.

The map shows the distribution of some 1,800 Kerr families in 1992. Ten dots represent 1% of the total. Greater Dublin, which has over a fifth of all Irish families, has exerted little attraction on the Kerrs. Only 8% live there. A quarter of all the families live in the Belfast, Lisburn and Antrim area, more than twice the national average and confirmation of the strongly Scottish antecedents of the name. The distribution shows much the same density extending over most of Northern Ireland and continuing into Monaghan and north eastern Donegal. It thins in Cavan. There is a cluster in Longford and some settlement in Leix. This is not subject to comment by MacLysaght, but Longford was a King James I plantation, as also were Offaly and north Leix.

A third of Irish families live in the North of Ireland. Three quarters of all Kerr families live there.

Kerrigan
470 families

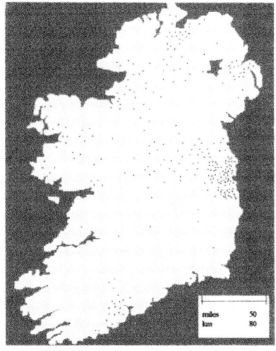

The sept of Ó Ciaragáin was one of the Hy Fiachrach group of north Connaught. There is a townland called Ballykerrigan in the parish of Balla, Co. Mayo. From Connaught a branch migrated to Co. Donegal, where Ballykergan is in the parish of Kilteevogue, near Stranorlar. Some also went to Armagh, where they were well established by the mid seventeenth century.

The surname Kerrigan has been confused with Carrigan in Fermanagh and with Corrigan in Mayo, particularly around Westport. These two names are etymologically related to each other but not to Kerrigan. Kerrigan has gained ground also in Leitrim, where the unrelated small sept of Ó Ciocharáin adopted it. On the other hand, the name has lost ground in Roscommon. There, Ó Ciaragáin was mistakenly thought to be derived from ciór, a comb, to produce the surname Comber. In fact, the name derives from ciar, meaning black.

The map shows the distribution of some 270 Kerrigan families with telephones in 1992. Allowing for homes without telephones, there were probably 470 families altogether.

As is usual with many names, Greater Dublin is now the most important location for the Kerrigans. Their representation there is about the same as the national average of 22%. Only 4.5% live around Belfast.

The name is not now found in Armagh or in the Stranorlar area of Donegal. Families around Balla in Mayo are equalled in numbers by those around Westport. The name is strong in Leitrim. Unusually, it is strong in areas with which is not historically associated. Longford and Westmeath stand out, as does the area around Derry. There is also a cluster in Co. Cork. the reason for the presence of Kerrigans in these areas is unclear.

Northern Ireland has around a third of all Irish families. It has 17% of the Kerrigans.

Kidd
300 families

MacLysaght considers Kidd in Ireland to be a name of English origin. Reaney puts its origin in England mainly to 'kide', Middle English for 'kid', but sometimes to a form of Kitt, a nickname for Christopher. Black, on Scottish surnames, considers Kitt to have been a more important origin than kid, north of the border. It is a common name in Dundee and Arbroath. In both countries it is recorded from the twelfth century.

The map shows the distribution of some 215 families with telephones in Ireland in 1992. Allowing for homes without telephones, there are likely to have been about 300 families altogether. Cos. Antrim and Down are the most important areas of settlement. A third of all the families live in the Belfast, Antrim and Lisburn area, which is three times the national average representation. Many of the rest live in areas immediately adjacent.

Greater Dublin has been a major destination for internal migration in relatively modern times and now accounts for over a fifth of Irish families. Some 15% of Kidd families live there. This is a high proportion in comparison with some other Ulster families, but the origin of Kidds in the capital may be more local. Around 15% of them live around Carlow. This cluster is unexpected for an Irish name that has been described as almost exclusively Ulster. The explanation may date back to the Cromwellian land confiscations which were particularly high in Co. Carlow.

Northern Ireland has about a third of all Irish families. It has two-thirds of all Kidd families.

Kieran
210 families

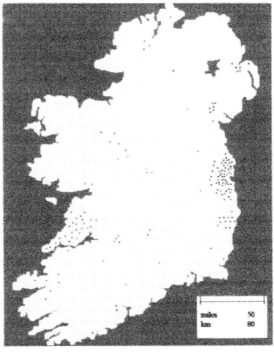

The Irish sept of Ó Céirín, from ciar, meaning black or dark brown, was in early times in possession of the greater part of the barony of Costello, which straddled the Mayo and Roscommon county borders. From a paramount position in the Middle Ages they declined in importance. An inquisition of 1609 found them as erenaghs of Killaghtee in the diocese of Raphoe, Co. Donegal. A census of 1659 found them numerous in Co. Sligo.

In 1420, an influential branch moved to what is now Co. Clare where they subsequently became prominent.

According to MacLysaght, Co. Mayo remains the most important location for members of the sept, but families there have anglicised the name to Kearns by the adoption of a terminal 's' so often found on English surnames. There are six variants with the 's' today, including Cairns. There are four variants without the 's', shared by a total of 149 families. These are shown on the map. Allowing for homes without telephones, there were likely to have been 210 families altogether. Only 30% of the families have the citation form of the name, Kieran. Kerin families account for 36%; Kearon families account for 26%; and Kerrane families for 8%.

Apart from a mixture in Dublin, the variants are strongly regional. Kearon is the variant in the south east. Kerin is exclusively the western part of Co. Clare. Kieran is the form in Dublin and Northern Ireland.

McKillop
100 families

The Gaelic origin of this name is Mac Fhilib. It means 'son of Philip', though the identity of the Philip who first gave the name is unknown. The aspirated pronunciation of 'F' in the genitive produces the sound and spelling of the anglicised version of the name. McKillop is a branch of the Scottish Clan MacDonell or MacDonald of Keppoch, though some of the name are said to have been standard-bearers of the Campbells of Dunstaffnage and the name also occurs on the Scottish island of Arran.

Co. Antrim was not one of the counties planted at the beginning of the seventeenth century, but MacLysaght notes that McKillop was recorded in the 'census' of 1659 among "the principal Irish names with some Scotch in the barony of Glencarn". He was unable to find when it was established in Ireland, but practically all early birth registrations, wills and other references to the name have been in Co. Antrim. He says that Killops and Kellops are variants.

The map shows the distribution of some 79 McKillop households with telephones in 1992. Allowing for homes without telephones, there would probably be just over a hundred families altogether. They remain overwhelmingly Co. Antrim families. Unusually, there is no pronounced cluster around Belfast. In addition there are 16 Killops families with telephones, say 20 altogether. They live in much the same area as the McKillop families. There are no Kellops families at this time. Despite their long standing presence in Ireland, there are no McKillop families in the Republic.

Mother Mary MacKillop, founder of the Australian order, the Sisters of St. Joseph, was of a Catholic family of the Scottish Highlands.

King
2200 families

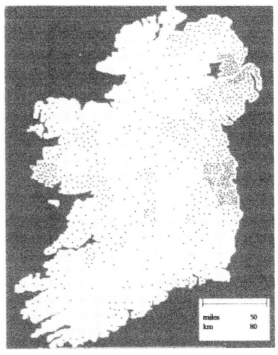

The surname 'King' is derived from the Old English 'Cyning' or 'Cyng'. It would have been a nick-name for someone of kingly qualities or appearance, or for someone who had appeared as a king in a play or pageant, or who had been King of Misrule or 'king' of a tournament. The name was in widespread use and is found in Scotland from the mid 13th century.

King families in Ireland may be of English or Scottish origin, brought into the country by settlers from Britain. It may also be Irish, as a translation or pseudo-translation of Gaelic names containing the element 'rí', meaning 'king': Conry, Conroy, Cunree in Connaught; MacAree and MacKeary in Oriel, and even sometimes Gilroy and MacKinn. There is also a rare name, Ó Cionga, now King, which belongs to Lough Ree.

The map shows the distribution of some 2,200 King families in 1992. Ten dots represent 1% of the total. A quarter live in Northern Ireland, which has a third of all Irish households. This is a low proportion for a plantation name and is explained by the popularity of the name in the Republic. The various sources of the name are evident. The main clusters are around Dublin and Belfast, where the density of settlement is much the same. In neither urban area is the proportion of King families at the national average level for all families. Greater Dublin has 17% as compared to 22%; and Belfast has 9% as compared to 11%. A further 2% live in Ards, adjacent to the Belfast area. This is characteristic of Protestant settlement.

The Irish source areas are apparent, in Connaught and also in Oriel, by the density in Co. Cavan. There are clusters around Athlone and Roscrea. Though the name is widespead, there are extensive parts of both Northern Ireland and the Republic in which it is rare.

McKinley
460 families

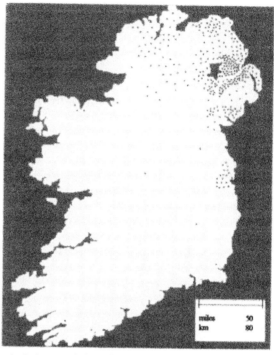

McKinley, with an occasional spelling of McKinlay, is from the Scots Gaelic Mac Fhionn Laoich, meaning 'son of the fair hero'. Unlike most Scots names with a 'Mac' prefix, McKinley is not a common name in Scotland. It is found mainly in Glenlyon and Balquihidder. The Irish Gaelic Mac an Leagha, son of the physician, usually rendered as McAlee, was sometimes anglicised as McKinley in Co. Antrim.

McKinley is not a numerous in Northern Ireland either. The map shows the distribution of some 330 families with telephones in 1992. Adjusting for homes without telephones means that there are about 460 families altogether. Families of Mac an Leagha origin amongst them are likely to be few. The distribution pattern has typical characteristics of the Scottish settlement of Ulster. About a quarter of all the families live in the Belfast, Antrim and Lisburn area, more than twice the national average proportion of 11%. The cluster extends south eastwards into Lurgan and Portadown, where another 9% live. The coast of Antrim and the Ards peninsula of Down stand out and there is a cluster in south Down and south Armagh. There is representation throughout the rest of Northern Ireland. About 10% of the families live in north Donegal.

The presence of the name in Donegal recalls the Irish Gaelic Mag Fhionnghaile, a Donegal family, meaning 'fair valour', which produced McGinley. Historically, the two names were seldom used as synonyms. McGinley is much more numerous in Donegal than McKinley. It may be that some Mag Fhionnghaile families, closer to the Scottish influence of east Ulster, have been rendered into English as McKinley.

With the exception of Donegal, the name is virtually unknown in the Republic. Greater Dublin has attracted about 22% of all Irish families. Only 5% of McKinley families are to be found there.

Lacey
600 families

The name Lacey in Ireland may have one of two origins, Anglo-Norman and Irish. The first Anglo-Norman, Hugo de Lacy, was granted the whole of the Kingdom of Meath, comprising Co. Meath and additional territory. Another Anglo-Norman family in Limerick had a name first recorded as del Essé, which evolved into Lacy. De Lacy was hibernicised as de Léis and Léiseach and sometimes was rendered into English as Leash.

The Irish origin of the name Lacey is from an early form Ó Flaithgheasa, descendant of flaith, prince, which became Ó Laitheasa

The map shows the distribution of some 330 families with telephones in 1992. Making allowance for homes without phones, there are probably 600 Lacey families altogether, with a minority having the spelling Lacy. In common with many families in present day Ireland, the main location is Greater Dublin. About 40% of Lacey families live there, almost twice the national average. The high proportion in Dublin is typical of both Anglo-Norman names and Leinster names generally.

The fact that Lacey representation today is very thin in areas associated with Anglo-Normans of the name suggests the Anglo-Normans were landlords with little demographic impact. Co. Wexford shows up clearly. About 17% of Lacey families live there. Wexford was the site of Maurice FitzGerald's landing in 1169 and many Anglo-Norman names are to be found there. Nevertheless It is safe to assume that the relative strength of Lacey representation in Wexford is due to the local Gaelic sept. In proportion to the total population however, Lacey numbers are very few. Even in Wexford, they are only a fifth of 1%. The low representation in Northern Ireland, about 4%, is typical of Anglo-Norman names.

Lacey is a rare name in Ireland. With only one family in 2,500 having the name, the profile it has achieved well exceeds its numbers.

McLaughlin
2600 families

Mac Lachlainn or Mac Lochlainn is one of several Irish septs which took their surname from a Norse personal name. As McLachlan, it is also found in Scotland, where its chief seat was in Cowal in Argyll.

The McLaughlins are a senior branch of the northern O'Neill. Their territory was in Inishowen in northern Co. Donegal. They were continuously mentioned in Ulster in the Irish Annals until they lost their ascendancy after a battle in 1241. The modern spelling in the home territory of the name is usually McLaghlin. McLoughlin is also found and is numerous. This variant is however more dispersed and more likely to have an origin other than Mac Lachlainn. Some will be of the O'Melaghlins of Meath. A spelling variant McGloughlin is found in Dublin.

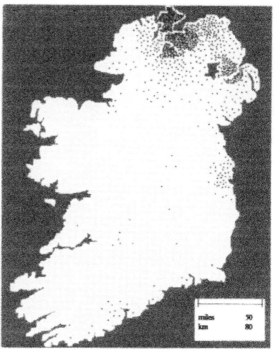

The map shows the distribution of some 2,600 McLaughlin families in 1992. Ten dots represent 1% of the total. Inishowen still stands out for the density of McLaughlin settlement. A fifth of all the families live in this small area. The same density extends into Derry and Tyrone, where over a third of the families live.

Greater Dublin has over a fifth of all Irish families. It has only 4% of the McLaughlins. Representation in the Republic generally is thin. The urban areas of Cork, Waterford, Limerick and Sligo are just discernible, perhaps because of migration in relatively recent times. Representation in the Belfast area is slightly higher than the 11% national average.

The McLaughlin population thins out markedly outside its historic core, even within Donegal. It is plentiful in the area of Co. Derry opposite Inishowen. Though most Ulster families will be of Irish origin, some will be Scottish. It is not clear from the map whether the density in western Antrim is due to expansion from the Irish core area or from Scotland. The Glens of Antrim are more thinly settled than western Antrim. For this name, the border between the Republic and Northern Ireland is irrelevant.

Lavelle
465 families

Lavelle is an anglicised form of the Irish Ó Maolfábhail, meaning descendant of the devotee of (St) Fabhail. There were two Irish septs of the name. One was based at Carrickabraghy in the north west of Inishowen, Co. Donegal. The other was originally seated at Donaghpatrick in the barony of Clare in Co. Galway.

The families in Donegal generally adopted McFaul or McPaul for their anglicised surnames, perhaps influenced by Scottish families called McFall in Ulster. Those in Connaught adopted Lavelle. Both anglicised forms are adaptations of the Gaelic. In Donegal, the 'O' was dropped and the Maol became Mac. In Connaught, the 'O' was dropped, the 'l' of Maol was retained, and the 'f' was aspirated.

In the mid 19th century O'Mullawill was common, but Lavelle was recorded as coming into use. The names O'Lawell, O'Lowell and O'Lavell were recorded in the 17th century Money Hearth Rolls for Co. Armagh.

The map shows the distribution of some 260 families with telephones in 1992. Adjusting for homes without telephones means there are probably 465 families altogether. About 22% of the Lavelle families live in Greater Dublin, the same as the national average. The barony of Clare is north of Galway City. The name is not numerous in Galway, or in the adjacent part of Mayo. The densest settlement, apart from Dublin, is in Mayo. There are a few families in Belfast, no doubt attracted by job opportunities.

There is a third cluster of families centred on Louth and south Armagh, presumably descendants of those recorded in the 17th century Hearth Rolls. This is hard to explain in terms of a Mayo or Donegal origin and it may be that it is yet another sept.

The McFaul/McPaul variant is much rarer than Lavelle. Like Lavelle, it also is scarce in the barony of its reputed seat.

Leahy
1200 families

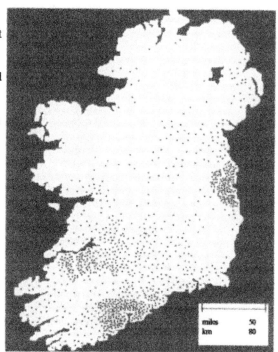

In Irish this surname is Ó Laochda, from 'laoch', a hero. It has long been associated with Munster, being well recorded in the Fiants, the Ormond deeds and the Money Hearth Rolls in the sixteenth and seventeenth centuries. Some Leahy names are more properly Lahy, being from the south Galway and Clare names of Ó Laithimh and Ó Lathaigh, themselves derived from flaitheamh, a lord or ruler. Other names from this source have been Lahiff and Flahy.

The map shows the distribution of some 1,200 Leahy families in 1992. One dot represents 0.1% of the total. The thin scatter in Galway and Clare indicates that the proportion of the families with a possible Lahy origin is relatively small.

For most families in modern times, Greater Dublin is the most important location. With its origins remote from Dublin, the proportion of Leahys living in the Republic's capital area is, at 14%, substantially less than the 22% national average. Munster remains more important. There are two main concentrations. Co Cork has 27% and a further 21% live in Kerry and Limerick. Leahy families will have a larger proportion of all families in the Kerry and Limerick border area than they do in the heavily populated Dublin and Cork areas. Historically associated with Cork, Kerry, Limerick and Tipperary, the sept now extends into Waterford and Kilkenny.

Northern Ireland has about a third of all Irish households. It has under 3% of Leahy families. Northern families are more likely to have names with a more English appearance than those in the Republic. This is true also of Leahy families. A quarter in the North have the spelling Leahey.

O'Leary
5400 families

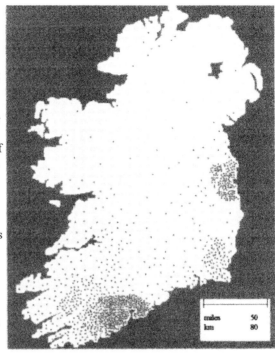

In Irish Ó Laoghaire, from the Gaelic for calf keeper, the O'Learys were originally chiefs of the coastal country around Rosscarbery in south west Cork. At the time of the Anglo-Norman invasion they were moved about twenty miles further north, where, under the MacCarthys, they became lords of a territory between Macroom and Inchigeelagh. The head of the family resided at Carrignacurra, about a mile to the east of the village of Inchigeelagh.

This local migration has meant that the O'Learys are still concentrated in the south-west. The map shows that the area around Carberry is still less densely settled than that around Macroom and Inchigeelagh. Both are now overshadowed by the O'Leary numbers in the urban area of Cork city itself.

The map shows the distribution of some 3,000 O'Leary families in 1992, including a very few with the Irish spelling Ó Laoghaire and the simplified form Ó Laoire. Almost half of them live in Co. Cork where they make up about 1½% of the population. Just over 10% live in Co. Kerry, where they account for 1% of the population. They are almost 1% in Co. Wexford.

Greater Dublin has long been a destination for internal migration. This is particularly so since the Famine and because of industrialisation. For many families the concentration of their numbers in Dublin is the biggest in the country. Only 14% of O'Leary families live there. For the O'Leary families, the most important location is Cork.

O'Leary remains a name associated with the southern half of the country. Northern Ireland has a third of all the households in Ireland. Fewer than 1% of the O'Learys live there.

Lee
1200 families

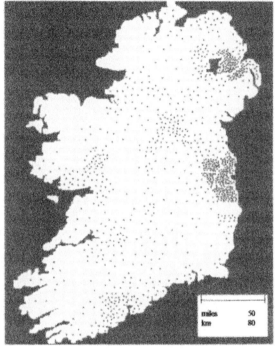

In Irish the source word is Laoidhigh, the genitive of laoidheach, the adjective formed from laoidh, a poem. This produced two forms with the Ó prefix, and two with Mac. Ó Laoidhigh is the form around Cork and Limerick, and Ó Laidhigh is around Galway. MacLaoidhigh was the form in Leix. Mac an Leagha was found in Ulster, which Woulfe gives as son of the physician. With few exceptions, these have become anglicised as Lee.

In the English language, Lee, Lea, Leigh and Ley are names derived from nominative or dative cases of the Anglo-Saxon 'leah'. Originally it meant a wood, glade or clearing. It is related to 'light' - a clearing in the woods. It is certainly the most common topographical suffix in English place-names. It is rare in Scotland. In simplex form it was an early surname. Woulfe indicates that names from this source appeared in the Anglo-Norman era in Meath, Kildare and Kilkenny. MacLysaght says by the beginning of the 17th century this English name was well established in plantations in Tipperary and elsewhere.

The map shows the distribution of the 1,370 families with the surname Lee in 1992. Each dot represents 0.1%. The areas associated with Anglo-Norman settlement are apparent through the south and west. Leix is an area of sparse settlement, but Cos. Cavan and Longford appear as a definite settlement cluster. Lee is most numerous in Cavan, at about one family in 250. This may indicate planter origin.

About 10% of Lee families live in the Belfast area, about the same as the national average. This would be a high proportion for a Gaelic name, which suggests that the area includes people of English origin. About 22% of the families live in Greater Dublin, the same as the national average.

Northern Ireland has a third of all Irish households. It has 23% of Lee families.

Logan
940 families

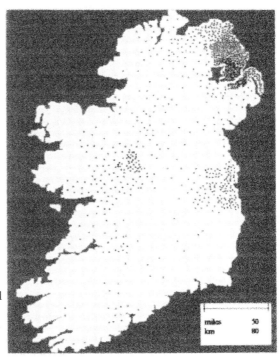

The name Logan may be of one of three origins in Ireland. Along with Lohan, it is a derivative of the Irish Ó Leocháin. The chiefs of this sept were lords of Gailenga Mór, now Morgallion, Co. Westmeath, until driven west of the Shannon by the Anglo-Normans. Less exalted Ó Leocháin families however remained in their homeland. A number of Logans and O'Louchans appear as names of parish clergy in the early fifteenth century Armagh and Down.

The Norman invasion also brought a Norman family called de Logan. They were recorded occasionally in medieval documents in Carrickfergus, Co. Antrim, the first as early as 1190. Norman settlement in Ulster was slight and bearers of this name may be presumed to have been rare.

Most Logan families in Ireland today are of Scottish origin. Logan was the original name of the clan Maclennan. Petty's 'Census' of 1659, half a century after the Plantation of Ulster, records Loggan as one of the principal names in four baronies of Co. Antrim. In three of them it was classified as Irish, but there is little doubt that these were Scottish Logans.

The map shows the distribution of some 940 families in Ireland in 1992. Eighty-two percent of them have the spelling Logan. The remainder are Lohan. Ten dots make up approximately 1% of the total. There are also 10 Loughan families, of whom eight live in the Belfast area. Northern Ireland has a third of all Irish households. It has three quarters of the Logans but none of the Lohans.

The areas historically associated with the name appear clearly on the map. The predominance of the Scottish origin name is evident from the density of settlement in Antrim and in the uniformity of spelling in Northern Ireland. Apart from Dublin, where families of both spellings have converged, Lohan as a name is now almost entirely west of the Shannon.

O'Loughlin
780 families

When Norwegian Vikings settled in Ireland during the Dark Ages, a kind of creole Norse emerged as the races mingled. Their fjord-country Scandinavian homeland became known as 'loughland'. In the Irish language, the settlers were called Lochlanns, Lochlainn in the genitive, and the Irish Annals refer to them as such in describing the subsequent Norse-Irish settlement of north western England in the late ninth century. Woulfe says that Lochlainn became a personal name.

At first, a sept in north Donegal was called O'Loughlin, but they adopted the 'Mac' prefix in the twelfth century. McLaughlin is the usual spelling today.

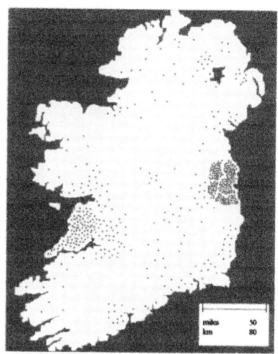

The map shows the distribution of some 540 O'Loughlin families with telephones in Ireland in 1992. Allowing for homes then without phones, there would be 780 families altogether. About 8% of them live in Northern Ireland, where the Donegal origin may provide an explanation. Another sept arose in Dalcassia, which is the pre-eminent historic location today for the O'Loughlins. Their strength in west Clare is evident. Almost a fifth of O'Loughlin families live there. A few in addition use the spellings O'Loghlin or O'Loghlen.

Though the name is now found throughout Ireland, it remains strongest in areas nearest the sea. Greater Dublin has 22% of the population of Ireland, but O'Loughlin strength there is 30%. This is a high proportion, though being a rare name it means few families. O'Loughlin strength in Dublin is probably the result of recent economic migration, but it recalls that Dublin was once a Norse city which must have been the most important staging post from which the Lochlainn settlement of England was launched.

Loughman
420 families

MacLysaght sees this surname as a variant of Ó Lachtnáin, the name of several small Connaught septs. It means descendant of Lachtnán, diminutive of lachtna, gray. Numerous mediaeval bishops and abbots of the name were all Connaught men. The usual anglicised form of the name is Loughnane or Loughnan.

Ó Lachtnáin is an example of the tendency for a rare Gaelic name to be changed to a well known name of a similar sound. In Meath it has become O'Loughlin, whilst Loftus is found in Connaught and Lawton in Cork.

The map shows the distribution of 224 families with telephones in 1992. Allowing for homes without phones, there are probably about 420 Ó Lachtnáin families altogether. A third of the families have the name Loghman. The remainder are Loughnane families, including some with the spelling Loughnan. From the locations indicated, it appears that the those of the clan living to the south and east of the main cluster chose the form Loughman, whilst the two-thirds living to the north and west preferred Loughnane. Perhaps because they are closer to Dublin, a third of the Loughmans now live in the Republic's capital area, whereas only a sixth of the Loughnanes live there. The high proportion of Loughmans in Dublin is a characteristic of Leinster names.

Loughman is a very rare name. In 1991 Ireland had 1.56 million households. Loughman families therefore account for only one in 12,000.

Love
280 families

The surname Love may be of Anglo-Norman, English or Gaelic origin. Black found it long established in Scotland in the Monklands area, near Glasgow, where he had little doubt of its derivation from the Old French for 'wolf'. This was 'louve' in the feminine and 'loupe' in the masculine. The surname Lovell is from a diminutive of 'louve'. There is an Old English source in 'Lufu', meaning 'love', which was a popular and widely distributed woman's name. The masculine 'lufa' was also found.

Woulfe has Love as a translation of the Gaelic Mac Ionmhain, son of beloved. In Scotland, some McKinnons in the Western Isles anglicised their name as 'Love' in the erroneous belief that McKinnon was derived from Mac Ionmhain. The Gaelic for love is 'grádh', which has meant that some McGraths, in Ulster pronounced McCgraw, have also translated their name as Love.

The map shows the distribution of some 200 families with telephones in 1992. Allowing for homes without telephones means there will be about 280 families altogether.

As McGrath is widely distributed through Ulster and elsewhere, a McGrath origin does not account for the concentrations of the Love surname. The Belfast, Lisburn and Antrim area has been a destination for internal migration. It has 11% of all Irish families and 15% of all Love families. This high proportion suggests Scotland as the main origin of the name. North Londonderry and Fermanagh also appear as areas of high density of settlement by Love families, again suggesting a pattern of the Plantation era.

Greater Dublin has about 22% of all Irish families. It has only 8% of Love families. Northern Ireland has about a third of all Irish families. Over two-thirds of Love families live there.

Lynch
5700 families

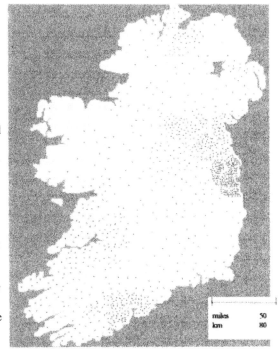

The surname Lynch has two origins: the Gaelic Ó Loingsigh and the Anglo-Norman de Lench. The Gaelic Lynches, formerly called O'Lynch, comprise a number of septs, notably in Sligo, Breffny (Cavan), Dalriada (North Antrim), Thomond (Clare), and Corca Loaidhe (south west Cork). The sept of Donegal was more correctly MacLoingseacháin, or Lynchehaun.

After the Anglo-Norman invasion, the de Lench family first settled in Meath. At the beginning of the fourteenth century a branch of them migrated to Galway, where they became the most influential of the 'Tribes'. Their predominance in the affairs of Galway city until the end of the Jacobite wars has meant that the Anglo-Norman Lynches have been more prominent nationally than their Gaelic namesakes.

The map shows the distribution of the 5,700 Lynch families in 1992. One dot represents 0.1% of the total. As with most names today, Greater Dublin is the most important cluster. It has 18% of the Lynches, compared to 22% of all families.

Descendants of the Gaelic septs are apparent in Cos. Cork, Clare and Donegal. Cavan is the county in which the Lynches have the highest proportion of the population: they account for almost 2%. There are few now in north Antrim, whence came the forebears of the eighteenth century American Col. Charles Lynch, remembered for 'lynch law'.

The fame of the Anglo-Norman Lynches of Galway is not matched by high numbers of families with the name in the county.

Lynch representation in Northern Ireland is sparse. Only 8% of families live there, as compared to 31% of all Irish families.

Lynn
470 families

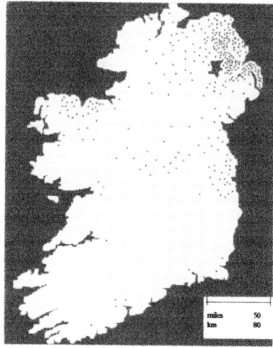

The surname Ó Floinn appeared in several parts of Ireland from the Gaelic personal name Flann, meaning ruddy. Modern Ulster Irish aspirated the initial 'F', thus producing the surnames Lynn and O'Lynn. Septs originating elsewhere in the country evolved into the surnames Flynn and O'Flynn. Lynn and O'Lynn make up around 7% of the Ó Floinn derivatives.

The map shows the distribution of 317 families with telephones in 1992. Adjusting for telephone ownership puts the estimate for all families at 470. Lynn accounts for 96% and O'Lynn for 4%.

For many names the urban areas take the lead in the restoration of the 'O' prefix, but this does not apply to the modern versions of Ó Floinn. The O'Lynns are clustered around Larne, and the O'Flynns around Cork. The capitals, Belfast and Dublin, are unimportant.

The presence of Lynn the east coast down to Dublin may be put down to economic opportunities in relatively recent times. The name is virtually unknown in the southern half of the country, and also in Leitrim where the Flynns have their strongest representation at 1¾% of the population. It is intermixed with Flynn in Westmeath and in Mayo and Sligo.

The Lynn cluster in Mayo and Sligo is clearly separate from the main cluster in east Ulster. It accounts for about 10% of all Lynns now. It may be of Ulster origin. Because the West has suffered severe depopulation since the Famine and Antrim and Down have grown, that the proportion of the sept that moved to Connaught could have been 20% or more.

Magee
1570 families

Magee is the usual spelling of the Gaelic Mag Aoidha, meaning son of Hugh. The 'c' of 'Mac' often became 'g' before a vowel. There are other spelling variants, including MacGee and McGhee, the forms with a 'c' being more common in the west of Ulster.

Magee has two origins, Irish and Scottish. The Irish Magees belong to the country on the borders of Cos. Donegal and Tyrone. The Magees of Scottish origin are akin to the MacDonnells and claim descent from Colla Uais, making them too ultimately Irish. They are associated with Co. Antrim, where the large isthmus to the east of Lough Larne was once in their possession and is still called Island Magee.

The map shows the distribution of some 1570 families in 1992. Ten dots represent 1% of the total. The Donegal-Tyrone border area is discernible by density of settlement. Together with adjacent parts of Derry, this may be taken to be the area of the Irish origin Magee families. Fermanagh and Cavan appear prominently, which may be taken as evidence of Scottish settlement of the Plantation era. Scottish origin would also account for the density of Magee settlement in east Ulster. The Belfast, Lisburn and Antrim area has 28% of all the Magee families, compared to 11% of Irish families as a whole. The same density extends to Portadown, making a core area home to 37% of Magee families.

Magee is overwhelmingly an Ulster name. Its presence in Dublin and Cork is likely to be the result of recent migration. Greater Dublin has over a fifth of all Irish families. It has only 9% of the Magees.

Though not numerous, there is a cluster of families in Co. Kildare for which the origin is not clear.

Maguire
3700 families

Maguire is the most common anglicisation of the Irish Maguidhir. MacGuire is occasionally found. Mag is a form of Mac used before vowels and Uidhir means of the dun color.

Appearing in the tenth century in what became Co. Fermanagh, Maguires became predominant there in the fourteenth. Their chief was one of the most important in Ulster until the Plantation. They suffered severely by the confiscations of Cromwell and William of Orange. In the years following William's military successes of 1690 and 1691, Maguires were prominent among the Wild Geese in the service of France and Austria.

The map shows the distribution of 3,700 families in 1992. Each dot represents 0.1%.

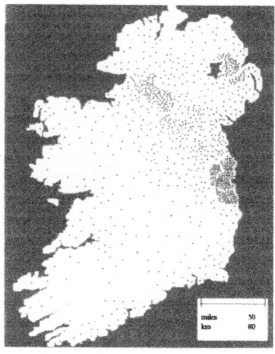

The Maguire area of origin, Co. Fermanagh, appears clearly. Some 10% of the families still live there, where they make up 2½% of the population. They are also strongly represented in neighbouring Co. Cavan where they are about 1%. The map also shows the two main destinations for the internal migration of recent years: Dublin and Belfast. In common with many families, the most numerous cluster of Maguires today is in Greater Dublin. About 22% of their families live there, the same proportion as of the all-Ireland population. About 8% of Maguires live in the area of Belfast, Antrim and Lisburn. About 11% of all Irish families live in this area.

Maguires are relatively thinly spread south of a line from Dublin to Donegal. About 29% live in Northern Ireland, slightly less than the national average.

Maher
2600 families

Maher is in Irish Ó Meachair, derived from meachar, the word for hospitable. It is the name of a family of the same stock as the O'Carrols of Ely-O'Carrol, who were lords of the barony of Ui Cairin, now Ikerrin, in the north of Co. Tipperary. O'Meachair resided at Druim Saileach, now the site of the castle of Moydrum, at the foot of the famous Devil's Bit mountain, about five miles south of Roscrea.

Shortly after the Anglo-Norman invasion Ikerrin was added to Ormond, but unlike some Gaelic septs, their chief was left in possession, though subject to the Butlers who had become Earls of Ormond.

The map shows the distribution of some 2,600 families in Ireland in 1992. Ten

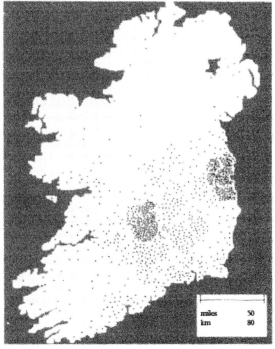

dots make up 1% of the total. Eighty-six percent of the families have the spelling Maher. The remainder spell the name Meagher.

Like many families today, Greater Dublin is now the most important location for the Mahers. About 24% live there, slightly more than the 22% national average. This may be due to depopulation in Tipperary since the Famine, where numbers in 1971 were little more than a quarter of the 1841 level. There has been a slight gain since then.

There remains nevertheless a striking concentration of Maher families around Roscrea. Some 14% of all the families in Ireland continue to live in this core area of the sept. The natural dispersal of the name appears to have been mainly to south and east into the rest of Tipperary, Kilkenny and Carlow.

The two spelling forms have different distributions: 34% of the Meaghers are in Dublin. The core area itself has 16% of the Mahers, but only 10% of the Meaghers. The Meagher distribution suggests it is largely a restored spelling. These are typically more urban and southern than earlier anglicised forms.

Mahon
1220 families

Mahon has two origins: Ó Mocháin means descendant of Mochán, a 'pet' form of an early name beginning with 'Moch'; and Ó Macháin, which means descendant of Machán, the youth. O'Mahon became much used for Ó Mocháin as well as Ó Macháin. The name also appears as Maughan. Mahon, Mohan and Maughan families, particularly in Connaught, anglicised their name as Vaughan, evidently from the genitive of Mocháin, Uí Mhocháin, which has the same pronunciation. Vaughan, from the Welsh 'fychan', small, has been in Ireland since the sixteenth century, though few of the name will be of Welsh extraction.

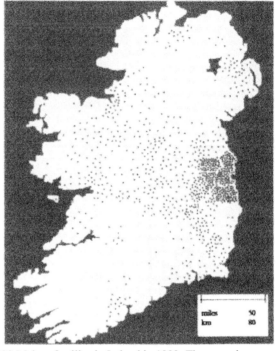

Neither Mahon nor Mohan suggests where the name ought to be found. The map shows the distribution of some 1,220 Mahon families in Ireland in 1992. The name is strongest in Leinster. This generally means that Greater Dublin appears at a higher than usual density. A third of Mahons live around the Republic's capital as compared to just over a fifth of all Irish families. The density in Dublin will reflect the build-up of population there in relatively modern times. Modern population build-up may also account for the presence of the name in Belfast, Derry, Cork and Waterford.

Outside Dublin, the density is strongest in the catchment area of the River Slaney, which rises west of Dublin and enters the sea at Wexford. Most of the remainder of the families live in the centre of the country from Greater Dublin west to Galway and Sligo.

The name is largely absent from the coastal area south of Dublin and from the Wicklow mountains. It is absent from much of Munster, much of Ulster, and the west of Connaught.

Northern Ireland has a third of all Irish families. It has only 6% of the Mahons.

O'Mahony
3250 families

O'Mahony is from the Irish Ó Mathghamhna, descendant of Mathghamhain, meaning 'bear', who was a grandson of Brian Boru. Mathghamhain's father, Cian, commanded the forces of Desmond at the battle of Clontarf in 1014, where Mathghamhain was slain with many other Desmond men. O'Mahony chieftains were powerful, controlling an extensive district in Co. Cork along the River Bandon, which became the barony of Kinelmeaky, and south to the coast. They were often described as princes. In modernised spelling, the name is Ó Mahúna,

MacLysaght, who often used data now a century old, said the name, usually without the prefix O, was among the hundred commonest Irish surnames. The map shows the distribution of some 3,250 families in Ireland in 1992. Ten dots make up 1% of the total. A minority have an 'ey' ending rather than 'y'. Where the prefix is reintroduced, it tends to be most numerous in the south and in urban areas. Of the families in Co. Cork, 96% have the prefix. In Dublin, those with the O are 67%, whilst of the few in Northern Ireland, only 18% are O'Mahony. Overall, 86% of the families now have the prefix.

The clan remains overwhelmingly south western. For most families, Greater Dublin is now their most important location, but only 11% of O'Mahonys and Mahonys live there. Co. Cork has 52% of the families, who make up 1½% of its population.

The name is virtually unknown in central and northern counties of Ireland. Northern Ireland has about a third of all Irish households. It has under 1% of the O'Mahony and Mahony families.

Marshall
800 families

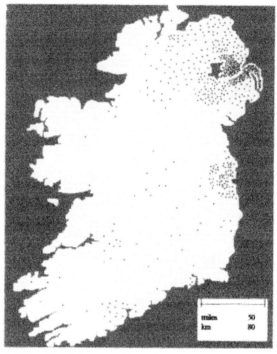

This is an occupational name of Frankish origin. It had a meaning of horse (mare) servant. Though the kindred Anglo-Saxon language could produce much the same word, Marshall as a name was brought to the British Isles by the Normans. Early examples in England may refer to a high office of state, most notably the Earl Marshal. Later the surname is equated with Smith and Faber. In Scotland, most Marshalls were of the latter type. Scotland was the main source of the name in Ireland, most probably from post-Plantation settlers.

The name in Ireland is rare. The map shows the distribution of some 580 Marshall families in 1992. Allowing for homes without telephones, there were just under 800 Marshall families altogether. Northern Ireland has over two thirds of Marshall families. It has one third of all Irish families. The six counties stand out as areas of high density settlement. The Belfast, Antrim and Lisburn area has 26% of Marshall families, compared with 11% of all Irish families. Another 9% live in Ards.

There are clusters of Marshalls around Cork and Limerick. This presence in the South is likely to pre-date the Plantation of Ulster and is probably from Anglo-Norman times. Greater Dublin has 11% of Marshall families, under half of the national average resident in the capital, but high for a Plantation name.

Martin
4600 families

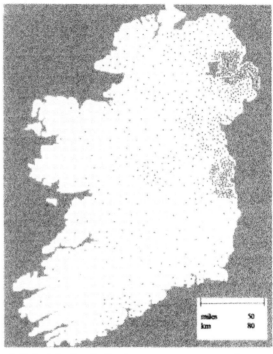

After calling 25 localities in Normandy after the military saint of France, the Normans introduced the name Martin to lands they conquered throughout Europe and the Mediterranean. It became a popular Christian name and an early surname.

Though the name came to Ireland with Strongbow's followers and a Martin family went on to become one of the celebrated 'Tribes of Galway', the distribution of 4,600 Martin families in 1992 does not show the typical Anglo-Norman settlement imprint. Each dot on the map represents 0.1% of the total. The most striking feature is the strength of the name in Antrim and Down. The area of concentration on the map accommodates about 14% of all Ireland's families. It contains 22% of all the Martins, indicating a strong presence of families of English and Scottish origin from the Plantation of Ulster. Martin would have been adopted by their forebears under Norman influence in Britain.

The name had also been adopted by native families in Ireland. These were mainly in the centre and north of the country. The name MacMáirtin was assumed by a branch of the O'Neills in Tyrone, where there was also a Gilmartin family. Ó Martáin was an established name in Westmeath in the sixteenth century. Martins today have about 0.5% of the population of Westmeath. They are at the same level over much of Ulster. Martins' strength in Antrim and Down does not exceed this. The cluster in the west of Westmeath means that the area where Martins make up the greatest proportion of the total population is probably around Athlone and Mullingar.

Economic opportunities in Greater Dublin in modern times have attracted Martins of all three origins. Their representation in the area at 15% is two-thirds of the national average.

Mathers
160 families

Mathers is derived from the Anglo-Saxon 'maethere', meaning a mower or reaper. It was first recorded as Alan le Mathere in the Wiltshire Assize rolls of 1249. Mather was the form in which it was first used as a surname and it was as such that it came to Ireland from Yorkshire. Like many English surnames, Mather later acquired a final 's'.

Mather appears in Dublin records from the early seventeenth century. By the end of that century it was well established in Co. Armagh.

The map shows the distribution of some 112 families with telephones in Ireland in 1992. Allowing for homes without telephones, there were probably about 160 families altogether. Some 82% of them have the final 's'. The remainder spell the name as 'Mather'.

It may be seen that there are two principal areas of settlement: Northern Ireland and Dublin with Kildare. Mathers is the normal form of the name in the North, whilst families in the Republic are almost all called Mather. About 13% of the families live in the Belfast, Antrim and Lisburn area. This is slightly more than the national average and is indicative of a British origin name.

In both the North and the Republic, the population in the capital city area is overshadowed by another area. A third of the Northern Ireland Mathers families live south of Lough Neagh around Portadown and Lurgan. Of the Republic's Mather families, almost half live in Co. Kildare.

Maynes
210 families

According to Black on Scottish surnames, Mains was the name of the principal or home farm on an estate. Reaney on British surnames sees Mains along with Main and Maine as spelling variants of Mayne and Maynes and from the French for 'strength' or 'hands', or from the province of Maine or the town of Mayenne. In Scotland the Old Norse Magnus became MacManus with MacManis recorded in 1506 and MacMaines in 1673. Ireland today has all the spelling variants noted by Reaney and also has Maines.

The map shows the distribution of 149 households with telephones in 1992. Allowing for homes without phones, there are likely to be 210 families altogether. Those with the 's' were in a minority of 17%.

Much the most common spelling is Maynes. There were only two Mains families, one in Belfast and one in Dundonald. There was only one with the spelling Maines. The distribution for Mayne includes three spellings of Main and three of Maine. With one exception, those in the Republic's capital all have the spelling Mayne.

Both Maynes and Mayne are heavily represented in the Belfast, Lisburn and Antrim area with 26% of their number there, more than twice the national average. To some extent this may reflect that this was a destination for jobs in industry with relatively recent settlement. The origins of the forms without the 's' are mainly Antrim and Down. Those with the 's' are mainly south Londonderry. The spelling Mains may indicate a different history from Maynes, or it may be that families detached from the south Londonderry cluster adopted a simpler and more anglicised form.

The proportion of the families in Dublin at 18% is higher than would be expected of a Northern origin name. It may be that some families there moved directly from England rather than from Ulster.

Mee
116 families

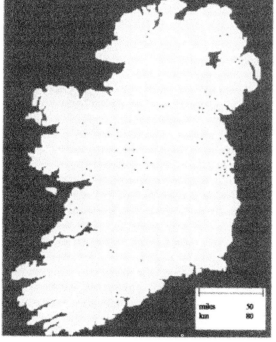

The surname of the sept of Ó Miadhaigh was first anglicised as O'Miey and later as Mee and Mea. It was located in Teffia, Co. Westmeath, where the name Clonyveey, Cluain Uí Miadhaigh, (O'Mee's meadow), bears witness to their presence. The name is derived from miadhach, meaning honourable.

As happened with many Irish septs in that area, the O'Mees were dispossessed by the Anglo-Normans. The Fiants of the sixteenth century show that they continued in the area only as peasants. Some moved north-westwards. MacLysaght states that Mee and Mea are the usual modern forms of the name and that it is mostly found in Sligo and neighbouring counties.

According to MacLysaght, families in Munster are likely to be of different origin. Those in Tipperary were from Mac Máighe, where the pronunciation is closer to McMawe. Mee has also been found as an abbreviation of MacNamee, another originally Westmeath family, of whom record was made in Clare and in south Down. Mee in south Down could also be an abbreviation of Meehan.

The map shows the distribution of some 76 families in 1992. Allowing for homes without telephones, there were probably 116 families altogether. The spelling Mea is not to be found in Ireland today. There appear to have been at least three septs. East Connaught is the location of the main historic cluster. The settlement pattern confirms a movement from Westmeath to the north west, but it does not extend as far as Sligo. There are families in Clare, but if there once was a cluster in south Down, it has moved westwards and southwards to Armagh, Louth and Monaghan.

The proportion of the families in Greater Dublin is around 20%, slightly less than the national average in this area.

Meek
90 families

Meek is an example of a surname based on the disposition of the person in whom the name originated. In Britain two languages contributed to the word, 'mjúkr' in Old Norse and 'meke' in Middle English. The name means 'humble' or 'meek'.

Historically, there have been several spellings of the name. In 1229 in England, there was Richard Mek in Somerset and in 1300 Robert le Meke in York. Scotland in the fourteenth century had Mek and Meyk. In the fifteenth it had Meik and Meyk, and thereafter Meike made an appearance.

The map shows the distribution of some 68 families with telephones in Ireland in 1992. Adjusting for homes without telephones means there are likely to have been about 90 families altogether. The spelling of the surname has now standardised on to two forms: Meek with 44% of the families and Meeke with 56%.

The Belfast, Antrim and Lisburn area is of greatest important to the Meek and Meeke families. About 11% of all Ireland's families live in the area, but it has a third of Meek and Meeke families. About 80% of the families live in Northern Ireland as a whole. Dublin, which has over a fifth of Irish families, has only 6% of Meek and Meeke families.

The remaining families are scattered over the Republic. Fermanagh, a county in which Plantation names are usually well represented, does not have any Meek or Meeke settlement.

Mills
800 families

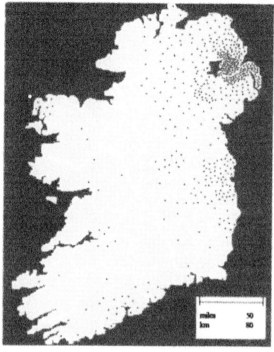

Mills were a feature in the Irish landscape from the Dark Ages. St Columba, who was later to found the abbey on Iona in 563 AD, had a mill constructed in Raphoe, Donegal, earlier in his life. It was evidently a water mill, as the reason it was recorded was that the saint had revived a man who had drowned during its construction.

The surname Mills in Ireland may however be of English rather than Irish origin. As an Irish name, Mills would be derived from An Mhuilinn - of the mill. As an English name, Mills, where not a patronymic from Miles or Mill, means dweller by the mills. A dweller by a single mill would be Milne.

The map shows the distribution of some 526 Mills families with telephones in 1992. Adjusting for telephone ownership by the rates prevailing in Ireland's two states produces an estimate for all families of about 800. With the map showing an overwhelming concentration in the area of Belfast, Lisburn and Antrim, the majority of Mills families may be assumed to be of English origin.

Some 53% of them are in Northern Ireland, as compared with 31% of all Irish families. The three counties of Ulster in the Republic also appear as important areas of Mills settlement.

It is outside of Ulster, that the name is more probably derived from an Mhuilinn. The cluster in Dublin may be expected to have arisen from recent internal migration to urban employment opportunities, from Ulster as from the rest of the country. The south coast area from Cork to Dungannon may have a similar explanation. It remains to be seen whether the presence of mills during the period of Irish surname formation accounts for the clusters of Mills families in north west Mayo; Limerick; Wicklow and Arklow; Kildare; and Westmeath/Longford.

Molloy
1900 families

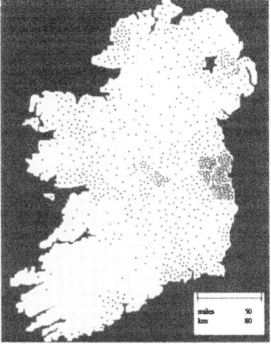

Malloy is a variant of Molloy, which also appears occasionally as Maloy and Mulloy. MacLysaght records five variant spellings. The original sept was called Ó Maolmhuaidh, descendent of Maolmuadh, noble chief. They were of the southern O'Neills and were important in Fercal in mid Offaly. The O'Molloys were hereditary bearers of the British standard in Ireland. There was another sept in Co. Roscommon. In addition, Molloy has officially been recorded as a synonym of Mulvogue in Connaught, of Logue in Co. Donegal., of Mullock in Offaly, Mulvihill in Kerry and Slowey in Monaghan. Maloy has been used for MacCloy in Co. Derry.

The map shows by the distribution of some 1,900 Molloy families in 1992. Ten dots represent 1% of the total. In addition, there are a few families with spellings of Malloy, Maloy and Mulloy families, mainly in Belfast or Dublin.

As is usual with many names, Greater Dublin is now the most important location for the Molloys. Some 22% live there, the same as the national average in that area. Elsewhere, the settlement pattern of the Molloys reveals the influence of the historic sources of the name. Following Dublin, the Tullamore area in mid Leinster has the greatest density, but Waterford and Galway emerge as important. West Donegal also has high density settlement. Only 4% of the families live in the Belfast, Antrim and Lisburn area, little more than a third of the national average. This is usual for an Irish Gaelic name.

Northern Ireland has a third of all Irish families. It has only 13% of the Molloys.

Montgomery
1350 families

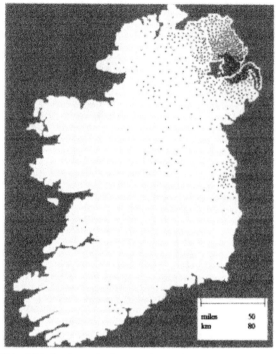

Montgomery is a place-name in Calvados, Normandy. The connection with Ireland began well before the 1170 Anglo-Norman invasion, as Arnulf de Montgomeri had married a daughter of Murtagh O'Brien in 1100. Montgomery appears frequently in the records of the Anglo-Norman ascendancy in Ireland in the thirteenth and fourteenth centuries. The families were prominent in counties Dublin, Meath and Louth, but MacLysaght believes them to be extinct.

The Montgomery families now so well known in Ulster first came to Ireland in 1603. Sir Hugh Montgomery, a Scot from Ayrshire, acquired part of the lands of Con O'Neill. These became the nucleus of a collection of estates amounting by 1878 to 113 square miles. Some 23% of this land was in Co. Antrim, 17% was in Co. Donegal and 14% in Co. Leitrim. The remainder was spread over another ten counties.

The map shows the distribution of some 1350 Montgomery families in Ireland in 1992. Ten dots represent 1% of the total. A third of the families live in the Belfast, Lisburn and Antrim area, three times the national average. A further 8% live in Ards. This concentration is confirmation of a Scottish origin. The name is absent from Leitrim and scarce in Donegal, suggesting that land ownership did not necessarily mean settlement.

The northern cluster thins out into Longford and Westmeath and there are families in the far south of Ireland. The presence of Montgomery families in the Midlands may still be explained by plantation settlement. In the south their presence could be due to recent dispersal, or it could date back to the Anglo-Normans.

Montgomery today is overwhelmingly an Ulster name. Some one third of all Irish households live in Northern Ireland, whereas 88% of Montgomery families live there.

Moore
5100 families

A family of this name could be of any one or more of three origins. The distribution of the 5,100 families of 1992 helps to tell the story. Each dot on the map represents 0.1%

The dispersed settlement from Wexford, site of Maurice FitzGerald's landing in 1169, along the south coast and into the South West, is a typical Anglo-Norman feature. 'Maur' in old French meant someone of a dark or 'Moorish' complexion. There was a sixth century St. Maur. Christian and surnames evolved. Those taking their surname from this source became de Móra in Irish.

The concentration around Belfast indicates the importance of British settler origin from the Plantation of Ulster. The area accommodates 11% of all Irish families, but 18% of the Moores. 'Moor' is an English word meaning wasteland of mountain or marsh.

Underlying these settlements is the Irish Ó Mórdha, descendants of Mórdha, himself twenty-first in descent from Conal Cearnach, hero of the Armagh based Red Branch order of chivalry. The meaning of mórdha is stately or noble. This family was the leading sept of the Seven Septs of Leix.

Economic opportunities in the Greater Dublin area in modern times will have attracted Moores of all three origins, but their representation there is only two-thirds of the national average of 22%.

Over a third of Moore families live in Antrim and Down, where they make up almost one percent of the population. The few in Leix make up the same proportion. Anglo-Normans as aristocrats may be expected to be scarce in relation to the population they ruled. Moore families in Co. Waterford have only half the representation of those in east Ulster and Leix.

Northern Ireland has a third of all Irish households. It has just over half of the Moores.

Moorhead
300 families

MacLysaght describes Moorehead as a variant of the Scottish Muirhead. According to Black's 'Surnames of Scotland', the name is derived from one or more localities called Muirhead in the southern counties of Scotland, perhaps from Muirhead in the barony of Bothwell. The first record of the name was a Sir William Muirhead of Lachope in the late 14th century.

The map shows the location of some 211 families with telephones in Ireland in 1992. Allowing for homes without telephones, there are likely to be around 300 families altogether. Moorhead accounts for 62%, Moorehead for 33%, and Muirhead for 5%. Despite the Scottish origin, English spellings in Ireland have therefore almost entirely replaced the Scottish.

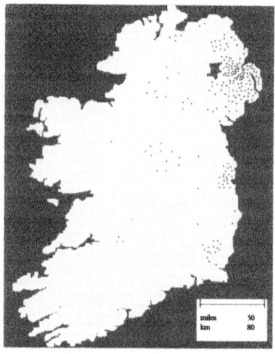

The concentration of the name in the Belfast, Antrim, Lisburn area is twice the national average of 11%, which confirms the Scottish ancestry. The name is as much Co. Down as Co. Antrim. It also appears across the south of Ulster, on both sides of the present international border. About 12% live in the Dublin area. This is a high proportion for a Scottish name. The strength of the name in Dublin is likely to be the result of internal migration from two clusters of the name in the Republic, one in central Wexford and one in Longford and Westmeath.

Longford and Wexford were areas included in the Plantations of King James I of England. The clusters of families in these areas here suggest a presence in Ireland of almost 400 years. Moorehead is the minority anglicised form everywhere except in Wexford. Rare as it is, from first introduction, the name has evidently never been confined to Ulster.

Moran
2500 families

Found throughout the country, Moran is essentially a Connaught name. Several distinct families lived in Galway, Leitrim, Mayo and Roscommon. They had two Irish surnames which were anglicised to Moran.

With a name possibly derived from mór, great, Móran was a chief based at Ardnaree, near Ballina, Co. Mayo, who held sway on both sides of the River Moy. His descendants became Ó Móráin. There were Ó Moghráin chiefs in Cos. Galway and Roscommon. In its early form, Mugróin, their name meant slave's seal, indicating a commitment to a head of a church establishment. Mugron, co-arb, or heir of St Columba in Ireland and Scotland, died in 979 AD. There were Moran families recorded in the sixteenth century in Clare and north Tipperary, and over much of Leinster.

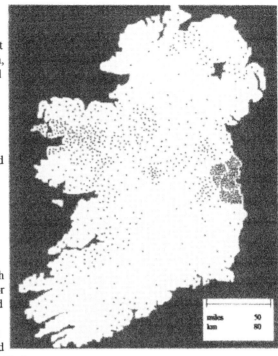

The map shows the distribution of some 2,500 Moran families in 1992. Each dot represents 0.1% of the total. Greater Dublin has just over a fifth of all the families of Ireland. It has the same proportion of Moran families. The four counties of origin - Mayo, Leitrim and Roscommon, stand out clearly by the density of Moran settlement.

In Fermanagh, Moran is also an anglicised form of the Scottish MacMorran, which, like Ó Moghráin, is a derivative of Mugron. Though representation of the name in Fermanagh is weak, it is notable that there is a distinct cluster in Derry. Despite this, the Moran name is relatively scarce in the north. Northern Ireland has a third of all Irish families. It has only 6% of the Morans.

Moreland
140 families

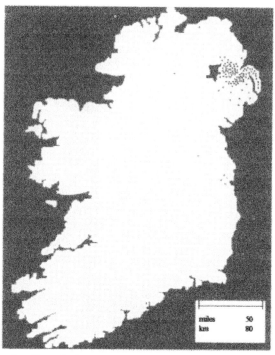

Moreland is a name derived from a dweller on or at a moor. 'Moor' meant barren land either excessively wet or dry. It was one of the origins of the surname 'Moore'. In the North of England and in parts of Scotland a Norse word 'lund' was assimilated with 'land'. It had the meaning of a small wood. England had place-names of Morland, Somerset; Morelonde, Surrey; and Moreland Sussex which produced surnames from the fourteenth century. Scotland had Moreland, Kinross, Morland, Skelmorlie; and Moorland, Gretna.

In Ireland, Woulfe has Murland in Co. Down as a surname derived from the Gaelic Mac Murghaláin, from 'murghal', sea warrior. Murland is not found as a surname in Ireland today.

Although England and Scotland have had several spellings of 'moor', which survive in variants of the simplex surname 'Moore', Moreland is virtually the only spelling of this name in Ireland. There is one exception only, a family in Belfast using the spelling Moorland. This consistency may be due to the apparently close-knit cluster in which the name is found in Ireland.

The map shows the distribution of some 106 families in Ireland in 1992. Allowing for homes without telephones, there are likely to be 140 families altogether. Almost two-thirds of them are found in the Belfast, Antrim and Lisburn area. This is six times the national average representation for this area and strongly suggests a Scottish origin for the name. Another 17% live in the area of Bangor and Ards Peninsula.

Very few families live outside Cos. Antrim and Down. Only six families live in the Republic, four of them in Dublin.

Morgan
1200 families

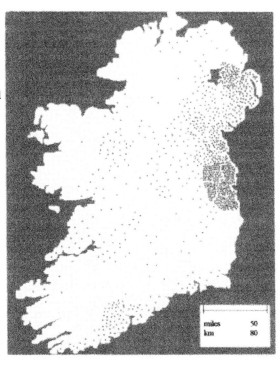

The early Celtic 'mori-canto-s', meaning 'sea-bright', is the origin of the name appearing in modern Welsh as Morgan and in Old British, Old Breton and Old Cornish as Morcant. Scotland would have known the Pictish form, Morgunn. Historically, Morgan and Murgan were found in Aberdeenshire and among the Sutherland Mackays.

In Ireland, MacLysaght found Morgan numerous in Dublin and Belfast, and also Oriel - an area consisting of Cos. Armagh and Monaghan, southern Co. Down, and parts of Cos. Louth and Fermanagh. He considered Morgan to be of Welsh origin, though it had absorbed several Irish surnames, notably Merrigan and Morahan. Merrigan was originally of Westmeath and Longford, and Morahan was of east Offaly.

The map shows the distribution of some 1,200 Morgan families in Ireland in 1992. Some 30% of the families live in Greater Dublin, very much more than the 22% national average of families in this area. Belfast, Antrim and Lisburn have 9%, which is slightly below the 11% national average in this area.

The main cluster shown on the map does not extend into Fermanagh, but it very definitely covers the area between the two main cities. The concentration in Dublin of this name is surprising. The most numerous Welsh name, Walsh, dating from Anglo-Norman times, has 20% of its families in Greater Dublin, and only 3% in the Belfast area. Morgan in the Belfast area is therefore plentiful for a Welsh name, but as Plantation families usually exceed 11% in the Belfast area, it seems low for a later name from Britain.

Elsewhere, there is a notable Morgan cluster in Co. Cork, one in Co. Clare, and one centred on north Roscommon. Fermanagh does not feature. These southern and western families could be from Welsh settlement, but perhaps the other names that merged with Morgan are responsible.

Morton
420 families

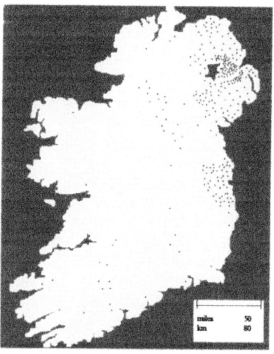

Morton appeared in Ireland in the thirteenth century. It had appeared in England a century earlier where may have been derived from any one of many place-names so called. Its first presence in Ireland coincides with Anglo-Norman invasion of Ireland. Families in the Dublin area therefore may be of early English origin.

There was little penetration of the North by the Anglo-Normans, so that families in Ulster may be assumed to be of Scottish rather than English origin and to have settled there from the Plantation. There were two principal origins of Scottish Mortons. One was Morton in Dumfriesshire. The other was Morton in the parish of Kemback in Fife, which had originally been Myrton or Myretoun. This was the locality from which the most famous family, the Mortons of Cambo, took their name. It is said to have been derived from the office of 'mair' of the barony of Crail which an ancestor had held in the fourteenth century, and whose own lands were designated Mairtoun. It is likely however that both this land and the surname took their meaning, like the other sources, from an old English term for a settlement by a moor or a marsh.

The name is rare in Ireland. The map shows the distribution of some 280 families called Morton who had telephones in 1992. Allowing for homes without phones, there were likely to have been 420 families altogether. Some 22% of the families lived in Greater Dublin, which was the same as the national average.

The distribution reveals an uneven settlement in the North. There were two clusters of settlement: the main one in the four easternmost of the nine counties of Ulster; and a smaller one in Fermanagh and Cavan. Some 60% of all the families lived in Northern Ireland. The Belfast, Lurgan and Antrim area alone had 23%, which was twice the national average and indicative of Protestant settlement.

Mullan
1200 families

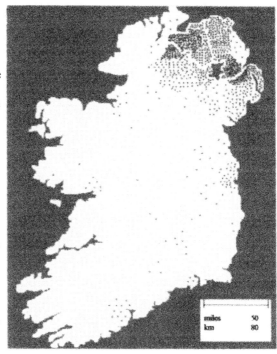

In the early Christian period, a child born on a saint's day was baptised as the 'mael', later 'maol', meaning bald or tonsured servant or devotee of the saint. This produced many compound names. Ó Maoláin is a diminutive of 'maol'. Derivatives of Ó Maoláin are found throughout the country as Mullane, Mullen, Mullin, and Mullins. But for this diversity, they would add up to one of Ireland's most numerous names.

Woulfe considers that though there were no doubt several distinct families, the only one that was apparently dynastic was that of O' Kane's country in Co. Derry. There was a historic sept in Co. Galway, where the ancestor, Mullan, was descended from a King of Connaught. A third sept lived in Co. Cork, where the name has usually been rendered into English as Mullane.

In Ulster there have been two additional possible origins of the name. Some families of Ó Mealláin, a sept of Tyrone whose name is a diminutive of 'meall', pleasant and in English O' Mellon, have lost their separate identity. The name may also be an abbreviation of McMullan, a Scottish surname borne by many seventeenth century settlers in Ulster.

The map shows the distribution of some 1,200 Mullan families in Ireland in 1992. Ten dots make up 1% of the total. The areas historically associated with Mullan and Mellon stand out by the density of settlement. The name is also strong in Antrim which is the main McMullan county.

In the North of Ireland Mullan is much the most numerous variant of Ó Maoláin. In the Republic, the majority have the spelling Mullen. Though Mullen is numerous also in the North, the boundaries of the Mullan spelling are particularly abrupt. This may be a standardisation influenced by education authorities.

Northern Ireland has about a third of all Irish households. Some 90% of Mullan families live there.

McMullen
1400 families

McMullen. along with McMullan, McMullin and McMullon, derives from the Gaelic Mac Maoláin, meaning son of maolán, a diminutive of bald or tonsured one. These names, along with McMillan, in similar spelling variants, are all versions of the Scottish clan McMillan. Most of these Scottish families came to Ireland at the time of the Plantation, though McMullen was recorded in Upper Ards before the Plantation.

The name was not found in Scotland as McMullen. Its preponderance in Ireland as McMullen may be due to the presence in North Antrim of the Irish name O'Mullan, which may more remotely be the origin of the Scottish McMillan.

The map shows the distribution of 1,400 McMullen families of all spellings in 1992. Ten dots represent 1% of the total. Some 86% of them live in Northern Ireland. Over a fifth of their total live in the area around Belfast, which is twice the national average. The Ards peninsula has same high density of settlement. Dublin, which for many Irish families is the most important cluster, has only 10% of the McMullens, which is less than half of the national average.

In addition to McMullen, Ireland has 500 McMillan families. McMullen families therefore outnumber McMillans by about three to one. The McMillan settlement pattern is much the same as McMullen. It differs in that at 90%, slightly more of McMillans live in Northern Ireland than the McMullens, McMillan is even more concentrated around Belfast and Ards than is McMullen; and Central Antrim is more important to the McMillans than the north coastal area.

Mulvanny
450 families

This name was first recorded as Ó Maoil Mheana in 1164 in the Annals of Ulster in recording a descent of Eoghan, son of Niall of the Nine Hostages. Woulfe and Ó Raifertaigh consider it probable that the name is associated with the Meana (now Main) river in Co. Antrim. If so, the name would mean 'devotee of the Main'.

The map shows the distribution of some 265 families with telephones in 1992. Adjusting for homes without telephones, there are probably about 450 families altogether. Mulvaney, Mulvany and Mulvanny families make up 72%. Mulvenna families 26%; and Mulvenny families 2%.

A name of an area of origin is usually carried by people who leave it rather than those

who remain. Just as families called Delaney, Ó Dubhshláine, meaning 'descendant of black of the Slaney', are not found in the Slaney river system, but in the neighbouring system of the Barrow and Nore, so the Mulvennas and Mulvaneys are clustered in localities other than the Main system. The Mulvenna heartland is in the Glens of Antrim, whilst the Mulvaneys are clustered in the Navan and Kells area of Meath. There is virtually no intermixing in the heartlands and representation in Dublin is almost entirely Mulvanny.

The 12th century Annals of Ulster were referring to a third area, the O'Cahan country of what became Cos. Tyrone and Derry. Before the destruction of the Gaelic Order in the 17th century, the Mulvennas were hereditary ollavs, or learned men, of the O'Cahan. By the time of the 1659 census, Mulvennas were no longer to be found in this area. They were recorded in Glenarm in the Glens of Antrim.

The name is rare. With 1.56 million households in Ireland in 1991, Mulvaneys and Mulvennas account for only one family in 6,000.

The name may however be of great antiquity and have counterparts on the continent. The German River Main has the town of Mainz on its banks. Both words were originally Celtic, and were Latinised as Moenus and Maguntiacum. The town was an early ecclesiastical centre and bishopric. Much the same may be said of Cenomanica, which became Le Mans, close to the river Mayenne in the French province of Maine. The root meaning of these words is not clear, but they recall Ballymena, An Baile Meánach, a town on the Antrim Main river system, a the meeting point of a number of roads, and which is translated as middle town

Murphy
16100 families

Derived from murchadha, a sea warrior, the surname Ó Murchadha arose independently in several parts of Ireland, though its more probable form in Ulster was MacMurchadha.

A sept once centred in Tyrone is still significant in Ulster, but now more so in Armagh. A sept in Sligo were dispossessed and scattered in the thirteenth century. Much the most important are the septs of Leinster, centred on Co. Wexford; and Munster, centred on Muskerry in Co. Cork, which is said to be a branch of the Kinsella section of the Wexford sept.

The map shows the distribution of some 16,100 families in 1992. Each dot on the map represents 0.1% of the total. Murphy is the most numerous surname in the country.

The areas where Murphys make up the greatest proportion of the population are the two areas historically most associated with them. In both Cos. Wexford and Cork the Murphys account for almost 4% of the total population. There is a concentration of Murphy families in Greater Dublin. At 16% this is less than the quarter of Irish families generally that are resident there, but Murphy numbers mean they make up approaching 1% of the Dublin population there, similarly to the major east Leinster family of Byrne.

The modern trend to restore O and Mac prefixes has not taken place with Murphy. Some families are now using Murchú as a simplified Gaelic form.

About 12% of Murphy families are in Northern Ireland, as compared with 31% of the population of Ireland as a whole.

Murray
6200 families

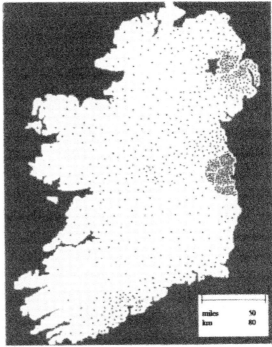

The old Irish muireadhagh had a meaning of seaman, and also lord. It produced the surname Ó Muireadhaigh, which was formerly anglicised O'Murry, but now is now almost always Murray. There were several distinct families in different parts of the country. The O'Murrays of Mayo, Roscommon, Westmeath and Cork were dynastic families who once had extensive landholdings, but who were dispossessed and dispersed. The only sept to remain important after the Anglo-Norman invasion was that of Úi Maine, or Hy Many, in what became Cos. Galway and Roscommon. Based in the barony of Athlone, the seat of its chief was at Ballymurray.

A member of the sept of O'Murrihie in Ballywidden, in the barony of Carbery, Co. Cork, produced an Archbishop of Tuam in the fifteenth century, who founded a unique ecclesiastical jurisdiction, the Wardenship of Galway.

The map shows the distribution of the 6,200 Murray families in Ireland in 1992. One dot represents 0.1% of the total. Athlone and Cork remain discernible by density of Murray settlement as locations of former septs. About 22% of Murray families live in Greater Dublin, and 9% in the Belfast/Lisburn/Antrim area. These proportions are about the same as all Irish families living in those areas.

Many of the Murrays living in Northern Ireland will be of Scottish extraction. Despite this, Murray representation in the North is lower than the national average. Some 25% of the Murrays live in the North, as compared to 31% of all Irish families.

McMurray
350 families

The old Irish muireadhagh had a meaning of seaman, and also lord. It produced the surname Ó Muireadhaigh, formerly anglicised as O'Murry, but now is now almost always Murray. In addition, there was a family, Mac Gille Mhuire, son of a devotee of Mary, which was also anglicised as Murray and which was found in the north of Co. Down. At about 6,300 families, Murray is one of the most numerous Irish surnames

MacMuireadhaigh, son of MacMuireadhach, was common personal name in the Annals of the Four Masters. It became a surname in Galloway, Scotland, where it was first recorded in 1530. It was reintroduced to Ireland with settlers of the Plantation era. Some of the McMurrays may
have lost the 'Mac' prefix by assimilation with Murrays of Irish and Scottish extraction in Ireland.

The map shows the distribution of 257 families with telephones in 1992. Allowing for homes without telephones, there are likely to be about 350 McMurray families altogether. They are outnumbered by Murray families by 20 to one. Whereas the Murrays are less well represented in the North of Ireland than the Irish population as a whole, few McMurrays are found in the Republic. Within Ulster, two-thirds of the families live in a single cluster in south Antrim and north Down.

A probable Plantation era origin Scottish origin is strongly suggested by the strength of the name in the area centred on Belfast, Lisburn and Antrim. This area contains 11% of all Irish families. It has over 40% of the McMurrays.

McNamara
2100 families

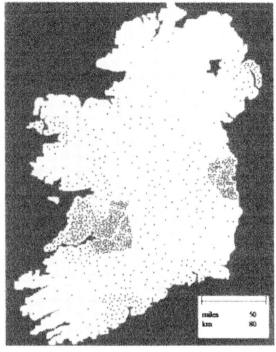

MacNamara was the most important Dalcassian sept after the O'Briens, to whom they were marshals. The Dalcassians comprised the main septs of Thomond, an ancient territory approximating to most of what is now Co. Clare, with adjacent parts of Cos. Limerick and Tipperary. The Gaelic is Mac Conmara, or 'son of the hound of the sea'.

The name appears in Black's 'Surnames of Scotland'. Black points out that 'hound of the sea' means 'shark'.

The map shows the distribution of some 2,100 MacNamara families in Ireland in 1992. Ten dots make up 1% of the total.

The MacNamara concentration in their heartland is typical of that of many other well known families in their historic areas. Their strong presence in Clare and Limerick means that despite the small size of the MacNamara clan nationally, they nevertheless account for 1½% of the population of these counties.

Greater Dublin now accounts for 22% of all the families of the island of Ireland. It accounts for 16% of the MacNamaras. The size of the MacNamara cluster in the Cork area is small considering the proximity and importance of Cork.

Northern Ireland has about a third of all Irish households, but only 4% of the MacNamaras live there. The distribution in the North is unexpected, in that recent arrivals from Clare would be expected to be to job opportunities in the industrial area of Belfast. The cluster on the coastal area around Bangor and Ards in north Down is likely to be older. A Scottish origin might be a more likely explanation

O'Neill
8100 families

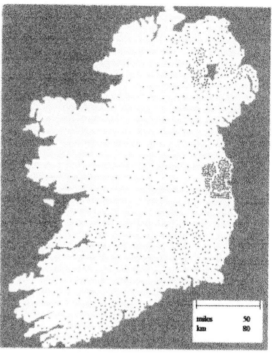

Even before Ó Néill was adopted as an Irish surname in the mid-tenth century, the Old Irish Niall, meaning a champion, was taken from Ireland as Njáll by the Vikings. It went with them to France. The Norman conquest brought it to England where it later produced the surnames Neilson and Nelson.

The were several O'Neill septs. The most famous was that of Ulster. The chief family of Cinel Eoghan, the territory of the O'Neills of Tir Eoghan comprised not only the modern Tyrone, but also most of Derry and part of Donegal. Descended from the early fifth century Niall of the Nine Hostages, they took their name from a later Niall, a King of Ireland killed in battle against the Norsemen in AD 919. The O'Neill Red Hand emblem is at the centre of the arms of Ulster. The O'Neills of Decies, now west Waterford, claim descent from the Ulster sept. Those of Thomond were centred on Bunratty, Co. Clare; and those of Co. Carlow on the barony of Rathvilly.

The map shows the distribution of some 8,100 O'Neill families in 1992. One dot represents 0.1% of the total. As with most surnames, the most important cluster is now Greater Dublin. This is because of internal migration to the capital and depopulation in much of the rest of the country since the Famine. At about a fifth, O'Neill families are as strongly represented there as Irish families generally. Elsewhere in the country, areas historically associated with the O'Neills are still apparent. They account for the highest proportion of the population in Co. Carlow, where, at around 1½%, the O'Neills have twice the strength they have in Tyrone and Derry, or in Dublin.

Some 29% of O'Neill families live in Northern Ireland, compared with 31% of all Irish families. About 7% of them live in the urbanised area of Belfast/Lisburn/Antrim, which contains 11% of all Irish families.

Nolan
3900 families

Woulfe has five Irish names which were anglicised as Nolan.

Ó Nualláin, derived from nuall, noble or famous, is the most important. There were two families with the name, one in Co. Carlow and one in Co. Cork. The Carlow family was the much the more prominent. Long associated with that part of the county around the barony of Forth, in pre-Norman times the head of the family had the hereditary privilege of inaugurating MacMurrough as King of Leinster. Woulfe does not indicate a particular location for the diminutive form, Ó Nuallacáin.

In Fermanagh, Nolan may be a derivation of Ó hUltacháin, descendent of the Ultonian - someone from another

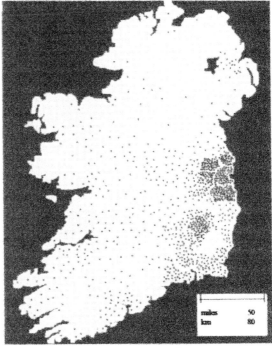

part of Ulster. In Mayo and Roscommon, it may be an anglicisation of Ó hUallacháin, from Uallachán, proud, which elsewhere became Houlihan. Mayo also had a form MacNualláin.

The map shows the distribution of 3,900 Nolan families in 1992. Each dot represents 0.1%. Like many families, Greater Dublin is now the main cluster. About 29% of Nolans live there, compared to the national average of 22%. Only about 3% of the families live in areas where names other than Ó Nualláin are likely to account for their presence.

Some 10% of all the Nolans live in Co. Carlow, where they make up almost 3% of the population. This is one of the highest concentrations of an individual name in the country. They are approaching 1% in the neighbouring counties of Wexford and Kilkenny. In the sixteenth century, migrants from Carlow moved to Galway and Mayo. Connaught landlords called Nolan owned 12,000 acres in 1878, but no significant landholding was held by a Nolan in Carlow.

Northern Ireland has around a third of all the households in Ireland. It has under 3% of the Nolans.

McNulty
1000 families

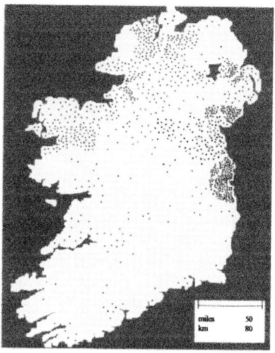

Ultach was a territory in the north east of Ireland after which the much larger province of Ulster was named. Mac an Ultaigh therefore means 'son of the Ulsterman', or more specifically, 'son of the Ulidian'. It has always been primarily associated with the west of Ulster. Woulfe describes MacNulty as a Donegal family who are probably a branch of the Dunlevys.

The map shows the distribution of some 1,000 families in 1992. The early anglicised form of McAnulty acounts for 6%. McNulty accounts for 81%. Families who have dropped the 'Mc' prefix account for 13%.

The name is rare in the southern half of the island. As may be expected, apart from the Belfast, Lisburn and Antrim area, which has attracted population from the surrounding areas since the industrial revolution, it does not feature strongly in the former Ultach itself. The settlement is densest in west and south Ulster and in north Connaught. It is very strong in Donegal, but is absent from the barony of Boylagh, the O'Boyle country.

The two minority forms are contained within the overall pattern. In some localities they outnumber the McNultys. McAnulty is clustered in south east Ulster and Nulty in Co. Cavan and north Leinster.

Greater Dublin has 22% of all Irish families. McNultys are less strongly represented at 14%, but as over a third of the Nultys live in the Republic's capital area. Northern Ireland has a third of all Irish families. It has a quarter of the Mac an Ultaighs.

Orr
900 families

The surname Orr is of a Scottish origin. It may be from a place-name, the parish of Orr in Kirkcudbrightshire. There is an old Renfrewshire family of the name. Its origin may be from the Gaelic 'odhar donn', 'odhar' meaning sallow of complexion and 'donn' meaning brown. Alternatively, it may be an anglicisation of the Scottish Gaelic Mac Iomhair, 'son of Ivar'. If the latter, it would be of the same family as MacIver, MacIvor, MacUre and Ure. The Ures were a sept of the Clan Campbell and the name Orr is prominent in Kintyre, particularly Campbeltown.

The presence of the name in Ireland is relatively recent. MacLysaght found the first reference to it in 1646, concerning an officer in Ormond's army, who may not have been Irish born. The next written record was in 1655, a Thomas Orr, who lived in Church Street, Dublin.

Many families called Orr appear in records in Derry and adjacent areas in 1665, which suggest that settlement had begun several years earlier and before 1655.

The map shows the distribution of some 900 families in 1992. The settlement pattern is extremely concentrated: 45% of them live in the cluster in south Antrim and north Down. The proportion in the Belfast, Lisburn and Antrim area, at a third, is three times the national average.

Dublin, for many Irish families the main modern day location, has attracted under 10% of the Orrs. The representation of the name in the Republic's capital is therefore less than half the national average. The rest of the Republic has only 6% of the Orrs, and two thirds of those are in Donegal. With the exception of the small presence in north Donegal, the boundaries of Northern Ireland are evident from the density of Orr settlement.

Pierce
600 families

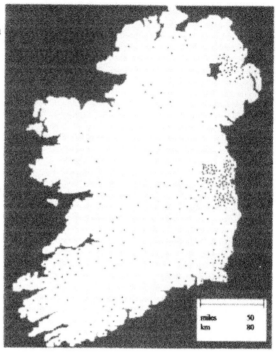

Pierce in its various spellings is derived from Piers, an Anglo-Norman form of the Latin Petrus, Peter, by way of the Irish Piaras, or Mac Piaras.

The map shows the distribution of some 340 families with telephones in 1992. Adjustment for homes without phones produces a total of about 600 families.

Pierce numbers are small compared with other Anglo-Norman names. There are 5,800 Burke families and 3,900 FitzGeralds, whilst Walsh families, descended from Welsh retainers of the Anglo-Normans, number 10,900. Nevertheless, in most respects the Pierce distribution follows the familiar pattern of Anglo-Norman settlement. It has the concentration in Greater Dublin - over a quarter live there compared with the national average of 22%. There is a concentration in Wexford, site of Maurice FitzGerald's landing in 1169. There is the trail along the south coast and the penetration into the West. Where Pierce differs from the Anglo-Norman pattern is in the high proportion of its families - some 14% - resident in Northern Ireland. Other Anglo-Normans have only 2% - 7%. A half of the Northern Pierces are in the urbanised area of Belfast, Lisburn and Antrim.

The Pierces of Kerry, who played an important part in the Desmond wars, and who are still an identifiable cluster, were a branch of the Fitzmaurices.

Pierce has more spelling variants than other Anglo-Norman names. Overall, Pierce accounts for almost three-quarters of the total. With the exception of a handful spelt Pears, the remainder are split almost evenly between Pierse, Pearce and Pearse. Pierce is over 90% in Northern Ireland and the South East, but the minority spellings account for a third to a half in Munster, Connaught and north Leinster. Internal migration from these areas to Greater Dublin probably accounts for the relatively low proportion there - only 80% - with the spelling Pierce.

Quinn
5500 families

There are several distinct Quinn families. The best known are those of Co. Clare, descendants of a tenth century lord called Conn; those of Co. Longford; those of Co. Tyrone; those of the Glens of Antrim; those of Raphoe, Co. Donegal; and those of the neighbourhood of Castlebar, Co. Mayo.

The Irish personal name Conn could mean head, sense, reason and intelligence, and also a freeman. It produced the surname Ó Cuinn, from which Quinn is the main anglicised form. Ó Cuinn is pronounced O'Coyne in the south of the country, and has given rise to the much rarer surname of Coyne.

The map shows the distribution of 5,500 Quinn families in 1992. Ten dots represent 1% of the total. The

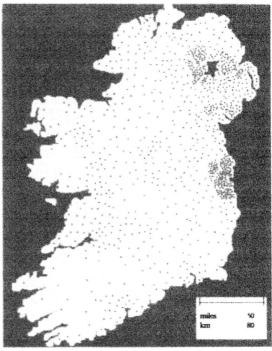

main cluster is now in Greater Dublin. About 16% live there, compared to the national average of 22%. Elsewhere, much the most important group are the Quinns of Tyrone. Their distinctive settlement pattern around Lough Neagh is shared by their kindred, the much less numerous O'Hagans. Though the cluster in south Down and south Armagh is second only to Lough Neagh, neither Woulfe nor MacLysaght refer to Quinns in that area.

The Quinns have much the same proportion of the population in many of their areas of origin. Most numerous in Co. Tyrone, they are about 1% of the population there. They are also 1% in Cos. Clare, Donegal, Longford and Fermanagh. They are half that strength in Co. Mayo, and less than half in the populous Co. Antrim. Typically of Irish Gaelic names, their share in the area of Belfast, Antrim and Lisburn, at 7%, is well short of the 11% of all Irish households living in this area.

About a third of all Quinn families live in the six counties. This is the same proportion that Northern Ireland has of Irish families as a whole.

Rea
820 families

Rea is a contraction of the Scottish Gaelic MacRea or MacCrea. The Irish Gaelic of the same meaning would be MacRaith, which has usually been rendered Magraith and has become anglicised as MacGrath or Magrath. The meaning is son of grace or prosperity. Reay is a minority spelling.

The great majority of families with these names live in Cos. Antrim and Down. Though they are Scottish, they are not newcomers to Ireland. The place-name Ballymacrea in Co. Antrim, together with mention in the Fiants of 1600 - 1601, show that they were established before the Plantation of Ulster.

There are other origins for Rea and Reay in Ireland but they are much less common. In Co. Cavan there were Ulster plantation settlers called Rea. In Kilkenny and Cork there are families called Rea, where the name is a derivative of the Irish Riabhach, meaning swarthy or grizzled. The name O'Rea featured as a principal Irish name in the barony of Owney in Co. Limerick in the Fiants of 1550 - 1600.

The map shows the distribution of some 570 families with telephones in 1992. Allowing for homes without phones, there were probably about 820 families altogether. Rea accounts for 97% and Reay for the remainder. Three quarters of all the families live in Northern Ireland, with over a third living in the Belfast, Lisburn and Antrim area alone. This distribution is strongly indicative of Scottish origin. Greater Dublin, which for many families is now the most important location and which has 22% of all Irish families, has under 5% of the Reas and Reays.

The families whose origin is Riabhach are relatively few. Only 7% of the families live in Cork; 5% in Co. Limerick; and 3% in Kilkenny.

O'Regan
2100 families

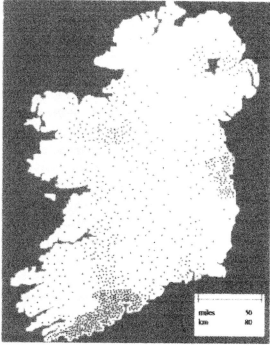

The surname O'Regan originated independently in several parts of the country. There were two leading Ó Riagáin families. One, a branch of the southern O'Neill and one of the four tribes of Tara, were lords in Meath. After the Anglo-Norman conquest they migrated to Co. Leix and have now largely disappeared. The other main O'Regan sept, descended from Riagán, nephew of Brian Boru, were based in the Limerick area.

The meaning of Riagáin is obscure. The English written form 'Regan' apparently led to the pronunciation 'Raygan', but the resultant spelling 'Reagan' is very rare in Ireland.

The map shows the distribution of some 2,100 families in 1992. Ten dots make up 1% of the total. The Meath and Limerick areas associated with early Regan history are not the main areas of settlement today. The main clusters are now in Cork and north Connaught.

In 1595, several O'Regan families were recorded in Carbery as kinsmen of the MacCarthys. This remains an area of dense settlement. Some 39% of all the families live in Co. Cork, where they make up almost 1% of the population. The 5% living in Co. Roscommon make up the same proportion of that county. For many families, internal migration in modern times has made Greater Dublin the most important location. The Republic's capital area has 22% of all the families in Ireland. It has only 8% of the O'Regans and 15% of the Regans.

Over 60% of the families have now restored the 'O' prefix. The lead of the far south of the country in this trend is striking. Of the many in Cork, over 95% have the prefix. In Dublin, just over half have it. Northern Ireland has a third of all Irish households. Only 5% of the Regan families live there, and of those, over 95% do not have the prefix.

O'Reilly
7800 families

Ó Raghailligh means descendant of Raghallach, a leader who fought and died alongside High King Brian Boru at Clontarf in 1014. The name is derived from 'ragh', meaning race, and 'ceallach', meaning gregarious. Raghallach was a great-grandson of Maolmordha, reputed to be of the family of the O'Conor kings of Connaught.

The O'Reillys were chiefs of an area which comprised the greater part of what became Co. Cavan. In the thirteenth and fourteenth centuries their control extended over the whole of Cavan and parts of Meath and Westmeath. Sometimes they were chiefs of the whole of Breffney. They had extensive landholdings until the Cromwellian confiscations.

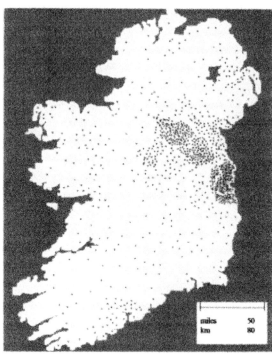

The map shows the distribution of some 7,800 families in 1992. Ten dots make up 1% of the total. Typically of a Leinster name, a high proportion of the families live in Greater Dublin. Some 31% live in this area which contains about 22% of the all-Ireland population.

There is a high density of settlement from Meath through Cavan to Longford. Some 10% of all the families live in Co. Cavan, where they make up about 5% of the population. In Longford the clan has about 3% of the population.

A minority in the recent past, families with the 'O' prefix are now the majority. Families with the prefix account for 59%. In addition there are a very few, mainly in the North, with the spelling Riley. Some 74% of families in Greater Dublin have the prefix. Northern Ireland has only 8% of the O'Reillys and Reillys. In the area centred on Belfast, Lisburn and Antrim, about 53% have the prefix, as compared with just less than half in the six counties as a whole. For the North, the proportion having the prefix is unusually high.

Rutherford
225 families

The surname Rutherford is listed in MacLysaght's "More Irish Families" amongst names of English and Scottish origin already found in Ulster in 1659, though not numerous enough to be classified as 'principal' names in the census of that year. He indicates that the name is of Scottish origin.

Though it is rare for Irish surnames to be taken from placenames, in England it is quite common. There are, or were, three small settlements called Rutherford in Britain. One is in Yorkshire. There is a 'lost' Rutherford in Devon. In Scotland, Rutherford is in Roxburghshire, close to the English border.

The placename is derived from the Old English 'hýthera ford'. 'Ford' is probably

the second most frequently used topographical term in English placenames after 'leah', (now 'ley'). Whilst it was unusual for the Old English to call fords after livestock, where they did so, they distinguished between types of cattle. Hýthera, or híthera, had a meaning of 'horned cattle'; Sturford, Wiltshire, and Stafford, Sussex, contain the word 'steor', steer. The most famous example is Oxford.

Surnames first began to appear in Scotland in the early twelfth century. Rutherford achieved prominence by its adoption later in the century by a powerful Border family. As well as people from a place being given a name when they moved elsewhere, tenants in Scotland often took the name of their landlords, sometimes being given incentives by their lords to do so.

The map shows the distribution of 159 families with telephones in 1992. Over 80% of them live in Northern Ireland. Allowing for homes without phones, there are probably 225 Rutherford families altogether. This is a rare name, accounting for only about one family in 2,300 in Northern Ireland, and one in 7,000 in the country as a whole. The mainly Northern Ireland Irwin and Irvine families outnumber Rutherford families by about 10 to 1.

Ryan
9700 families

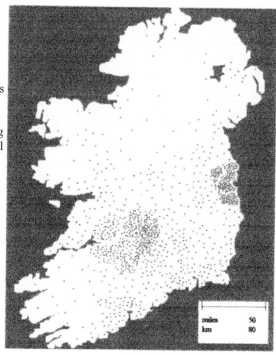

The Irish Ó Riain is properly the name of a small Leinster sept, but Ryan is now also the normal abbreviation of the Ó Maoilriain families of Tipperary. Possible cognate forms of the element 'Rian', in Irish and other languages, suggest links with water, or kingship, or setting in order. As O'Connor and O'Neill are derived from words which were applied to champions, the sense of king or ruler may be appropriate, but Rian is so ancient that no connection may be made with certainty to any of the options.

The Ó Riains, who were chiefs of Idrone, settled in Cos. Carlow and Wexford. The Ó Maoilriains, chiefs of Owney, held the rich pasturelands of the Golden Vale bordering Cos. Tipperary and Limerick. This area appears clearly on the map, which shows shows the distribution of some 9,700 Ryan families in Ireland in 1992. One dot represents 0.1% of the total.

As with most families, the main present day cluster is the Greater Dublin area, where almost a fifth of Ryan families live. The Golden Vale heartland of the former Mulryans remains the area in which the sept has the highest proportion of the population: Ryans account for around 5% of all families in Co. Tipperary.

Ryan remains a name associated with the southern half of the country. Northern Ireland has a third of all Irish households, but under 2% of Ryan families live there.

Salmon
350 families

The surname Salmon in Ireland may be of several origins. It may be from the Gaelic Ó Bradáin, from 'bradán', meaning a salmon; or from the English names, Salmon or Seaman.

The location of the surnames provides an indication as to which origin produced the name. In Leix and the Midlands it is often a corruption of Seaman. In Connaught and Clare and probably also in Kildare it is from the Gaelic. It was often rendered as Sammon. This phonetic spelling remains the most numerous to the present day.

The map shows the distribution of some 194 families with telephones in Ireland in 1992. Allowing for homes without phones, there would probably be 350 families

altogether. Over half of them, about 56%, have the spelling Sammon. It may be that Sammon had an even greater majority in years gone by. Today, it is the predominant spelling in the west of the country and rural areas. Salmon on the other hand is much more urban, and is dominant in Dublin and Belfast. Only a quarter of the Sammons are to be found in Dublin as compared with a half of the Salmons. Some 9% of the Salmons live in Belfast, a figure almost as high as for all Irish families. There are no Sammons in Belfast. It may be that families in these large towns were more exposed to English influence and so were more likely to adopt the English spelling. Families in these towns are there largely because of internal migration in relatively recent years. It would follow that if families there opted for Salmon rather than Sammon, so too would emigrant families on leaving Ireland or on arrival in the English speaking New World.

Ó Bradáin was also rendered into English as Fisher in the Glenties district and as Bradden and Bradan in Leitrim.

Scott
2400 families

The Old English word 'Scott' originally meant an Irishman. Later it meant a Gael from Scotland. In the English border counties, it came to mean a man from Scotland, not necessarily a Gael.

The Scottish gallowglasses who came to Ulster between the 13th and 16th centuries were sometimes called Albanach, from Alba, Scotland. Later Albanach became Scott.

The Scotts were one of the most powerful riding clans of the Scottish borders, based in West Teviotdale, Ewesdale and Liddesdale. When the power of these clans was broken by King James VI after he became also James I of England in 1603, many riding clan families moved to Ulster to escape persecution. Fermanagh was a popular destination and Scott was registered as a 'principal name' there in 1659.

The map shows the distribution of some 2,400 families in Ireland in 1992. Ten dots represent 1% of the total. The families are very concentrated in the Belfast, Antrim and Lisburn area, where a third of them live. This is three times the national average. The cluster extends at the same density into the Ards Peninsula, so that these two adjacent areas accommodate 42% of all the Scotts in Ireland. Northern Ireland is home to 74% of the Scotts and another 5% live in the three Ulster counties in the Republic: Cavan, Donegal and Monaghan. Greater Dublin has 22% of all Irish families. It has only 8% of the Scotts.

Despite early prominence in Fermanagh, Scott differs from some families of Scottish origin in that this county does not stand out as an area of intensive settlement. The dense settlement in the area around Belfast and in Ards is typical of many Scottish families.

McShane
355 families

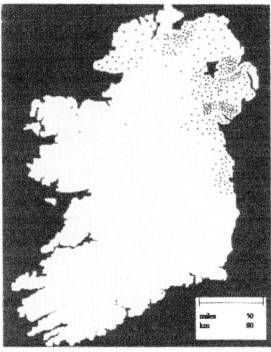

Shane is from the saint's name which transliterates from the Hebrew as Jehohhan and which in modern English is John. The Anglo-Norman word 'Jean' is the precursor of Shane. The letter 'J' being late construct, earlier Celtic forms were Eoin, Ian and Owen. McShane is from the Irish Mac Seáin, son of Seán. McShane is thus the equivalent of Johnson.

According to MacLysaght, the McShanes of Ulster and Louth were a branch of the O'Neills and those of Kerry, thought to be extinct, were FitzMaurices. The Shane families of Westmeath were a branch of the O'Farrells.

The map shows the distribution of some 355 families with telephones in 1992. Allowing for homes without telephones, there would be about 500 families altogether. There is no representation of the name today in either Kerry or Westmeath. Greater Dublin has been a destination for internal migration and today has 22% of all Irish families. It has only 7% of the McShanes. The Belfast, Antrim and Lisburn area has 15% of the families, more than the 11% national average in this area. Unusually, this is not the most important cluster in Ulster. The south Armagh and south Down area has 16% of the families. The area around Derry at 14% is almost as important as Belfast. Louth, together with adjacent parts of Cavan and Monaghan, has 11%. Donegal has 9%. The name is represented in Antrim but not the Glens of Antrim. It is represented in Donegal, but ironically not in Inishowen, a placename featuring an older form of John. It is sparse also in Tyrone, a place name of the same derivation.

In common with other names derived from saints, whether biblical or vernacular, McShane is a name of the northern parts of the island. Northern Ireland has a third of all Irish families. It has two-thirds of the McShanes.

Shannon
1000 families

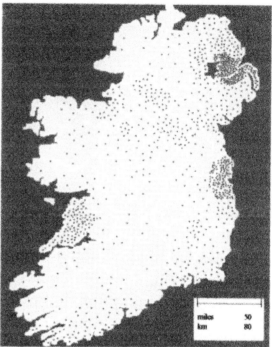

Three Gaelic families were anglicised as Shannon. One, Ó Seanáin, descendant of Senan, a personal name, was a family associated with Carlow and Wexford. Another, Mac Giolla tSeanáin, or Giltenan, son of the follower of St Senan, became Shannon in Co. Clare. Its variant in Tyrone and Fermanagh was Mac Giolla Seanáin, Gilshenan. This produced O'Seanan as one of the principal names around Enniskillen in the 1659 census. The third, Ó Seanacháin, O'Shanahan, was rendered by English surveyors as Shannon around Belfast and also in Clare. O'Shanahans of Clare were dispossessed by the MacNamaras in the fourteenth century and were scattered around the rest of Munster.

The map shows the distribution of some 1,000 Shannon families in 1992. Ten dots make up 1%. Carlow and Wexford stand out, at low density. The Gilshenan origin sept is still centred on Fermanagh, but it extends into Cavan and Connaught rather than Tyrone. This may be due to population movement after 1659. The Giltenan origin sept stands out clearly in west Clare, and there is a scatter of Shannons through the rest of Munster, presumably from the dispersal of 600 years ago.

The most striking feature is the concentration around Belfast. Some 15% of Shannon families live there against an average of 11% for all Irish families. The concentration of 18% in Greater Dublin, though the biggest single concentration, is less than the national average.

Shannon is nowhere a numerous name. It accounts for one family in 300 in Clare, and one in 400 in Fermanagh.

Ptolemy recorded the name of the longest river in Ireland in the second century AD as Senos. It is thought to be from a root word with the sense of age, seniority and wisdom. The three Gaelic family names are from this root, but evolved independently, not from the river, nor from each other.

Sheehan
2200 families

Possibly derived from siodhach, peaceful, Ó Siodhacháin was the name of two distinct families. One of them was a sept in the Galway area which in medieval times were hereditary trumpeters to the O'Kelly, the O'Lonergans being harpers. The other sept was based in Lower Connello, Co. Limerick.

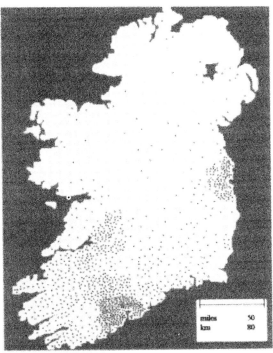

The map shows the distribution of some 2,200 Sheehan families in 1992. Each dot represents 0.1% of the total. Internal migration to Greater Dublin in modern times has made that area the main location for many families. Some 22% of the population of Ireland lives there. As is frequently found with families whose heartlands are remote from the Republic's capital area, the Sheehan representation is low. The 12% of Sheehans in Greater Dublin are far exceeded by those in and around the city of Cork, where over a fifth of the families live.

The Galway sept is not distinguishable from the present day distribution. The Limerick sept's centre of gravity has moved southwards from its historic base. Almost 40% of Sheehan families live in Co. Cork.

The South West of the country often has the highest proportion of families who have restored the 'O' prefix. With some names, notably Murphy, this has not occurred. Sheehan is another example. There are hardly any O'Sheehans.

Around a fifth of the families spell their name 'Sheahan'. It is almost exclusively a Munster, and now Dublin, variant. The small percentage in the North and West are almost all Sheehans. If the siodhach derivation is correct, then the spelling should be Sheehan rather than Sheahan.

Northern Ireland has about a third of all Irish households. It has under 2% of the Sheehans.

Sheehy
900 families

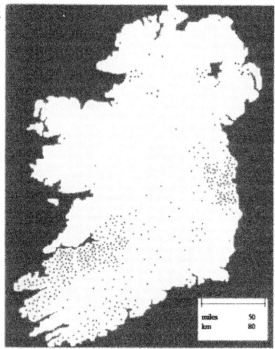

The name Mac Shíthigh came to Ireland in the fourteenth century from Scotland where the families were a branch of the MacDonnells. At the battle of Ballysodare, Co. Sligo, in 1369, they took part in a conflict between two factions of the O'Connors. In 1420 they came to Munster and settled in Co. Limerick as constables to the Earl of Desmond and built a castle at Lisnacolla, near Rathkeale. Woulfe indicates 'siteach', peaceful, as the origin of the name, but Black's later derivation from an old Gaelic word for wolf seems more suitable given their galloglass history.

The map shows the distribution of some 490 households with telephones in 1992. Allowing for homes without phones, there were probably about 900 families altogether. Sheehy accounts for 95% of the Mac Shíthigh derivatives. There are no McSheehys. There are some Sheehy families west of Lough Neagh, but the others in Ulster have evolved into distinct spelling forms. With the exception of one McShee, the old spelling of M'Shee has now become McShea, which now accounts for four-fifths of the variants. The one fifth with spellings Seay or Seaye are in or around Belfast. In Ireland, the more numerous O'Shea has perhaps influenced both spelling and pronunciation of the variants. In America, Seay is pronounced 'See'. In Scotland the initial 'Sh' sound became aspirated thereby producing MacHeath and MacKeith.

The importance of west Limerick remains clear. Greater Dublin has 22% of all Irish families. Under a fifth of Sheehy families live there, reflecting the remoteness of the main cluster from the Republic's capital.

Simpson
1200 families

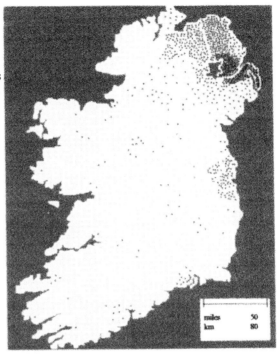

Simpson is a derivative of Simon, a Hebrew personal name made famous through Scripture and adopted widely throughout Christendom. Sim was a popular diminutive. It became a surname as Simson and acquired an intrusive 'p'. Simmons, Simmonds and Simms are other examples from the same source. Where there were variants, families, or persons keeping records, were not always consistent in the form they chose.

The various derivatives of Simon are well known in England and Scotland and came to Ireland from those countries. Simpson and Simms were both recorded in Antrim in the early sixteenth century.

The map shows the distribution of some 1,200 Simpson families in Ireland in 1992. Ten dots make up 1% of the total. There is a dense cluster of settlement around Belfast, Lisburn and Antrim, in which 26% of the families live. This is over twice the national average for this area and is confirmation of the British origin. The same density extends into the Ards Peninsula. Taken altogether, the dense cluster accounts for a third of all the Simpsons in Ireland. Most of the remainder live in the six counties of Northern Ireland, and particularly in Cos. Antrim and Derry. In total, 77% live in Northern Ireland.

The Greater Dublin area, which has 22% of all Ireland's families, has only 7% of the Simpsons. Families there may be as a result of direct migration from England, as also may be the small clusters in Waterford and Cork. That in Inishowen, north Donegal, will be of the same origin as the rest of Ulster.

Sinclair
250 families

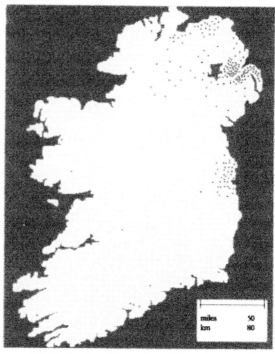

Sinclair is a name of Norman origin. In England, Hugo de Sancto Claro was recorded in the Domesday Book of 1086. The tenants of Eudo Dapifer came from Saint Clair sur Elle, La Manche, Normandy. The name appeared in southern Scotland in the reign of David I, 1124 - 1153. A Sinclair with an origin in Saint Clare l'Évêque, in Calvados, Normandy, became Earl of Caithness in 1379. The frequency of the name in Caithness and Orkney is due to the adoption of by tenants of the name of their overlord. It is not therefore a clan in the true sense of the word.

On the west coast of Scotland there was a name Mac na Cearda, 'son of the smith'. The particular trade varied with the local industry, but here meant 'brassworker'. The trade eventually became debased and the word 'tinkler', a Scottish version of 'tinker' was used for it. With a softened 't', 'tinkler' became Sinclair. There was also a sept of the Sinclairs called Cairds. Around 1900, Sinclair and Cairdie were still being used interchangeably in Ballycastle, Co. Antrim.

The name is rare in Ireland. The map shows the distribution of some 190 families with telephones in 1992. Allowing for homes without telephones, there were probably 250 families altogether. A third of them live in the Belfast, Antrim and Lisburn area, with a further 9% in the adjacent area of Ards. A secondary area of settlement extends from north Co. Antrim, where 10% of the families live, across to north Co. Londonderry which has 5%. The origin of the families could be in any of England, western Scotland or northern Scotland.

Some 17% of the families live in Dublin and 8% live elsewhere in the Republic.

Smith
11000 families

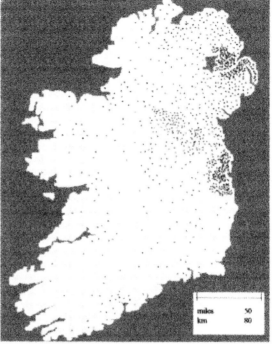

Smith families may be in Ireland either from the Plantation of Ulster and disbanded Cromwellian soldiers; or by translation from McGowan, Irish MacGabhann or Mac an Ghabhainn, meaning Smithson. The Co. Cavan homeland of the latter is clearly visible on the map. Some in Cavan are descended from families transplanted there from Antrim and Down because they had sided with the O'Neills in the reign of Elizabeth I.

Though in medieval times the Ghabhainns of Clare and Tipperary were historians to the O'Loghlins of Burren and the O'Kennedys of Ormond, these areas are not distinguishable today by density of settlement by Smith families.

The map shows the distribution of some 11,000 families in 1992. Smith accounts for 47%, Smyth for 44% and McGowan for 9%. Ten dots of any color make up 1% of the total. The McGowans remain a large proportion only in Sligo, Leitrim and Donegal. Some 31% of all Irish families live in Northern Ireland. The McGowans have much the same proportion at 29%. The Smiths have 24%; whilst 46% of the Smyths are north of the border.

About a fifth of the total live in Greater Dublin compared with 22% of all families of Ireland. About 15% live in the Belfast, Lisburn, Antrim area, compared with 11% of all Irish families.

Almost 5% of Co. Cavan families are Smith, Smyth or McGowan.

Stewart
3300 families

Stewart, like the less numerous Stuart, is derived from the Old English 'Stiward' or 'Stigward', meaning 'keeper of the house'. After the Norman Conquest it was used for the manager or steward of an estate. In both England and Scotland, every bishop, earl and manor had a steward. The Lord High Steward of Scotland was the first officer of the Scottish King. In 1371, Robert the Steward became King Robert II of Scotland. The form 'Stuart' was a French spelling adopted by Mary, Queen of Scots. The final 't' is Scottish.

Andrew Stewart, Lord Ochiltree, of Ayrshire, was one of the nine Scottish chief undertakers of the Plantation and was granted lands at Mountjoy in Tyrone. His grandson, after whom Stewartstown in Tyrone was named, was made Lord Mountjoy in 1683. Two other Scottish chief undertakers were Stewarts and six of the fifty Scottish undertakers were Stewarts. They were granted lands in Donegal, Cavan and Tyrone.

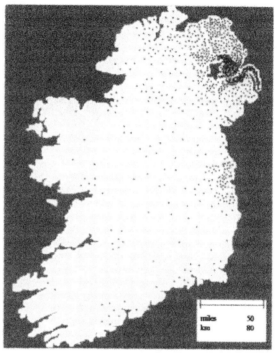

The map shows the distribution of some 3,300 families in 1992. Ten dots represent 1% of the total. Stewart is much the majority form. The more families there are, the relatively weaker Stuart is. Northern Ireland has 78% of all the families. Only 5% of them use the spelling 'Stuart'. Stuarts make up 18% in Dublin. Of the few families in Munster, almost half use the spelling Stuart.

The settlement pattern has the hallmarks of a Scottish origin. The nine counties of Ulster have about 85% of all the families. 32% live in the Belfast, Antrim, Lisburn area alone, three times the national average. Another 7% live in Ards, the whole making a distinct core of almost 40%. Only 7% live in Dublin, just a third of the national average in this area. Plantation settlements may be discerned not only in Ulster, but in the rest of the Republic.

Stitt
160 families

Stitt, Stutt, Stout, Stoute and Stoutt are pronunciation and spelling variants of the same name. For most families, the origin is likely to be from the Middle English 'Stout', which is from the Old French 'estolt' and 'estout' meaning stout or bold. Old English origins seem much less likely. 'Stut' could mean a rounded hill - Henry atte Stoute, 1330. It could also mean a gnat. This meaning survives in the Wiltshire placename Stitchcombe.

Stitt and Stutt reflect Northern English and Scottish pronunciation whilst Stout has become southern and therefore standard English. Stitt does not appear in Reaney's 'A Dictionary of British Surnames', but it has equal ranking with Stutt in Black's 'Surnames of Scotland'. MacLysaght includes only Stout. All three variants are found in Northern Ireland.

The map shows the distribution of 114 Stitt, Stout and Stutt families with telephones in Ireland in 1992. Allowing for homes without telephones, there are likely to be 160 families altogether. Stitt families account for two thirds. All spellings of Stout make up 27%. Stutt families make up 5%. These are rare names.

The Belfast, Antrim, Lisburn area appears as the main area of settlement, suggesting a Scottish origin, and the Stitt and Stutt variants there indicate Scottish pronunciation. They are not found in the Republic. 'Stout' is the variant in the Republic. It is not found in Ulster. The distribution is surprising in that Greater Dublin has a low proportion of all the families and there is such an important cluster in Co. Cork.

O'Sullivan
9800 families

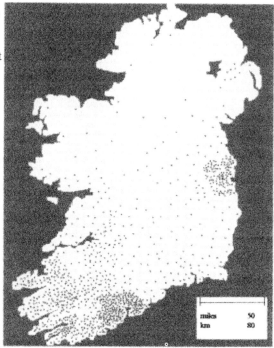

The full meaning of the Irish Ó Súileabháin is uncertain. Súil means eye, but there is disagreement over the second part of the name. It could be hawk-eyed, or one-eyed. Reaney has it as black-eyed.

Some O'Sullivans will be descendants of O'Sullahans who changed their name. O'Sullahan is from Ó Súileacháin, probably meaning quick-eyed, which was once found in south Ulster and the Midlands. The map shows these would have been few. There are no telephone directory entries for Sullahan today.

Originally of south Tipperary, the O'Sullivans were forced westwards by the Anglo-Norman invasion. They became one of the leading septs of the Munster Eoghanacht and the most numerous name in Munster. There were several sub-septs, of which the most important were O'Sullivan Mor and O'Sullivan Beare.

The map shows the distribution of some 9,800 families in 1992. Ten dots make up 1% of the total. Some 89% of them have the 'O' prefix. The greatest number of O'Sullivan and Sullivan families is in Co. Cork, where they make up almost 4% of the population. Their greatest proportion is in Co. Kerry where they are around 6%.

For the Sullivans as for others, the prefix 'O' fell into disuse with the strengthening of English rule from the early 17th century. By 1866 only 4% used it. The last century has seen the trend reversed, though the prefix has not been equally restored in all locations, O'Sullivans are 96% in the Cork area, whilst in nearby Bantry they are 80%. In the Dublin area they are about 83%. There are clusters of the name without the prefix in the Bantry and Belfast areas.

Only 12% of the families live in Dublin. Little more than 1% of the clan's families live in Northern Ireland, and of these, only a third have the prefix.

Tate
280 families

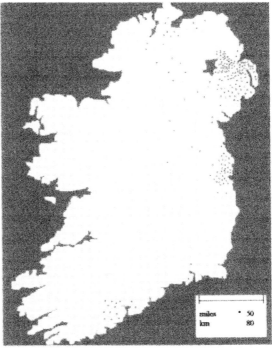

MacLysagh includes Tate in his list of surnames of English origin which were present in Ulster at the time of the 'census' of 1659, though which were not sufficiently numerous to be regarded as 'principal names' at that time.

The name survives in Ireland to the present day, though it remains rare. The map shows the distribution of some 200 families with telephones in 1992. Allowing for homes without telephones, there were probably about 280 households altogether. Tait, Taite and Taitt account for 30% of the total.

The settlement pattern of the families is distinctly urban. The Belfast, Dublin and Cork areas stand out clearly. Londonderry has a small cluster.

The Belfast, Lisburn, Antrim area has 11% of all the families of Ireland. It has three times that proportion of Tate and Tait families. This is usually an indication of Scottish or English origin. Greater Dublin has over a fifth of all Irish families. It has 15% of the Tate families. The Republic as a whole has a third of the families, so that this is not a typical Ulster only name.

Half of the families in the Republic use the spelling Tait. In Northern Ireland, only 18% do.

Thompson
3700 families

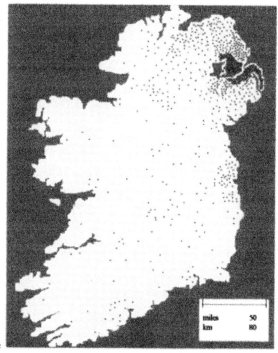

Thompson is one of many name forms derived from the Hebrew personal name Thomas, meaning a twin. As the name of one of the twelve disciples, it became popular throughout Europe with the spread of Christianity. In Gaelic, the aspirated 't' of MacThom produced the surname McComb. Likewise Thomas, pronounced 'homas, became Holmes by assimilation with the English name of a different origin. These names in Ireland or Scotland, could become Thomson, then Thompson by pronunciation.

Though it appeared in Ireland relatively recently, Thompson is now well established and numerous. The map shows the distribution of some 3,700 families in 1992. Ten dots make up 1% of the total. The presence of the 'p' is said to be English, but as only 3% of the families do not have this letter, many Thompsons in Ireland must also be of Scottish origin.

The Belfast, Lisburn and Antrim area alone has 37% of all the families, more than three times the national average and a sure indicator of Scottish origin. A further 10% of the Thompsons live on the Ards Peninsula. Northern Ireland has about a third of all Irish households. It has 81% of the Thompsons. For the most part, the settlement pattern reveals the border of the six counties. Whatever their origin, surnames based on saints' names tend to be northern.

Concentrated as Thompson families are, their concentration is less than that of the McComb families, four-fifths of whose number live in the Belfast area and 96% in Northern Ireland. Thompson is one of the most numerous Protestant names in Ireland. For every 1000 Murphy families, there are 229 Thompson.

Todd
530 families

'Tod' or 'todde' has been a nickname for a fox since the Middle Ages in England, mainly in the north, and in Scotland. It has been applied to people since the thirteenth century. The second 'd' has always been used in England. It began to appear in Scotland in the seventeenth century. Tod survives today mainly on the west coast of Scotland.

'Tod' for fox still survives in dialects in Britain. The Irish for fox is 'sionnach'. Around 1900, families called Shinnahan, an Irish name derived from Sionnach, were using Todd interchangeably with their own names, around Ballycastle in Co. Antrim.

The map shows the distribution of some 390 Todd families with telephones in 1992.

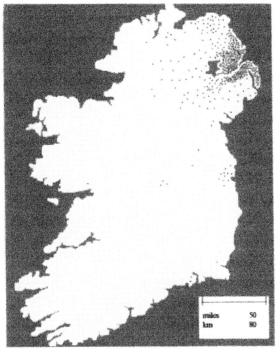

Allowing for homes without telephones, there are probably about 530 families altogether. As has often happened in Northern Ireland, where English and Scottish traditions merge, the English spelling tends to predominate. There is only one entry for Tod in the directories.

A third of all the families live in the Belfast, Antrim and Lisburn area. This is three times the national average representation. The Ards Peninsula accounts for another 10%. Strong representation in these areas strongly suggests a Scottish origin. To the west, the cluster continues to Portadown.

Outside the core area, Todd representation falls off rapidly. There is a slight increase in density in north Antrim. This could be further influence from Scotland, but is perhaps supplemented by former Shinnahan families.

Because of internal migration in relatively modern times, Greater Dublin has become the most important location for many Irish families. Over a fifth of the population lives there. It has only 3% of the Todds. Northern Ireland has a third of all Irish families. It has 89% of the Todds.

O'Toole
1500 families

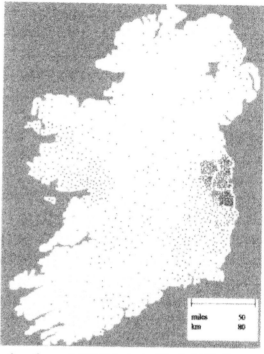

Tuathal was the personal name of a King of Leinster who died in 956. The word means people mighty. The Leinster sept of Ó Tuathail derives its name and origin from this King. Their clan name was Ui Muireadhaigh, which later became the name of their territory, in what is now the south of Co. Kildare. They were driven from this territory by the Anglo-Normans and settled in the mountains of Wicklow. They managed to retain considerable property until the confiscations of Cromwell and William III. A branch of the family settled in west Connaught at an early date, where, according to Hardiman, there was also a distinct sept, an offshoot of the O'Malleys. An Ulster family of the same name is said by MacFirbis to be a branch of the Cinel Eoghan.

The map shows the distribution of some 1,500 O'Toole families in 1992. Ten dots represent 1% of the total. The density in Co. Kildare remains the same as in much of Wicklow and much the same density is apparent in west Connaught. There are relatively few families in Ulster and those in the province are widely dispersed.

In common with many names, Greater Dublin is now is home to the most important cluster. Because of the proximity of the original O'Toole homeland to the capital, the representation of the name in Greater Dublin is, at approaching 40%, about the highest of all Irish surnames.

Northern Ireland has a third of all Irish families. Despite being home to a sept of the Cinel Eoghan, it has only 4% of the O'Tooles.

Treacy
1350 families

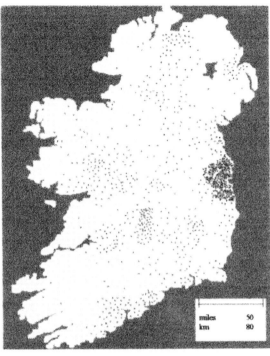

The Irish Ó Treasaigh, descendent of Treasach, fighter, was the name of three distinct families. One was of south east Galway, akin to the O'Maddens, and was dispersed at an early date. Another was in west Cork, of the same stock as the O'Donovans, a branch of which settled in Co. Limerick. The third was in Co. Leix, where Tracys were lords of Ui Bairrche, a territory including the barony of Slievemargy on the Carlow border. This sept was dispersed by successive invasions.

The map shows the distribution of some 1,350 Ó Treasaigh families in Ireland in 1992. Ten dots make up 1% of the total. Two-thirds of them have the spelling Treacy, including a few spelt Treacey. Of the remainder, 87% are spelt Tracey and 13% are spelt Tracy.

There are still concentrations of the name in east Galway and west Cork. The dispersal from Leix seems to be associated with a build up in the adjacent counties, with a definite cluster around Roscrea. There is a further area of settlement, from Fermanagh through Tyrone to Derry, which does not feature in the works of MacLysaght and Woulfe.

MacLysaght indicates that the form Treacy is unusual outside Ireland. It may be a recent development in Ireland following the introduction of literacy and education as to the origin of the name. Typically, the North has been less affected and its spellings are more likely to be unreformed. A fifth of the Tracey/Tracys are in Northern Ireland, whereas only 5% of the Treacy/Treaceys live there.

About 29% of the Treacy/Treaceys live in Greater Dublin, which is a typical proportion. Traceys have over 50% in the area, whilst two-thirds of Tracys are in the Republic's capital. These are high figures. The explanation is probably from Tracy, Viscounts of Rathcoole in Co. Dublin. Their name may have been adopted by local people, whose descendents are staying with or close to the Anglo-Norman spelling.

Tracy appears in two place-names in Normandy. They would have been called after landowners in the Gallo-Roman era, and in Latin would have been Traciac(um). The Gaulish possessive suffix '-ac', similar to the Irish, is contracted to 'y' in northern France. The name Tracy therefore is ultimately Celtic, whatever its spelling and origin.

Vernor
65 families

Black's 'Surnames of Scotland' is the only authority to have an entry for this name. It appears in fifteenth and sixteenth century records as Vernour. Verner and Vernor appear in the seventeenth century. Black quotes Harrison as saying the name is a French form of the Old Germanic personal name Warenheri. Reaney's 'Dictionary of British Surnames' does not cover the name, but Warner is given as a derivative of Warenheri, along with Garner and Guarnier. The root of the name appears to be akin to the English element 'war' in 'wary' and 'beware'. Warenher (i) was a common Norman personal name. As Warner and Garner, it appeared in English records from the twelfth century.

The absence of any Irish commentary on this name leads to a presumption that it came to Ireland by way of Scotland.

The map shows the distribution of 46 families with telephones in 1992. Allowing for homes without telephones, there were likely to be 60 - 65 families altogether. About 30% of the families lived in the Belfast area. This is almost three times the national average and may be taken as an indicator of a Scottish origin. The scattered distribution elsewhere is unusual. There are clusters of families on the western and eastern fringes of Co. Tyrone; in central Co. Down, and along the north coast of Co. Antrim around Bushmills. Four of the families have the spelling Vernor, the remainder being Verner. The Vernors are scattered amongst he Verners. Apart from a lone one in Londonderry, there was a Vernor in Dublin, one in Belfast and one in Bushmills. The intermixture of the spelling forms suggests a relatively recent common source.

The families living in the Dublin area amount to about 9% of the total. Northern Ireland has about three times the proportion of Verners and Vernors than it has of the Irish population as a whole.

Walsh
10900 families

Walsh was not initially a surname, but the name given to many unconnected Welsh families who came as retainers of the Anglo-Normans. It is now one of the most numerous surnames in Ireland; the most numerous of those resulting from the Anglo-Norman settlement; and the most numerous of the principal names meaning foreigner.

The map shows the distribution of some 10,900 Walsh families in 1992. Ten dots represent 1% of the total. As with most families, Dublin is now the most important settlement cluster. Some 19% of the Walsh households live there, as compared to 22% of all Irish households.

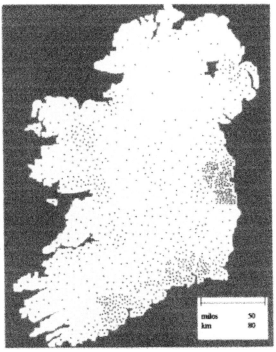

With the exception of Greater Dublin, Walsh families are not densely concentrated in any locality. Their distribution is distinguished by a band of medium density about 30 miles wide running along the south coast from Wexford, the site of Maurice FitzGerald's landing in 1169, through to and beyond Cork. Such are the high total numbers of Walshes that even at medium density, they make up almost 2% of the total population of the south coast counties.

There is another area of medium density settlement in Galway and Mayo. In Galway, Walsh families make up almost 2% of the total population, whilst in Mayo they are are about 2½%.

Like Doyle and McDonald, both names of groups that migrated into the country, the distribution of Walsh households reveals the original area of settlement. The name is sparsely represented in Ulster. Only 4% of Walsh families live in Northern Ireland, as compared to about a third of all Irish families.

Warden
50 families

Warden is an English surname. It has two origins. One is from the Anglo-French 'wardein', Old French 'gardein', meaning one who had the office of a warden or guardian. The other is from the place-name 'ward dun', meaning 'look-out hill'.

As 'the surname is late with us', Black considers that the most likely origin of Warden in Scotland is from a place-name in Northumberland. He points out that John Wardein was admitted a burgess of Glasgow in 1627. This date was not long after the union of the crowns of England and Scotland. Many families on both sides of the border lost their livings, whether in security, trade or contraband, when the union came into effect. They therefore moved out of the area. Northern Ireland was a destination for some of them. Warden-on-Tyne lies at the foot of an abrupt hill of 593' which dominates the confluence of the North Tyne and South Tyne Rivers and the road from Hexham to Scotland. It is the kind of location whose role would have diminished after the union. This may be the origin of the Wardens of Ireland as well as of Scotland.

The map shows the distribution of some 35 families with telephones in 1992. Allowing for homes without telephones, there were likely to have been about 45 - 50 families altogether. The name is rare in Ireland and is extremely localised. Well over half of the families lived at the northern end of the Ards Peninsula. Despite its proximity, Belfast has had little attraction for them. The name is not found in Dublin and is virtually unknown in the Republic.

Warke
80 families

In his work on Scottish surnames, Black states that Wark is probably from Wark-on-Tweed. This is on the English side of the river, in Northumberland. It was variously spelt as Werk and Werke. MacLysaght also gives Warke as a Northumberland place-name. He found it fairly numerous in the seventeenth century Hearth Money Rolls of Cos. Donegal and Derry.

The word is English and is a variant of 'work'. It is often used as a place-name, sometimes in compound form as Aldwark or Newark. Aldwark, 'old work', would be buildings, often fortifications, that could have been long established when English settlers first arrived in an area. The town of Newark, 'new work', was built close to the site of a Roman fort, which in medieval times was known as Aldewerke.

The map shows the distribution of some 60 families with telephones in Ireland in 1992. Allowing for homes without phones, there were probably 80 families altogether. Those with the spelling Warke accounted for 92%, whilst families spelt Wark made up the remainder.

The area around Belfast and Lisburn accommodated a third of the Warke families. For many Irish families, this area has been a destination for migrants in relatively recent times. The high proportion of Warkes living there, at three times the national average, is indicative of a Scottish origin of long standing. Co. Donegal does not now feature in the settlement pattern of the Warkes. The name continues to be found in Co. Derry and the adjacent part of Co. Antrim. It is virtually unknown in the Republic.

Whelan
4400 families

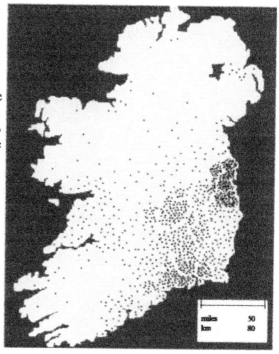

The map shows the distribution in 1992 of 4,400 families with names derived from the Gaelic Ó Faoláin, from faol, a wolf. Ten dots amount to 1% of the total. The majority have been anglicised as Whelan, who make up 62% of the total. The remainder are Phelan families. MacLysaght sees Whelan as a variant of Phelan.

Before the Norman invasion, the Ó Faoláin chief was Prince of the Decies, a territory approximating to west Waterford which existed from prehistoric times to the break up of the Gaelic order in the sixteenth century.

The families are still strong around the historic core, but are just as well represented in much of the entire south eastern quarter of the country. From Waterford through to Leix they make up almost 2% of all families. Though the two spelling forms are interspersed, Phelan in found in a broad spine down the middle of the cluster. Whelan is predominent to the east, in Wexford, Wicklow and Carlow, and begins to be the stronger again in Tipperary and west Waterford and beyond.

Because of growth in the Dublin area and depopulation in much of the rest of the country since the Famine, Greater Dublin is now the main cluster for Whelan and Phelan as it is for most surnames. Some 32% of Whelan families live there, double the Phelan proportion of 16%. This reflects the Whelan dominance in the eastern edge of the cluster. Both names are virtually unknown in Northern Ireland.

White
3500 families

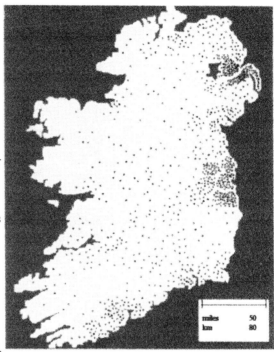

In England and the Scottish Lowlands, the surname White could be from the Old English 'wiht' a bend in a river, or from 'wait' a place for lying in wait. However, for the most part the name was from the Old English 'hwit' a nickname for someone fair haired or skinned.

In the Scottish Highlands, White was adopted for the Gaelic MacGhillebháin - son of the fair servant or lad. Along with Black and other names, White was adopted by McGregors and Lamonts when their own surnames were proscribed.

In Ireland from the Anglo-Normans, White was gaelicised as de Faoite. This produced MacFaoitigh which in turn produced McWhite, McWhitty and McQuitty. By translation of bán, white and geal, bright, White has often been adopted instead of Bane, Bawn, Galligan and Kilbane.

The map shows the distribution of some 3,500 families in Ireland in 1992. The spelling 'White' accounts for 80% of them, with the remainder being 'Whyte'. Ten dots of either color make up 1% of the total.

The Belfast, Antrim and Lisburn area is home to some 11% of the Whites and 8% of the Whytes. Names of more completely Scottish origin tend to be more strongly concentrated in this area. The medium strength representation suggests mixed Irish and Scottish origins. Greater Dublin is home to 17% of families of both spellings.

White is slightly more popular in the north and east and Whyte in the south and west. Some 35% of White families live in Northern Ireland, much the same as the proportion of all Irish families living there. Only 25% of the Whytes live in the North. The bias of the spellings contrasts with Smith and Smyth, where the 'y' variant is more popular in the North.

Whitley
85 families

There are seven place-names in England with the name of Whitley or Whiteley and one with the spelling Whitleigh. It is likely that the surname Whitley was associated with one of these, though there is a possibility that one of another seven Wheatley locations produced the name, or an unknown minor location. The 'ley' part of the name is the most widely used place-name element in England. It is from the Old English 'leah', a word related to 'light' and originally meaning a clearing. It later came to mean pasture. 'Whit' means white. The Whitleigh place-name is in Berkshire and the Whitleys and Whiteleys are in Cheshire, Northumberland, Wiltshire, Warwickshire and Yorkshire.

Black's 'Surnames of Scotland' has an entry for Whitlie, saying it is of recent introduction from England.

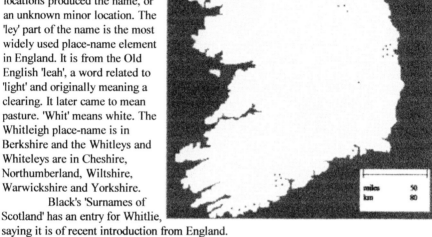

The map shows the distribution of some 59 Whitley families in Ireland in 1992. Allowing for homes without telephones, there are likely to have been about 85 families altogether.

The location of the families suggests the history of their settlement in Ireland. The cluster around Belfast and Ards is usual for Scottish or English origin families. Co. Fermanagh likewise often stands out as a plantation area. Co. Cork was an early settlement centre from England. Several of the Whitley locations were in counties that sent settlers to Ireland

Whitley remains a rare name in Ireland, whether North or Republic. It is nevertheless primarily a Northern name, as only 30% of the families live in the Republic.

McWilliams
450 families

Like the many times more numerous McDonalds, the McWilliams are a family of mixed Scottish and Norwegian descent. The family name Mac Mhic Uilleim means descended from William's son William. The senior William was the fifth Chief of MacLeod.

The Leod of MacLeod is a Scandinavian name, from the Norse settlements in the Western Isles of Scotland. Uilleim was from the Teutonic root that produced William in England and Wilhelm in Germany. The Gaelic family name Mac Uilleim was established in the Highlands and Isles of Scotland as early as the twelfth century. Anglicisation produced McWilliam and a number of other Mac variants.

In Ireland, Scottish influence met English as well as Irish. A terminal 's' was often added to a name after the English fashion. McWilliams is now the more usual form in Ireland. The map shows the distribution of 327 families with telephones in 1992. Allowing for homes without telephones means there are about 450 families altogether.

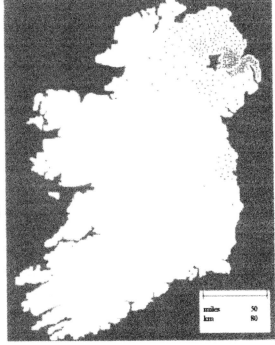

The distribution shows the relatively recent Scottish origin of the name. There has been very little dispersal outside what are now the six counties of Northern Ireland. Under 10% of the families live in the Republic. Most of those are in Dublin.

The McWilliams total will have lost some of its number over time as the 'Mac' prefix was sometimes 'translated', thereby adding to Williamson and Williams families of non-Gaelic origin. There may also have been some additions. McQuilliams in south Derry has become McWilliams. McQuillan has become McWilliam, particularly in Co. Down and McCollyums in the Toome district of Co. Antrim. These instances are unlikely to have been numerous.

Wilson
4500 families

Wilson is second only to Williams as one of several surnames to be derived from the personal name, William. It evolved independently in many places in England and Scotland. MacLysaght says that it is by far the most common English name in Ireland, though it has been estimated that four fifths of the Ulster Wilsons are of Scottish ancestry.

The name was common over the Scottish Lowlands, especially so in the Glasgow area in the sixteenth century. Where it occurs in Caithness and Sutherland, Wilson is derived from William, one of the sons of the fifteenth century George Gunn, Crowner, (Coroner) of Caithness. On the east coast they were a sept of the Clan Innes. The name appears in Ireland in the 'Census' of 1659.

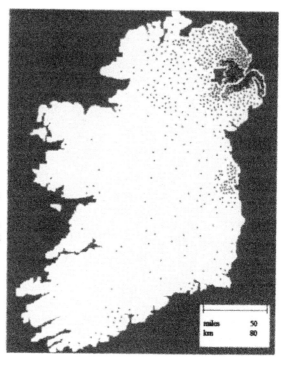

The map shows the distribution of some 4,500 families in 1992. Ten dots make up 1% of the total. Some 69% of the Wilson families live in Northern Ireland. The population is dense over all the six counties. Fermanagh stands out in the south west.

A third of the families live in the Belfast, Lisburn Antrim core area, which is three times the 11% share that this area has of all Irish families. This high ratio around Belfast confirms the importance of the Scottish origin. The same density of settlement extends into Ards, where another 6% live.

Only 31% live in the Republic. Of these, 4% live in the Ulster counties of Donegal, Cavan and Monaghan. Greater Dublin has over a fifth of all the families of Ireland. It has only 6% of Wilson families. The remaining 11% of families in the Republic are widely distributed. This may be taken to reflect the length of time the name has been established in Ireland.

Yeates
176 families

Yates, Yeats, Yeatts, Yetts, along with Yate are derivatives of the Old English 'geat', Middle English 'yate', a gate. The standard pronunciation took the hard 'g'. Reaney quotes Hereward de Jette in 1198. At that date the 'J' could be taken to be an ornamental 'I'. Philip del Yate, 1260. The terminal 's' appears in 1344 with Robert atte Yates. The meaning would be a dweller by one or more gates, or a gate-keeper. Black points out that in names derived from topographical features, a final 's' is not uncommon, that it may be either a plural or a genitive, it not being 'possible to say which from inspection'. He has Adam del Yate in 1347 and a Johannes Zett in 1479. The apparent 'Z' in this name is not the Greek 'Z' which now forms part of the modern

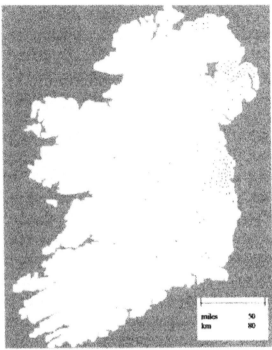

western alphabet. It is a runic letter resembling a 'z' which was pronounced like an aspirated 'g'. This is a useful indication of a pronunciation somewhere between the initial sound of gate and yate before they diverged.

MacLysaght says that Yeats has been recorded in Dublin since the seventeenth century; that the famous literary and artistic family of Yeats, which had formerly been in Dublin, moved to Sligo at the end of that century; and that the Yates and Yeates families elsewhere in the country are unconnected with them.

The map shows the distribution of some 127 families with telephones in 1992. Allowing for homes without telephones, there would be about 176 families altogether. Yeates accounts for 55%; Yates for 40% and Yeats for 5%.

Northern Ireland accounts for 43% of the families, and has all three spellings. As an individual location, Greater Dublin is slightly more important to the name than the Belfast area. All thre spellings are found in the Republic. There are no Yeats families in the telpehone directory for Sligo at the present day.

Index To Map Numbers

An index to the maps shown in this book, with the main spelling used. Be aware of other spellings of the name.

Name	#	Name	#	Name	#	Name	#
Adamson	1	Devine	52	Henderson	103	Moore	153
Alcorn	2	McDevitt	53	Henry	104	Moorhead	154
Archer	3	Doherty	54	Hogan	105	Moran	155
McAteer	4	Donaghy	55	Hogg	106	Moreland	156
Barrett	5	McDonald	56	Hopkins	107	Morgan	157
Bartley	6	ODonnell	57	Hough	108	Morton	158
Beattie	7	Donnelly	58	Hussey	109	Mullan	159
Beggs	8	ODonovan	59	Hynes	110	McMullen	160
Bell	9	Doran	60	Irwin	111	Mulvanny	161
Bergin	10	Doyle	61	Jennings	112	Murphy	162
Berry	11	Duff	62	Johnstone	113	Murray	163
Bonner	12	Duffy	63	Joyce	114	McMurray	164
Boyle	13	Duncan	64	Kane	115	McNamara	165
Brady	14	Dunlop	65	Keane	116	ONeill	166
Brennan	15	Dunne	66	Kelly	117	Nolan	167
McBride	16	Elder	67	Kennedy	118	McNulty	168
OBrien	17	McElroy	68	Kenny	119	Orr	170
Brown	18	English	69	McKeown	120	Pierce	169
Burke	19	McEvoy	70	Kerr	121	Quinn	171
Byrne	20	McFall	71	Kerrigan	122	Rea	172
Caldwell	21	Farrell	72	Kidd	123	ORegan	173
McCandless	22	Farrelly	73	Kieran	124	OReilly	174
McCann	23	Fitzgerald	85	McKillop	125	Rutherford	175
Carlin	24	Flanagan	74	King	126	Ryan	176
Carmody	25	Fleming	75	McKinley	127	Salmon	177
Carroll	26	Flynn	76	Lacey	127	Scott	178
Carson	27	Foran	77	McLaughlin	128	McShane	179
McCartan	28	Gallagher	78	Lavelle	129	Shannon	180
McCarthy	29	Gannon	79	Leahy	130	Sheehan	181
Carty	30	Garland	80	OLeary	131	Sheehy	182
McCay	31	McGarvey	81	Lee	132	Simpson	183
Clarke	32	McGee	82	Logan	133	Sinclair	184
McCleary	33	Geoghegan	83	OLoughlin	134	Smith	185
McClelland	34	Geraghty	84	Loughman	135	Stewart	186
Clifford	35	McGimpsey	86	Love	136	Stit	187
Cochrane	36	Given	87	Lynch	137	OSullivan	188
Collins	37	Glennon	88	Lynn	138	Tate	189
McComb	38	McGonagle	89	Magee	139	Thompson	190
McConnell	39	Gorman	90	Maguire	140	Todd	191
OConnor	40	McGourty	91	Maher	141	OToole	192
McConville	41	McGrath	92	Mahon	142	Treacy	193
Copeland	42	Greer	93	OMahoney	143	Vernor	194
Corrigan	43	Hackett	94	Marshall	144	Walsh	195
Costello	44	OHagan	95	Martin	145	Warden	196
Cowan	45	Harley	96	Mathers	146	Warke	197
Crowe	46	Harrington	98	Maynes	147	Whelan	198
McCullough	47	Hassell	97	Mee	148	White	199
Daly	48	Hasson	99	Meek	149	Whitley	200
Davison	49	Hayes	100	Mills	150	McWilliams	201
Delaney	50	Healy	101	Molloy	151	Wilson	202
McDermot	51	Heffernan	102	Montgomery	152	Yeates	203

Surname Index

An index to the surnames in this book. Be aware of other spellings of your name. Your family name may appear in this book under a slightly different spelling.

Acarson	39	Beattie	19	DeBurgh	31	McCarthy	60
Adam	13	Beatty	19	Burke	31	McCarthy	76
Adams	13	Begg	20	Burke	31	MacCarthys	143
Adamson	13	Beggs	20	Burke	182	McCartin	40
MacAdhaimh	13	OBeirgin	23	Burkes	124	Carton	40
Aidy	13	Bell	21	Burry	24	Carty	41
Alchorne	14	Bell	101	Bury	24	Carty	42
Alcoirne	14	Bergan	23	Byrne	32	Carville	38
Alcorn	14	Bergin	22	Byrne	88	McCaughey	120
Aldcorne	14	Berrigans	23	Byrne	174	Caulfield	70
Aldwark	209	Berry	23	Byrnes	32	McCaw	13
McAleary	45	Betagh	19	OByrnes	32	McCay	43
McAlee	138	Bigg	20	OCahan	127	MacCearbhaill	38
MacAnleagha	144	Biggs	20	McCahey	106	OCearbhaill	38
MacAntsaoir	16	OBirgin	23	McCahey	120	OCearmada	37
MacAnultaigh	180	Bissetts	131	Cahoon	57	Chapman	17
deAngulos	56	Black	211	Cairdie	196	Chattan	61
MacAnna	35	Blennerhass	110	Cairds	196	OCionga	137
MacAnnaidh	35	Boner	24	Cairell	36	Clarke	44
McAnulty	180	Bonner	24	Caldwell	33	Clarks	44
MacAodha	43	Bourke	31	Cameron	45	McCleary	45
Archer	15	Boyle	25	Campbell	45	OClearys	45
Archier	15	OBoyle	25	MacCana	35	McCleery	45
MacAree	137	OBoyle	180	MacCanann	91	McClelland	46
Armstrong	125	Boyville	25	McCandless	34	OClery	44
MacArtain	40	MacBradaigh	26	McCann	35	Clifford	47
McAteer	16	OBradain	189	MacCannon	51	MacCloskeys	127
McAteers	53	Bradan	189	Canny	35	OClovane	47
Atte Bell	21	Bradden	189	Capet	17	MacCloy	163
Auldcorne	14	Brady	26	Caradoc	41	OCluvane	47
McAvin	99	MacBradys	26	Carey	123	Cnaimhsigh	24
McAvoy	82	Bran	27	Carlin	36	MacCoan	57
Awldcorn	14	MacBranain	27	Carmody	37	Cochrane	48
Bane	211	OBraonain	27	Carol	36	Coen	57
OBaoighill	25	Brennan	27	OCarolan	36	OCoilean	49
Bareid	17	Brian	29	Carpenter	16	OCoinne	130
Baroid	17	MacBride	28	Carr	132	Colavin	33
Barrett	17	McBride	28	Carrigan	133	Collins	49
Barrette	17	McBride	50	Carroll	38	McCollyums	213
Bartholomew	18	OBrien	29	McCarrolls	38	Colquhoun	57
Bartholomew	19	OBrien	31	OCarrols	153	McCom	50
Bartley	18	OBrien	126	Carrragan	55	McComas	50
Bartley	18	OBriens	129	Carson	39	MacComb	50
Batey	19	OBroin	32	McCartan	40	McComb	50
Batty	19	OBroin	32	Cartans	40	McComb	202
Bawn	211	Brown	30	McCarthy	41	McCombe	50
OBeara	24	Browne	30	McCarthy	42	Comber	133

217   Names Arranged Alphabetically without the O' or Mac Prefix   217

Name	#	Name	#	Name	#	Name	#
McCombie	50	Cullivan	33	ODeorain	72	Doran	72
Comgan	57	McCulloch	59	ODermond	57	Dorcey	103
McComish	50	McCullough	59	ODermond	63	McDowell	73
McConaghy	67	McCullough	59	McDermot	57	Dowey	75
MacConaill	51	McCullow	59	McDermot	63	Doyle	73
MacCone	57	Cunovalos	51	MacDermots	56	Doyle	88
MacCongail	101	Cunree	137	Devin	64	Doyle	90
McConkey	67	Cyng	137	Devine	64	Doyle	207
MacConmara	177	Cynvall	51	ODevine	64	Duff	74
Connell	51	MacDaid	61	Devitt	65	Duff	74
McConnell	51	McDaid	65	MacDevitt	61	MacDuff	74
McConnell	51	MacDaids	65	McDevitt	65	McDuff	74
OConnell	51	Dalach	60	MacDevitts	65	Duffin	74
MacConnon	51	Daly	60	ODiff	75	Duffy	74
OConnor	24	ODaly	60	ODiorma	63	Duffy	75
OConnor	52	MacDarcy	103	Doherty	66	Duhig	75
OConnor	63	Davidson	61	ODoherty	65	ODuinn	78
Connors	52	Davies	61	ODoherty	66	Dullope	77
OConnors	31	Davin	64	MacDomhaill	68	Duncan	67
OConnors	60	Davis	61	McDonagh	67	Duncan	76
OConnors	96	Davison	61	McDonaghs	76	Dunlop	77
OConnors	194	Davitt	65	Donaghy	67	Dunlopp	77
Conroy	137	MacDavitt	61	Donaghy	67	Dunn	78
Conry	137	Dawson	61	MacDonaghy	67	Dunne	78
McConville	53	De Brun	30	Donald	69	Eadie	13
McConwell	53	De Burca	31	MacDonald	69	Elder	79
Copeland	54	De Burgh	31	MacDonald	136	MacElduff	74
Corcoran	48	De Carsan	39	McDonald	68	McElduff	80
Corrigan	55	De Faoite	211	McDonald	207	Elliott	125
Corrigan	133	De Gernon	92	McDonalds	213	McElroy	80
Corsan	39	De Harlea	108	MacDonnell	136	McElwee	82
Corson	39	De Jorse	126	ODonnell	24	MacEnchroe	58
Costello	56	De Lacey	139	ODonnell	69	English	81
MacCostello	56	De Lacy	121	ODonnell	101	MacEoin	131
Costelloe	56	De Leis	139	MacDonnells	94	Ervine	123
Coueran	48	De Lench	149	MacDonnells	151	Erwin	123
Cowan	57	De Logan	145	MacDonnells	194	McEvoy	82
MacCowan	57	De	164	McDonnells	51	McEvoy	82
McCoy	43	De Mora	165	ODonnells	66	McFall	83
Coyne	57	De Nangle	56	ODonnells	90	McFall	141
OCoyne	183	ODea	58	Donnelly	70	OFaolain	210
Craddock	41	Dehareleye	108	ODonnelly	70	MacFarland	18
McCrae	104	Del Esse	139	McDonnels	77	MacFarlane	18
Crampsie	24	Delahaye	112	ODonovan	71	Farley	85
MacCrea	184	Delaney	62	Donovans	71	Farrell	84
Crowe	58	Delaney	173	ODonovans	49	Farrell	108
Croy	58	Delaneys	23	ODonovans	116	OFarrell	84
Crozier	125	Delap	77	ODonovans	205	OFarrells	191
MacCuindlis	34	Dempsey	98	Doohey	75	Farrelly	85
OCuinn	183	ODempsey	24	Doohig	75	Farrelly	108

McFaul	83	McGilloway	82	Halket	106	Houriskey	33
McFaul	141	Gilmartin	157	Halkett	106	Houssaye	121
Ferrall	108	Gilroy	137	OHamergin	23	Howe	120
MacFiachains	58	Gilshenan	192	OHaras	45	Hugh	107
Fitzgerald	17	Giltenan	192	Harley	108	MacHugh	43
Fitzgerald	97	McGimpsey	98	Harrily	108	Hughes	112
Fitzgeralds	139	McGinley	138	Harrington	109	OHungerdell	109
Fitzgeralds	165	Givan	99	OHashea	110	Hurleys	108
Fitzhenry	116	Givans	99	Hassan	111	Hussey	121
Fitzmauric	191	Given	99	Hassen	111	Hyndes	122
OFlahertys	126	Givens	99	Hassett	110	Hynes	122
Flahy	142	Glenane	100	OHassia	110	MacIlduff	74
Flanagan	86	Glennane	100	Hassin	111	McIlduff	80
Flannagan	86	Glennon	100	Hasson	111	MacIlhair	132
Fleming	87	McGlennon	100	Haugh	120	McIlroy	80
OFlionn	88	Glynns	100	OHavergan	22	Innes	214
OFloinn	150	McGonagle	100	Hayes	112	MacIntyre	16
Flynn	88	McGonagle	101	OHea	112	Irvine	123
OFlynn	88	McGonigal	101	OHealihy	113	Irvine	125
Foran	89	McGonigle	101	Healy	113	Irwin	123
OForhane	89	Gorman	102	MacHeath	194	Isabelle	21
Fourhane	89	McGorman	102	Heather	24	Islay	21
Freeman	16	OGorman	102	Heffernan	114	MacIver	181
McGahey	106	MacGorth	103	OHeffernan	114	MacIvor	181
Gallagher	90	McGorty	103	Henderson	115	Jennings	124
Galligan	211	McGourkey	103	Hendry	116	Jocelin	56
Gannon	91	McGourty	103	Henry	116	Johnson	125
MacGannon	91	McGourty	103	McHenry	116	Johnson	131
Garlan	92	McGowan	79	OHenry	116	Johnson	191
Garland	92	McGowan	197	Heraghty	109	Johnston	125
Garner	206	OGradys	26	OHessedy	110	Johnston	131
Garrity	96	McGrath	104	Heugh	120	Johnstone	125
McGarrity	96	McGraths	148	OHeyne	122	Johnstone	131
Garty	96	McGraw	104	Hind	122	Joyce	126
Garvey	93	Greer	105	Hinds	122	Kane	127
McGarvey	93	Gregor	105	Hines	122	OKane	127
OGarvey	93	MacGregor	105	Hobbe	119	OKanes	52
Gearty	96	McGregors	211	Hobekinus	119	Kaufmann	17
MacGee	151	Grier	105	Hobigan	119	Kaupaland	54
McGee	94	Grierson	105	Hobkin	119	MacKay	43
MacGeehee	94	MacGuire	152	Hogan	117	Keane	127
Geoghegan	95	Gunn	214	Hogg	118	Kearns	135
MacGeown	131	Gwynn	94	Hogge	118	Kearon	135
Geraghty	96	Habkine	119	Holmes	50	Kearon	135
MacGeraghty	96	Hackett	106	Hopkins	119	MacKeary	137
Geraghtys	100	OHagan	107	Horish	33	McKee	43
Gerety	96	OHagan	118	Hosey	121	MacKeith	194
Gernon	92	Hagans	107	Hosie	121	Kellops	136
McGhee	94	OHagans	183	Hough	120	Kelly	128
McGhee	151	Haki	106	Houlihan	179	OKelly	193

Kennedy	129	Le Brun	30	Maguire	152	McMillan	172
OKennedys	197	Le Mathere	158	Maguires	55	Mills	162
Kenny	130	Lea	144	Maguires	64	Milne	162
MacKeon	131	Leahey	142	Maguires	121	Mohan	154
McKeown	57	Leahy	142	Maher	153	Molloy	163
McKeown	131	OLeary	143	Mahon	154	OMolloys	163
Kerin	132	Lee	144	OMahon	154	Montgomery	164
Kerin	135	Leigh	144	Mahoney	155	Moore	165
Kerr	132	Leiseach	139	OMahoney	155	Moore	168
Kerrane	135	McLellan	46	Main	159	Moorehead	166
Kerrigan	133	Lenglais	81	Maine	159	Moorhead	166
Kerrs	132	MacLennon	145	MacMaines	159	Moorland	168
Kersane	39	MacLeod	213	Mains	159	Morahan	169
McKevin	99	Ley	144	MacMairtin	157	OMorain	167
Kidd	134	Lochlainn	146	OMalleys	204	Moran	167
Kieran	132	Loftus	147	Malloy	163	Morcant	169
Kieran	135	Logan	145	Maloy	163	Mordha	165
Kilbane	211	Loggan	145	Maloy	163	Moreland	168
McKillip	136	OLoghlen	146	MacManis	159	Morgan	169
Killops	136	OLoghlens	60	OMaolain	171	Morgunn	169
King	137	OLoghlin	146	Marshal	156	McMorran	167
King	137	OLoghlins	197	Marshall	156	Morton	170
McKinlay	138	Loghman	147	OMartain	157	Mugron	167
McKinley	138	Logue	163	Martin	157	Muirhead	166
MacKinn	137	Lohan	145	Mather	158	Mulcahy	120
MacKinnon	50	OLonergans	193	Mathers	158	Mullan	171
McKinnons	148	Loughan	145	Maughan	154	McMullan	171
MacKintosh	45	OLoughlin	127	Maughan	154	McMullan	172
MacKintyre	21	OLoughlin	146	McMawe	160	OMullan	172
Kitt	134	OLoughlin	147	Maxwells	125	Mullane	171
Kneafsey	24	Loughman	147	Mayne	159	OMullawill	141
L'englys	81	Loughnan	147	Maynes	159	Mullen	171
Lacey	139	Loughnane	147	Mea	160	McMullen	172
MacLachlainn	140	Love	148	Meagher	153	Mullin	171
McLachlan	140	OLowell	141	Mee	160	McMullin	172
OLachtnain	147	Lynch	149	OMee	160	Mullins	171
deLacy	121	O'Lynch	149	Meehan	160	Mullock	163
Lahiff	142	Lynchehaun	149	Meek	161	McMullon	172
Lahy	142	Lynn	150	Meeke	161	Mulloy	163
Lamont	30	OLynn	150	Meik	161	Mulryan	188
Lamonts	211	Lynns	88	Meike	161	Mulvaney	173
OLaoire	143	OLynns	88	Mek	161	Mulvanny	173
Larcher	15	Mackays	169	OMelaghlins	140	Mulvenna	173
McLaughlin	140	OMaddens	205	Mergin	23	Mulvenny	173
McLaughlin	146	Magcanann	91	Merrigan	169	Mulvihill	163
OLavell	141	Magee	151	Meyk	161	Mulvogue	163
Lavelle	141	Maghimsey	98	OMiey	160	Murchu	174
OLawell	141	Magraith	184	Miles	162	Murgan	169
Le Archer	15	Magrath	184	Mill	162	Murland	168
Le Bell	21	Maguire	67	MacMillan	21	Murphy	128

Name	Page	Name	Page	Name	Page	Name	Page
Murphy	174	McPhail	83	McSheehy	194	Vernour	206
Murray	175	Phelan	210	Shinnahan	203	Walsh	17
Murray	176	MacPherson	45	Sim	195	Walsh	90
McMurray	176	MacPiaras	182	Simmonds	195	Walsh	182
McMurrays	176	Pierce	182	Simmons	195	Walsh	207
OMurrihir	175	Pierse	182	Simms	195	Walshes	17
MacMurrough	179	McQuillan	213	Simon	195	Walynus	17
OMurry	175	McQuilliams	213	Simpson	195	Wardein	208
OMurry	176	Quinn	183	Sinclair	196	Warden	208
Myretoun	170	Quinns	107	Slowey	163	Warenher	206
Myrton	170	McQuitty	211	Smith	197	Wark	209
McNamara	177	MacRaith	184	Smith	211	Warke	209
MacNamaras	110	Raygan	185	Smyth	197	Warner	206
MacNamaras	129	Rea	184	Smyth	211	Welsh	207
MacNamee	160	MacRea	184	Steward	198	Werk	209
Nangle	56	Reagan	185	Stewart	198	Werke	209
ONeil	46	Reay	184	Stigward	198	Wheatley	212
ONeill	107	ORegan	185	Stitt	199	Whelan	210
ONeill	127	Reilly	88	Stiward	198	White	211
ONeill	157	OReilly	186	Stout	199	McWhite	211
ONeill	178	OReillys	60	Stoute	199	Whiteley	212
ONeills	60	ORiagan	185	Stoutt	199	Whitleigh	212
ONeills	63	ORiain	188	Stuart	198	Whitley	212
ONeills	64	Rian	188	Stutt	199	Whitlie	212
ONeills	66	Rutherford	187	OSullahans	200	McWhitty	211
ONeills	70	Ryan	188	Sullivan	200	Whyte	211
ONeills	163	Ryans	114	OSullivan	200	McWilliam	213
ONeills	191	Salmon	189	Tait	201	Williams	214
ONeils	40	Salmon	189	Taite	201	McWilliams	213
Newark	209	Sammon	189	Tate	201	McWilliams	213
Nixon	125	Scott	132	MacThom	50	Williamson	213
Nolan	179	Scott	190	MacThom	202	Wilson	214
MacNoravaich	79	Seaman	189	Thompson	50	Wright	16
MacNuallain	179	Seay	194	Thompson	202	Wynne	94
McNulty	180	Seaye	194	Thomson	202	Yate	215
Obbykin	119	See	194	Tod	203	Yates	215
Oghy	95	MacSeinin	124	Todd	203	Yeates	215
Orchard	15	Senan	192	Todde	203	Yeats	215
Orr	181	OShanahans	192	Tommy	50	Yeatts	215
Oswald	121	Shane	191	OToole	204	Zett	215
MacParlan	18	MacShane	131	Tracey	205		
MacParland	18	McShane	191	Tracy	205		
MacParthalain	18	Shannon	192	Treacy	205		
Parthalan	18	McShea	194	OTuathail	204		
MacPartlin	18	OShea	194	Ure	181		
McPaul	83	Sheahan	193	MacUre	181		
McPaul	141	McShee	194	Vaughan	154		
Pearce	182	Sheehan	193	Vergin	23		
Pears	182	OSheehans	193	Verner	206		
Pearse	182	Sheehy	194	Vernor	206		

IRELAND 1841

Population
8,178,000

Six
Counties
1,649,000 - 20%

Co Dublin
373,000 - 7%

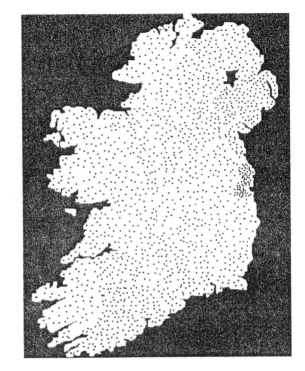

IRELAND 1991

Population
5,096,000

Northern Ireland
1,570,000 - 31%

Greater
Dublin
1,150,000 - 22%

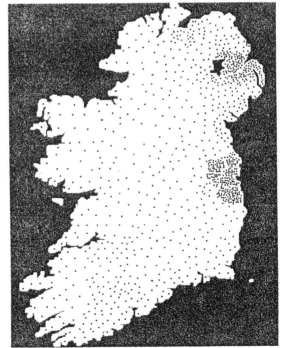

Works below made possible by members of the Irish Genealogical Foundation. Regular members receive our Journal of Irish Families 6 times yearly. Gold members receive the Journal 12 times yearly. Your membership is invited. Thank You.

Hardbound Works From Irish Families:
The Book of Irish Families Great and Small. 1992. 1999. (0-940134-15-2)
Families of Co. Kerry, Ireland. 1994. (0-940134-36-5)
Families of Co. Clare, Ireland. 1996. (0-940134-37-3)
Families of Co. Cork, Ireland. (0-940134-35 -7)
Families of Co. Limerick, Ireland (0-940134-31-4)
Families of Co. Galway, Ireland . (0-940134-00-4)
Families of Co. Dublin, Ireland. (0940134306)
Families of Co. Donegal, Ireland. (0940134756)
Irish Genealogies..from Keatings History (0-940134-49-7).
Complete Book For Tracing Your Irish Ancestors. (0-940134-02-0)
The Complete Book of Irish Family Names. 1987. (0-940134-41-1)
The Irish Book of Arms, Genealogy & Heraldry. 2000. (0-940134-86-1)
Irish Settlers on the American Frontier. 1985. (0940134-43-8)
Master Book of Irish Surnames. 1993. (0-940134-32-2)
Master (Atlas) & Book of Irish Placenames. 1994. (0-940134-33-0)

Other published works:
Beginners Guide to Irish Family Research. 1999.
Journal of Irish Families. 1986 - present. monthly. (ISSN 1056-0378)
Ortelius Map of Ireland 1572. (ancient map)
Gaelic Titles & Forms of Address. Duhallow. (0-940134-27-6)
Irish Knighthoods and Related subjects. (0940134-50-0)

County Genealogy and Family History Notes series.
Individual volumes available for the following counties:
Roscommon; Antrim & Belfast; Down; Tipperary; Waterford; Wexford; Derry; Sligo; Mayo; Tyrone; Cork; Kilkenny; Longford; Monaghan; Armagh.

Hardbound Rare Book Reprints Published by the I.G.F.:
Keatings' 'History of Ireland' 3 volume set. (0-940134-46-2)
The Poetry and Song of Ireland. O'Reilly. (1865). (0-940-134-43-8)
Irish Names and Surnames. Rev. Patrick Woulfe (0-940134-40-3)
Tribes/Customs of Hy-Many. O'Donovan. (orig.1873) (0-940134-39-X)
Tribes/Customs of Hy-Fiachrach. O'Donovan. (1874) (0-940134-38-1)
King James's Irish Army List. D'Alton. (0-940134-23-3)
A Social History of Ancient Ireland. Joyce. 2 v. set. (0-940134-24-1)

Write For Free Catalogue
Irish Genealogical Foundation
Box 7575
Kansas City, Missouri 64116 U.S.A.
© 2002 I.G.F. All Rights Reserved.
www.Irishroots.com

ISBN:0940134977